The closer we come to '92, the more you need our business connections.

As Europe progresses towards the single market, so Dan-Air Scheduled Services progresses towards the network of routes business travellers will rely on in 1992.

Indeed, we are already the second largest British scheduled airline to Europe.

We fly you direct from Gatwick to capital business centres like Paris, Madrid, Lisbon, Berne, Dublin and Zurich.

The prosperous South West of France is also Dan-Air territory, with flights to Toulouse, Perpignan, Montpellier, Lourdes and Nice.

Our new Class Elite business service is already in operation on all flights to Paris and Nice.

With special check-ins, custom designed seats, superb cuisine and complimentary champagne, Class Elite is our way of ensuring that business travellers arrive refreshed and ready for a day's work.

This service will be offered on many more routes during 1989.

But don't wait until 1992 to fly Dan-Air. Contact your travel agent for details of our European schedules. Or you can telephone Dan-Air Reservations on LinkLine 0345 100200.

You'll find we already have the right connections.

DAN-AIR
SCHEDULED SERVICES

The secret is service.

A TALE OF TWO CITIES
1789 - 1989

Execution Louis XVI, 21 January 1793, Musée Carnavalet, Paris

An International Exhibition to mark the 200th anniversary of the French Revolution

The Corn Exchange, Brighton
Next to the Royal Pavilion

4 May – 1 July 1989
Admission
Adults £3.00   Child/OAP £1.50

The Old Hall
Royal Horticultural Society

Vincent Square, London SW1
24 July – 15 September 1989
Admission
Adults £4.00   Child/OAP £2.00

The Exhibition

The exhibition tells the story of the French Revolution using millions of pounds worth of artefacts and special effects.

Witness an execution at the foot of the working guillotine.

See Marie-Antoinette walk into the Hall of Mirrors in a specially reconstructed room reflecting the splendour of Versailles.

What were the myths of the French Revolution – was there a Scarlet Pimpernel?

This fascinating story is now told through a spectacular collection brought together for the first time in this exhibition.

Opening Hours

Monday to Sunday 10.00am – 6.00pm
Wednesday 10.00am – 8.00pm

Group Bookings

Parties of ten or more persons are offered a discount of 10 per cent on the normal admission charge

Produce your 'Mutiny on the Bounty' ticket at 'A Tale of Two Cities' Exhibition and gain **ONE FREE ADMISSION** When an adult ticket is purchased

Manorial Research Plc

MUTINY
ON THE
BOUNTY
1789-1989

© 1989 👑 MANORIAL RESEARCH PLC, 104 Kennington Road, London SE11 6RE Telephone 01-582 1588

Registered in London No. 1644220

ISBN 0 9513128 2 0

Distributed by Comag, Tavistock Road, West Drayton, Middx UB7 7QE

Production, including typesetting and colour separations by Alphaprint, 3 Spicers, Ashdell Park, Alton, Hants GU34 2SJ

Designed by Pengilley Designs, 70 Frances Road, Windsor, Berks SL4 3AJ

Printed by McCorquodale Varnicote plc, Station Road, Pershore, Worcs WR10 2DN

CONTENTS

NEARLY EVERYONE has heard of Bligh, his mutiny and his epic voyage in an open boat – not so many are aware of his wider achievements. An accomplished disciple of Captain Cook, the great navigator, a determined commander in battle, commended by Nelson for his bravery in fierce action, protégé of Sir Joseph Banks, the President of The Royal Society and elected a Fellow of that learned body, colonial administrator – potentially a glittering career that should have assured Bligh of a respectable place in history, but all overshadowed because of a quirk of character that led to his failure to command the respect and obedience of his men at a critical time.

Leadership is best learnt from the example of one's superiors. Bligh had an abrasive personality, but could he have learned to keep this in check, shown the right way? At the age of 21 Bligh was chosen to be Captain Cook's navigator in HMS Resolution on his third voyage to the Pacific. Cook must have been in a position to make a great impression on young Bligh; a national hero famous for his dramatic voyages of discovery, he had a reputation as a leader who cared for his men, they would follow him literally to the ends of the earth. But sadly on this third voyage, Cook was a sick man. His illness manifested itself in irritability, indecision, violent bouts of temper and irrational behaviour, a complete change from his normal character. Those who had sailed with him on his earlier voyages, and they were many, could make allowances, but what of Bligh? Did he think that this was acceptable behaviour? Did this example lead him to give rein to his own aggressive instincts when ten years later he was in similar circumstances, in command on a long and demanding voyage to the South Seas?

I find it fascinating, if un-academic, to speculate on what might have been had Bligh been properly trained for command and had he been able to overcome or suppress the defects of character which led to the mutiny. The Bounty voyage would have been an outstanding success. Having delivered the Tahitian breadfruit to the West Indies, Bligh would have returned in triumph to England. His new discoveries would have added to the chart of the Pacific. Banks, a man of great influence, would have been delighted; his recommendation that Bligh should command the expedition vindicated. Bligh would have been seen to be inheriting the mantle of Cook. Thus when in 1791 plans were being made for a further expedition to the Pacific and to the North West coast of America Bligh would have been a natural choice for the command; familiar with the area from his voyage with Cook, leader of a second successful voyage to the Pacific, his navigational and hydrographic skills ably demonstrated, protégé of Banks, it would seem that there could be no more eligible candidate. But the Bounty voyage ended in mutiny, Bligh was sent to Tahiti in HMS Providence to try again to collect the breadfruit and the man chosen to lead the new expedition was Vancouver. He too had sailed with Cook but only as a young Midshipman. He had much less experience than Bligh. So, but for those fateful events on board HMS Bounty two hundred years ago the beautiful capital city of British Columbia might had had another name!

Evidently Captain William Bligh deserves to be remembered for more than the mutiny on the Bounty. I hope this exhibition and this catalogue will help to show his career in a wider perspective.

ADMIRAL OF THE FLEET LORD LEWIN KG CHAIRMAN OF TRUSTEES

Lewin of Greenwich

GAS
THE HEAT
OF THE
MOMENT

British Gas
South Eastern
ENERGY IS OUR BUSINESS

ACKNOWLEDGEMENTS

Exhibitions, like theatrical productions, are co-operative ventures involving the skills and expertise of a large number of people. Last year's Armada exhibition was made possible by loans from all over Europe, and by co-operation from Spain and Ulster in particular. This year's Mutiny on the Bounty exhibition has also relied on overseas loans and expertise, but in this case the assistance has come, appropriately, from Australia which has a number of links with Captain Bligh and Fletcher Christian.

We are particularly grateful to Alison Crook and Margy Burn of the State Library of New South Wales, and to John Thompson and Harry McCarthy of the National Library in Canberra, for lending some of their institution's most treasured possessions and for their support. The Queensland Museum has lent artefacts recovered from the wreck of the Pandora and we would like to thank Ron Coleman, Curator of Maritime Archaeology and his Director, Dr. Alan Bartholomai for their kind co-operation.

The design of the exhibition and much of the related publicity material has been the work of Desmond Freeman Associates, the Sydney-based firm which last year designed the museum's travelling exhibition *Captain James Cook, Navigator*. Desmond Freeman produced the most imaginative of the design proposals submitted to us for Mutiny on the Bounty, and has entirely justified our choice. His firm's professionalism and attention to detail has been extremely impressive, and has overcome the inevitable difficulties of long-distance communications. The project designers have been Rosemary Simons and Desmond Freeman, with assistance from David Spode and Quentin Mitchell. Graphic design has been by Michelle Hogan and draughting by John Caldwell and Mark Dyson.

The audio-visual effects in the exhibition have been masterminded by Philip Sugg and Robin Prater, and audio vidual production has been by Prater Audio-Visual Limited. The daunting task of fabricating the exhibition to a tight budget and to an equally tight timetable has been carried out by the exhibition contractors Kimpton Walker Limited. Transport of loans has been undertaken by MoMart Limited. We are indebted to Malcolm Wilson, Kenneth Britten, R A Lightley and Kelvin Thatcher for the production of specially commissioned ship models and for the expert restoration of existing ship models.

Many people have provided information about Bligh and the background to the Bounty mutiny. We are especially grateful to Stephen Walters who has given us the benefit of his expertise from the outset of the project, and introduced us to other experts in the field. We would also like to thank David Allan, Glynn Christian, Andrew David, Paul Epps, David Field, Yvonne Hayhurst, Gordon Huelin, David Mann, Christopher Sainsbury and Dorota Starzecka. We are also grateful to Robert Smith and the staff of Manorial Research plc for their support for the project and their patience during the production stages of the catalogue.

Within the museum, the project team for the exhibition has been led by Rina Prentice assisted by Helene Mitchell and Peter Ince. Project management has been in the capable hands of Elizabeth Cowell. Lionel Willis has played a key role in design aspects of the exhibition, and Ann Leane has co-ordinated the conservation input. Fredericka Smith has sorted out the complex loans arrangements. Other museum staff who have contributed to the exhibition include David Anderson, Robert Baldwin, Lawrence Birnie, Pat Blackett Barber, Andrew Bush, Bryan Clarke, Richard Clarke, Caroline Hampton, Eric Kentley, Roger Knight, Gillian Lewis, Margarette Lincoln, Ray Lunn, Chrissie MacLeod, Lindsey MacFarlane, John Palmer, George Spalding, Jim Stevenson, Gary Stewart, Peter Van Geersdaele, David Taylor and Jane Weeks. The museum relies heavily on the goodwill and hard work put into exhibitions by staff at all levels over many months, and it is a pleasure to record the debt which we owe to them.

David Cordingly
Head of Exhibitions

LENDERS

British Library

Trustees of the British Museum

Trustees of the British Museum (Ethnography)

Trustees of the British Museum (Natural History)

Exeter Maritime Museum

Trustees of the late Major General R H Goulburn

Herbert Art Gallery and Museum, Coventry

Hydrographic Department, Ministry of Defence

Mitchell Library, State Library of New South Wales, Sydney

Ministry of Defence Naval Library

Museum of London

National Library of Australia, Canberra

National Portrait Gallery

Borough of Poole Museum Service

Public Record Office

Queensland Museum, Brisbane, assisted by the Premier's Department of the Queensland Government

Trustees of the Royal Botanic Garden, Kew

Royal Geographical Society

Royal Society for the encouragement of Arts, Manufacturers and Commerce

Science Museum

Society for Promoting Christian Knowledge

R L B Wall

Desmond Weston

And several private owners who prefer to remain anonymous.

William Bligh's Royal Navy

Richard Ormond looks at naval organization and introduces the most famous mutiny at sea

■ MUTINY ON the *Bounty* is significant on three counts. First, as a confrontation between personalities and principles quite unique in the annals of the Navy; second, for the heroic consequences that followed on from the act of mutiny itself, in particular Bligh's open boat crossing (he sailed from Tofoa across the Pacific to Australia and entered the Timor Sea), and the establishment of the Pitcairn settlement; and finally for the light which the mutiny casts on the role of the Navy in the field of exploration and navigation.

The idea of mutiny appeals to the popular imagination, and most people assume it was a fairly common occurrence. In the Navy it was not. There were plenty of incidents that went by the names of mutiny during the 18th century; refusals to go to sea, occupation of ships and so on, but these were lower deck protests against pay and conditions. Seizing one of His Majesty's ships on the high seas and casting the captain adrift was an event almost without precedent. It explains the rapidity with which the Admiralty responded by dispatching a warship to bring the mutineers to justice. Such an act of flagrant disobedience struck at the very foundations of law and order on which the navy was built. The mutiny would never have taken place had it not been led by someone as senior as Fletcher Christian, for it required qualities of leadership to effect it. Interest in the mutiny has focused on the personal confrontation between Captain William Bligh and Mr. Fletcher Christian, his second in command. The increasingly tense and confrontational atmosphere on board ship, after the long stay in Tahiti, brought out the worst in both men, overbearing and bullying characteristics in Bligh, as he struggled to assert authority; suicidal tendencies in Christian. That this drama was played out on an overcrowded ship, many thousands of miles from home, and cut off for more than a year from European contacts, underlines its sensational aspects. In the unlikely event of such a happening in home waters, it would have been a tame event by comparison: no fierce gales around Cape Horn; no exotic Pacific paradise; no breadfruit; no danger in unknown seas; no aberrant psychological behaviour brought on by stress and confinement.

At the heart of the mutiny lies the issue of whether it was justified. It is no coincidence that its bicentenary coincides with that of the French Revolution. This was the age of Jean Jacques Rousseau, Tom Paine and *The Rights of Man*. Can the overthrow of a tyrannical authority be justified by an appeal to natural justice? Was Bligh's conduct sufficiently intolerable to excuse Christian's act of rebellion? It is the moral issues behind the dramatic incidents of the mutiny and the battle between opposing personalities that makes the story so compelling, and has brought out competing protagonists for one side or the other from 1790 to the present day. The failure to round Cape Horn, the long sojourn in Tahiti, the slow breakdown of relationships, the small size of the ship the absence of a second commissioned officer to support Bligh, the poor quality of the crew, all contributed to create an atmosphere favourable to mutiny. But the event, when it took place, appears to have been spontaneous and unpremeditated. Christian in the depths of despair was contemplating pushing off from the *Bounty* on a raft, so desperate was he to get away, when the midshipman Edward Young suggested that several of the crew were with him and would help him to take the ship instead. Like many great events with weighty consequences, the mutiny was a brief, casual and confused affair. Few people were clear what was happening, loyalties were divided, and the sequence of events leading to the dispatch of the launch was haphazard. Alone of the mutineers, Christian seems to have been aware of the enormity of the step he was taking, placing him beyond the bounds of society. The constant repetition of the refrain, "I am in hell", confirms that he was at breaking point and unable to help himself.

Bligh's 3,600 mile crossing of the Timor Sea in an open boat with 18 loyalists and a limited stock of food is rightly celebrated as one of the greatest feats of seamanship and navigation of all time. Bligh's confidence in himself, his unerring skills as a navigator, his continued control of his crew when in the last stages of exhaustion and destitution, demonstrate leadership of a high order. He was the right man for a crisis. The weather-stained log he kept in the launch is one of the chief treasures in the Exhibition. Seaman to the core, Bligh recorded the events of his voyage and surveyed the islands they passed as if he were carrying out normal duties aboard ship rather than struggling for survival.

The fate of the mutineers was no less dramatic than that of the loyalists. The seizure of those who remained in Tahiti by Captain Edwards of the Pandora, the shipwreck of that vessel off the Barrier Reef, and the adventures of the survivors, is a story in itself. The subsequent trial of the mutineers, and the execution of three of them, witnessed the start of the *Bounty* controversy. Bligh had returned to London in 1790 as the hero of the hour, the victim of a mutiny, who had survived an incredible ordeal against all the odds. By the time of the trial, he was aboard the *Provident*, completing the second and successful breadfruit voyage. Now was the time for the supporters of the mutineers to come forward, in particular Edward Christian, the barrister brother of Fletcher, and Nessy

Heywood, who secured a pardon for her brother Peter Heywood.

Edward Christian's, Appendix to Stephen Barney's Minutes of the Court Martial, based on interviews with the *Bounty* crew, and dressed up in legalistic form, was a clever piece of character assassination, building up a picture of a capricious and sadistic captain to explain, if not to excuse, his brother's conduct. From then on the battle was joined. Countless books and articles have been written and films produced to try and demonstrate what really happened on the *Bounty*, who was right and who was wrong, and what, in the final event, is the lesson to be learnt. The fate of the mutineers who escaped to Pitcairn is perhaps the strangest of all. The isolated settlement, beset by tensions between the whites and natives, became the scene for a sequence of murders the details of which remain unclear. From bloodshed was born a remarkable community, led by the sole white survivor, John Adams, who abjured alcohol and took to the Bible. The island was rediscovered in the early 19th century, and the evidence of the venerable patriarch helped to fill in a number of gaps in the *Bounty* story. The old mutineer himself was wisely left in peace.

The mutiny and its consequences dominate the foreground of the *Bounty* story. The wider context in which the voyage took place is often overlooked or misunderstood. Bligh had been commissioned to transport breadfruit plants from Tahiti to the West Indies as a new source of food supplies for the slaves there. The reasons for what may appear a rather bizarre enterprise require some explanation. In the first place, it is important to stress that the voyage of the *Bounty* was a naval expedition. You cannot understand the character of the voyage without understanding its specifically naval context. Whereas early voyages of discovery in the 16th and 17th centuries had often been privately financed, and undertaken in the expectation of profit, those of the 18th century had become the preserve of the Navy. No other body was capable of financing them, since they had no immediate commercial benefits. No other body possessed the specialized ships and equipment necessary to equip such voyages for long periods in unknown waters.

■ A remorseful Christian kneeling on Pitcairn, by Henry Warren, 1746-1831. *Private collection.*

No other body could provide the technological skills and know-how.

The Navy had various reasons for promoting voyages of exploration. In the first place, there was the disinterested scientific reason of finding out more about uncharted regions of the globe. There was also the desire to aid commerce and colonization. New lands might be a source of wealth and power to those who discovered them first; beating the opposition played no small part in naval thinking. Finally there were the strategic advantages that flowed from improved knowledge of sea-routes, navigable channels and straits, coastlines and ports. The surveying work of these expeditions formed no small part of that achievement. They made for safer and faster means of communication, and gave inestimable advantages to the naval power

that possessed them. By the end of the Seven Years War in 1763, the British Navy was pre-eminent in many parts of the world. Their warships, supplied by a succession of trading posts and colonial outstations, controlled the sealanes to the Indian Ocean and the Far East, across the Atlantic to the American colonies and the West Indies, and they constituted a formidable presence in the Mediterranean and the North Sea. The work of the naval explorers was an extension of the work of patrolling the seaways of the world, helping to defend British possessions and to extend her interests.

The most famous of the voyages were those undertaken by Captain James Cook. In little more than a decade his discoveries had totally transformed the state of European knowledge about the Pacific Region. It is no surprise to find that Bligh

had served with Cook on his third and final voyage, and had inherited his mantle as a pre-eminent navigator. Matthew Flinders, having served under Bligh, went on to survey the Australian coastline, and in his turn, inspired Sir John Franklin, the most famous of the early 19th century Arctic explorers. As the secrets of the Pacific unfolded, the new challenge was the discovery of the North-West Passage. It would be naval explorers and naval ships that would solve the riddle. The power of the Navy in the second half of the 18th century was formidable. The task of keeping the world's largest fleet in operation required a huge and complex organization. The Royal Dockyards, for example, represented industrial production and maintenance output on a scale unparalleled elsewhere in Britain. Supplying the ships, recruiting and training the crews, and laying down the conditions of service, called for a wide administrative network. The Navy prided itself on high professional standards, the calibre of its officers and seamen, and the quality of its leadership. Confidence in the effectiveness of the service was overwhelming.

That confidence had been shaken but not undermined by the experiences of the American War of Independence, 1778-82. Britain had entered a war for the first time without European allies, and faced a hostile combination of French, Spanish and Dutch navies that outnumbered her own. Defending her home shores, supplying the forces in North America, protecting trade and overseas possessions, proved too great a strain. The American colonies were lost, but in the closing stages of the war Britain countered the strategic threat in the Channel and the Caribbean, winning a series of engagements, most notably Rodney's victory at the Battle of the Saints in 1783. Britain had learned her lesson. The navy went through a process of strengthening and reorganisation which stood the nation in good stead when war broke out once more, in 1793 three years after the *Bounty* mutiny. It was the Navy which stood between revolutionary France and the subjugation of Europe, as Britain's European allies suffered successive defeats. It was naval successes which lit up a scene of prevailing gloom and defeat.

Captain Bligh was to play no small part in those heroic events of the Napoleonic period, and he ended his career with the rank of Vice-Admiral.

The mutiny had been merely a temporary slip in the career of an otherwise exemplary naval officer. It must have left its scars, but it affected neither Bligh's bouncy self-confidence in himself nor his ambition. It was he who received the surrender of the Dutch flagship at the Battle of Camperdown in 1797, and he who was commended by Nelson for his gallantry at Copenhagen in 1801 He later became Governor of New South Wales, and the victim of a new form of mutiny. His attempts to tackle colonial abuses were thwarted by a combination of corrupt military officers and self-interested local politicians. Bligh was simply out of his depth, and few useful parallels can be drawn with the earlier *Bounty* mutiny.

Bligh was over-zealous, a martinet and disciplinarian, with a blinkered view of human nature that flawed him as a commander. Nevertheless, he was a seaman of high abilities and an outstanding navigator, against whom circumstances conspired in 1789 to bring out his worst faults and blind spots. The story of the mutiny continues to revolve around this powerful and unpredictable personality.

Richard Ormond is Director of the National Maritime Museum.

Jolly tars were our men?

Life was hard in the 18th century Navy, but not as cruel as the stories suggest. Nicholas Rodger disposes of some myths

WE STILL know too little about the social life of the Navy in the 18th century. Only for the 1750s and 1760s has it been studied in any detail, and for the period of the Revolutionary and Napoleonic Wars from 1793 to 1815 we still depend largely on older studies derived from a limited range of secondary sources, usually the memoirs of old men with an axe to grind. It is therefore necessary to be cautious in painting the background to the Bounty mutiny: it seems likely that much had changed since the 1760s, and certain that much more was to change under the impulse of the French revolution which broke out just as Bligh and his men were in the Pacific: but we do not yet know exactly how much in either case. We can be sure that the Navy was not isolated from the currents of national life, and that in its own particular way it reflected the developments which were slowly transforming British society in the closing years of the century; yet it is well to remember that this was a peacetime expedition (though affected in the later stages of its preparation by a general mobilization), consciously modelled in most of its details on the precedents established in the 1770s by Cook, the man who had trained Bligh and was already, less than 10 years after his death, revered as the great master and exemplar of Pacific exploration. In most respects this voyage belonged to a settled pattern, and can be best understood in the context of an older social world which was soon to be fundamentally changed by the strains of war with revolutionary France.

That world was shaped by the sea, and did not much differ between the Navy and merchant ships. Men and officers moved easily from one service to the other as opportunity offered – Bligh and Christian had been shipmates in the West India trade before they returned to the Navy to sail in the Bounty. In both services, men experienced an alternation between the ceaseless exhaustion and dangers of seafaring, and quite long periods of relaxation in port. Even in wartime men-of-war spent barely half their time at sea, while merchantmen had always to spend long periods taking on and discharging cargo. When they did put to sea, they did not usually stay there for very long; even a transatlantic voyage would scarcely exceed two months, and most were shorter than that. Only the big East Indiamen were accustomed to make such long ocean passages as the Bounty undertook.

This was fortunate, for the physical and psychological strain of seafaring was considerable. He that would go to sea for

Taking Soundings: an etching by J A Atkinson (1808). A leadsman in the chains. In confined waters, a seaman had to take soundings continually. *National Maritime Museum*

pleasure, the proverb had it, would go to hell for a pastime. The handling of a ship at sea required precise teamwork, exhausting effort, agility, stamina, and hardiness. Almost all ships worked two watches, which meant that the crew, or more precisely the seaman part of the ship's company, were divided into two groups, one of which was always on deck. At sea, therefore, seamen never had more than four hours' sleep a night and frequently less. If the united strength of the ship's company were required for a manoeuvre, as it might often be in the smaller men-of-war or merchantmen, "all hands" would be called repeatedly, breaking the meagre sleep of the watch below decks. There was no way of heating a ship, and usually no way of drying wet clothes. In storms, according to one officer, "the spray of the sea raised by the violence of the wind is dispersed over the whole ship, so that the people breathe in water, as it were, for many weeks together". The seaman's berth was no place for the old, or even middle-aged: if a man was to acquire the agility and experience required to work aloft before he lost the strength and resilience of youth he had to start as a boy, and only those inured to it from boyhood, it was reckoned, could bear the hardships of the seafaring life. With limited exceptions among the officers and "idlers" (the non-seaman and non-watchkeeping specialists: such as the carpenter, cooper, sailmaker and armourer, who worked by day and slept at night) all ships were manned by young men and boys.

From the seaman's point of view, warships had the advantage of being much better manned than merchantmen. At least with full wartime complements, the numbers required to man the guns were far greater than those needed simply to handle the ship, so that the work in the Navy was lighter, and moreover there was more space to sling one's hammock on decks unencumbered with cargo. Nothing could make the seafaring life safe or easy, but it was significantly less

arduous in men-of-war, especially in big men-of-war. Within the Navy, however, there was a sharp contrast between the ships of the line, nearly two-thirds of whose ships' companies were seamen, and the small frigates, sloops, and armed vessels which might muster little more than one-third of their men seamen. Broadly speaking, the smaller the ship, the larger the proportion of her complement was taken by officers and idlers, and the more work there was for the rest. The little Bounty, with 45 men roughly the equivalent of an eight-gun fireship in establishment, sailed with only 13 working able seaman, one of whom was Michael Byrne the half-blind fiddler. As a merchant ship on the East Coast she would have been handled by even fewer, and with her hold full of coal there would have been even less room to berth in, but then she would have been at sea only a week or two at a time.

On the East Coast, moreover, the navigation for all its dangers was well-known. The Bounty was going into the vast emptiness of the southern oceans where little or nothing was known, and

she was going alone. No help could reach her in any difficulty. In an age when even the handiest vessels could only with the utmost difficulty claw off the land in the face of an onshore gale, when charts and pilots alike were extravagantly unreliable, and methods of fixing longitude were in their infancy, all seafaring was attended with innumerable perils. It was not unusual for ships to make landfall scores or even hundreds of miles out of their reckoning, and to be wrecked without ever knowing what coast they had been driven upon. When ships did go down few seamen could swim, ships' boats could not easily be hoisted out and were incapable of surviving a heavy sea. All this was true of European waters with which navigators were familiar and far more true of the remote vastness of the Pacific, still largely unexplored and uncharted by Europeans, and strewn with unreported reefs and islands.

For any ship which set out around the world to voyage in strange seas for months and years, the problems of food and health were as acute as those of navigation. For centuries, it had been accept-

ed by seamen that no long voyage could hope to escape fever and scurvy, and only the most fortunate would escape crippling losses. Well within the memory of older officers, Commodore Anson had returned in 1744 from his great voyage round the world with one ship left of a squadron of six, and of the Centurion's original compliment of 510, only 130 survived. Bligh was ordered to follow almost the same course in a single ship with 45 men. He had no reserves, no margin for error: he had to keep his men healthy if the expedition were to survive.

In fact, his chances of doing so were very much higher than they would have been even 40 years before. The great killers in ships, especially warships with their large crews living tightly packed together, had always been typhus and tropical fevers. These were well understood to be infectious diseases, although the actual mechanism of infection was unknown, and good officers like Bligh paid minute attention to cleanliness and

■ Model of The Endeavour showing stowage. *National Maritime Museum.*

hygiene to ward them off. Long passages out of contact with the land or other ships were themselves a good defence against infection, but they exposed the men to the terrible ravages of scurvy. Even with this terrifying and destructive condition, which remained into the 20th century mysterious to science, the situation had improved during the century. Naval (though not medical) opinion had come to believe almost unanimously that scurvy was a dietary disease, caused by the presence either of something harmful in the naval diet (salt was the obvious candidate) or the absence of something needful to health, and in either case to be combatted by issuing fresh food as often and long as possible. It was regular good practice by all captains and admirals to see their men fed fresh meat, bread, and vegetables not only in port but even at sea, for as long as they could be obtained. Fresh meat was regularly carried to sea on the hoof, and in addition to the ship's stocks, officers and men were encouraged to lay in their private supplies of fruit, vegetables and livestock. By this means scurvy, though never eliminated, could be kept at bay. The fundamental problem was that contemporary technology offered a very limited range of methods of preserving food, and those which did exist required the most rigorous care in the manufacturing process, and the best quality of raw food, to yield satisfactory results. It seems that the Victualling Board did meet these high standards, and the quality of what it issued was good, but no method existed by which vitamins could have been preserved even if their existence had neen known. Salt beef and pork, ship's bread (i.e. biscuit), butter and cheese, peas and oatmeal were the staples of shipboard diet once the fresh provisions had run out. The naval diet was plentiful, even luxurious by the standards of the labouring poor, who certainly did not eat meat four days a week ashore, and it provided more than sufficient calories for hard work. By modern standards it was monotonous and limited, but 18th century technology could do no better, and in the hands of a conscientious officer like Bligh it was adequate to preserve health even on very long voyages.

This was so even though Bligh, again following Cook, placed great faith in various medicines against scurvy which were in fact useless. It is now well known that Cook's judgment powerfully

influenced the Navy, and most European navies with it, against lemon juice and in favour of malt extract and sauerkraut. Had he been less conscientious and successful in guarding the health of his men, had he issued fresh provisions less often, the bad effects of this error might have become obvious, but as it was his unequalled authority, fully supported by Bligh, served to establish a new, erroneous orthodoxy. A previous generation of naval men, including the great naval physician James Lind, had been groping towards the recognition that fresh fruit and vegetables in general, and orange and lemon juice in particular, were unequalled remedies for the scurvy, but Cook's influence, coupled with revised opinions promulgated by Lind himself, turned inquiries for a generation into other and less fruitful courses.

From the perils of navigation, from the mysterious and unavoidable visitations of the scurvy, and simply from the exhaustion and debility of long voyaging in a little ship, the Bounty's expedition was attended from the start with enormous risk. It seems at first sight extraor-

■ Deal Castle by Thomas Hearn. The quarter deck of this 20 gun ship, about twice Bounty's size, looking forward. *National Maritime Museum.*

dinary that it should have been set on foot in such a casual, almost matter-of-fact manner, and still more remarkable that the confidence of its promoters should have been justified. But Bligh was perhaps the most brilliant pupil of the great Captain Cook, and he had thoroughly absorbed the methods of his master. From the start he kept the ship on three watches, so that the men had eight hours off and four hours on watch, or one

uninterrupted night in three (weather permitting). In even the worst weather off Cape Horn, he kept the galley stove alight and a man constantly attending it to dry clothes, so that, he boasted, no man ever went on watch or went to bed wet. To mitigate the damp and discomfort of the little ship he even berthed some men in his own cabin during the worst days off Cape Horn. He gave the men hot breakfasts (unknown at sea and indeed on land in those days), he insisted on the most rigorous cleanliness of men, clothes and ship, and he paid scrupulous attention to their diet, supplemented by fresh food whenever it could be had. Well aware of the connection between morale and health, he made sure to provide his ship with a fiddler so that the men could dance every evening. As a navigator, Bligh picked his way across uncharted seas and unknown dangers with a precise confidence unequalled by any seaman of the age. From all the predictable dangers, he brilliantly preserved his men and his ship.

To approach the unpredictable danger of mutiny, we need to look at the naval hierarchy of authority and rank. This was not in the 18th century as tidy and unambiguous as it was to become: there was no point at which a clear line could be drawn between officers and men, nor between gentlemen and their inferiors. The formal structure of ranks and ratings, and the informal realities of social status, were arranged haphazardly and by no means in parallel, so that there were many gentlemen who were not officers, and officers who were not gentlemen. The formal system of ranks and ratings distinguished commissioned officers (who were sea officers), warrant officers who were also sea officers and those who were reckoned only as inferior officers, petty officers with the status of inferior officers, and other petty officers who were not officers of any sort but simply ratings, slightly superior to the rest of "the people", the 18th century term for the ratings of the ship as a body. Officers and ratings were divided another way by their professions: seamen were the largest group, but there were many other trades among the idlers, and in each there were the qualified, the learners and the unskilled. Across these boundaries, affecting them all but coinciding with none, lay the invisible distinctions of social class, distributing gentlemen and tradesmen, noblemen and artisans with

careless impartiality among the ranks and ratings.

The most senior officers in the Navy were the commissioned officers. They were the only ones permitted to command combattant warships, and the only persons in the Service, with the significant exception of Midshipmen, who wore uniform. Commissioned officers and Masters were supposed to be the only watchkeeping officers, qualified to take charge of a warship at sea, but in practice ships as small as the Bounty had to use junior officers as watchkeepers. Commissioned officers were invariably reckoned as gentlemen, and most of them were gentlemen by birth, but a considerable minority had worked their way up from more humble origins. Bligh's patron and teacher James Cook was the son of a Yorkshire farm labourer, and his contemporary the mulatto Captain John Perkins may well have been born a slave. Besides the nine ranks of admiral, there were three commissioned ranks: in ascending order, Lieutenant, Master and Commander, and Captain – the latter often called Post-Captain to distinguish the rank from the title of "Captain" which was always accorded to the commanding officer of any vessel, however small. Bligh himself at the time of the Bounty mutiny was only a Lieutenant, but by contemporary conventions quite properly styled "Captain" Bligh. Master and Commander, though not formally established as the rank of Commander until 1794, was almost universally regarded as a necessary intermediate step between Lieutenant and Post-Captain.

Below commissioned officers came the warrant officers, who were the professional heads of specialist departments within the ship. They included the Mas-

1. A sailor in seagoing costume by Dominic Serres (1777).
2. A Midshipman.
3. A Master and Commander.
4. A Post Captain.
5. An Admiral
Officers' uniform of the pattern worn between 1774-1787 by Dominic Serres (1777).
National Maritime Museum.

ter, Surgeon, Purser, Boatswain, Gunner, Carpenter, Sailmaker, Cook, Armourer, and Surgeon's Mates. They were as a rule inferior in social status as well as in rank to the commissioned officers, but there were important differences in both within the warrant officers, who may be divided into three groups. First came the Master, responsible for pilotage and navigation; the Surgeon; and the Purser, who took charge of victualling (though the Bounty was too small to bear a Purser and Bligh had to do this himself). These three were sea officers like the commissioned officers and of more or less equivalent social status: in 1808 they were formally established as "wardroom officers": the social equals of the Lieutenants. The Boatswain, Gunner and Carpenter were also sea officers, but usually of lower social class and less education. All of them, however, had to keep accounts and produce reports in writing, and in small ships it was not uncommon for Boatswain or Gunner to stand watches. Bligh made Mr Peckover the Gunner one of his watchkeepers, and so exacting a navigator would not have given charge of the ship to an ignorant or incapable officer. There was a third category of warrant officers which included the Sailmaker, Cook, Armourer and Surgeon's Mates, who were not counted as sea officers but "inferior officers", meaning that they had only the standing of petty officers. Like all warrant officers, however, they took rank by their warrants: issued by the Admiralty or Navy Board in London, and could not be removed or disrated by their captain however much he disapproved of them. The limit of his authority towards even an inferior warrant officer was to put him under arrest and appoint another to act by order in his place.

There was another sort of inferior officer who did not have a warrant and was in principle just a petty officer, a working man chosen by the captain to take charge of some particular duties. But these inferior petty officers were very often the social superiors of all the warrant officers, for these ratings of Midshipman and Master's Mate were occupied by "young gentlemen" learning their profession with a view to becoming Lieutenants. In fact, the word "midshipman" was coming to be used loosely as a synonym for "young gentleman" or would-be Lieutenant. This was not yet true, for there were still many working petty officers in these ratings with no hopes of promotion: and many young gentlemen (especially the youngest, who might be no more than 10 or 12) in other ratings, including able seaman. In a ship a small as the Bounty, however, the Midshipmen and Mates (there were no fewer than eight of them, counting three rated as able seamen but considered and employed as Midshipmen) were the obvious source of additional officers, and it was his old ship-mate Fletcher Christian, Master's Mate, whom Bligh put in charge of one of the watches. A young man in his position was sometimes unofficially called a "Sub-Lieutenant", which accurately described his real position even though in theory he was only a rating. What is more remarkable is that Bligh appointed him an acting Lieutenant, something he could have no possible authority to do as there was no vacancy of Lieutenant to fill. If Bligh had achieved his ambition to be commissioned a Master and Commander, the Bounty would automatically have been allowed a Lieutenant, but as it was he was the only commissioned officer in the ship, and not even a commander-in-chief could have established another without Admiralty sanction. If Bligh had come home in normal circumstances he would undoubtedly have had a difficult time explaining Christian's irregular promotion. As a Lieutenant, Christian would have become First Lieutenant, Bligh's second-in-command and senior to Mr Fryer the Master, but it is not clear if he was regarded as such on board the Bounty. What is clear is that he was an officer, and within the little world of the Bounty a senior officer.

This brings us to the question of naval discipline in the 18th century, a subject about which probably more, and

more inaccurate, myths are in circulation than any other. To a large extent, naval discipline was a functional response to the necessities of seafaring, resting on mutual consent and enforced by public opinion. All seamen had been bred from boyhood in a world in which survival depended utterly on skilled teamwork; not simply on every man pulling his weight on the falls of tackle or halliard, but on the intelligent application of individual skill and initiative. In many manoeuvres the safety of the ship depended as much on the individual topman aloft as on the captain or master on the quarter deck. This bred a close, almost intimate world of shared dangers, in which the skilled seamen (and indeed the skilled idlers), enjoyed and expected to enjoy the respect due to key men on whom the whole company depended. This had nothing to do with any democratic ideas of levelling the social or naval hierarchy, which seem to have been still unknown in 1789; nor did it involve any challenge to the essentially autocratic nature of shipboard society, for all seamen knew that orders had to be given and obeyed at sea for the safety of all. What it did mean was that there was a natural alliance between the prudent officer and the responsible, skilled, and experienced part of the ship's company, against all slackers, drunkards, incompetents and troublemakers who threw more work onto their shipmates and made life in the crowded world of a ship more difficult or dangerous than it needed to be. Successful seafaring demanded a high degree of self-discipline, and those who did not or would not acquire it were a burden on their fellows.

In the hands of any reasonably capable and sensitive captain, naval discipline at sea was employed with the support of majority opinion to keep life as safe and comfortable as possible. The offences typically punished seem to have been idling and shirking, failing to keep oneself and one's berth clean, drunkenness and the like, and it is easy to see that responsible and hard-working men were positively keen to see the punishment of those guilty of such anti-social behaviour. Flogging was the usual punishment, and it enjoyed the tacit, sometimes the vocal support of majority opinion at sea, so long as it was done fairly and consistently. A weak man who punished too little, who did not live up to his threats, was liable to be less popular

than a severe but consistent captain. Most unpopular of all was the capricious officer, alternating cruelty and indulgence, whose men never knew where they stood with him. This seems to have been the character of Captain Pigot of the Hermione, the "black ship" whose bloody mutiny in 1797 is perhaps the best known in British history after the Bounty. Bligh's problem was different: there is no doubt that he was a humane and considerate commander who carefully followed the precepts of his mentor Captain Cook, but he was not a sensitive or perceptive man. It was typical of him to take pains to acquire a fiddler, knowing how valuable music and dancing were to morale and health; it was equally typical that when he was worried by sickness and depression he forced the men to dance with threats of punishment. He seems to have been ready with threats which he did not carry out; a mark of dangerous weakness in any commander. He often insulted and belittled people, ratings as well as officers, who from their rank or character should have been his natural allies in the preservation of discipline. His making Christian an acting Lieutenant was an example; not only was the promotion improper and unnecessary, it alienated Mr Fryer the Master over whose head Christian was advanced.

So far we have been considering naval discipline as it operated at sea, and to a considerable extent that alone was where it did operate. Once securely moored in port, the perils of seafaring passed, and with them the necessity of disciplined teamwork. Ships in port were notoriously disorganized, even chaotic, and the voice of authority was extremely weak. Released from the confinement and tensions of shipboard life, sailors became riotous and ungovernable. Their character on shore was of thoughtless, uncontrollable excess, and there was very little that officers could do about it. If officers were attacked on shore by drunken seamen, the Admiralty regarded it as a private matter of no official significance. Though in theory the provisions of the Articles of War could be applied to offences committed on shore when on duty, they seldom were even in wartime. The seafaring life was an alternation of disciplined teamwork and extravagant self-indulgence. When the time came to put to sea again (very often the moment at which they were paid), ships were

often immobilized for 24 hours or more until enough men sobered up to weigh the anchor. Then they fell, or had to be eased, back into the habits of their profession; a difficult moment for all captains, but seldom a dangerous one. The Bounty's stay at Tahiti was especially long, and the men's "run ashore" especially indulgent, but the necessity of easing every body back into the cramping routine of life at sea was nothing unusual, and it was not necessarily more difficult sailing from Tahiti, where the Bounty's men had been a tiny minority in a strange society, than it would have been leaving a home port.

The weakness of naval authority ashore and in port was no more than an aspect of the general weakness of central government in 18th century Britain. With feeble party structure in the House of Commons, a very small working Civil Service in Whitehall, few paid agents in the provinces and no police force, the authority of the government depended largely on cooperation and persuasion. Its powers to force people to act against their local interests were few. Moreover, most men still thought naturally in terms of local and personal loyalties which bound together the people of a village or locality regardless of differences of wealth or birth. There is no doubt that what we would call class identification was growing by 1789, especially in the new industrial cities, but it had a long way to go before it became the natural way in which most people thought of their common interests.

In the Navy, this made the ship the natural social unit, in which men looked to their captain as their patron and protector. Good captains were able to man their ships at least in part with those who had followed them from earlier voyages, and the better an officer, the larger and better his following, and the greater the professional advantage he reaped by a skilled and happy ship's company. Admirals were followed by officers in the same way, and in all cases the patron was expected to reward loyalty and good service by promotion. To a great extent the Admiralty had to delegate the promotion of officers, especially on foreign stations; to commanders-in-chief, and their authority was supported by their power to reward good service. Within ships the power to rate or disrate, and the power to recommend to comissioned or warrant rank, lay entirely in the captain's hands.

■ A detail of a John Webber engraving, showing naval dress in the 18th century. *National Maritime Museum.*

Thus the Service was bound together by vertical ties of patronage and service which owed very little to central authority or formal discipline.

It seems certain, however, that these ties were weakening by the time of the Bounty mutiny, and were to weaken much faster during the war years which followed. The reasons for this are still obscure, but it has something to do with the rise of Admiralty authority, progressively taking more and more powers of promotion into its own hands, undermining the influence of admirals and captains, and centralizing power within the Navy. The effect was to make naval discipline harsher, as a remote and impersonal authority substituted its unyielding power for the more flexible and personal bonds which had formerly held the Navy together. The sharp rise in class and political consciousness generated by the French revolution only speeded up changes which were already in progress, and injected a strong element of mutual antagonism and fear to divide quarter deck from lower deck. We should beware of exaggerating these changes; a recent study concludes that captains in the Navy administered their ships in much the same spirit that Justices of the Peace ashore dispensed justice in their districts, but there is no doubt that in both cases change was taking place, and that it was

tending to drive officers and their men slowly apart.

This brings us to mutiny, one of the several aspects of 18th century naval life in which Hollywood has so thoroughly distorted popular perceptions that an effort of imagination is required to recreate the original context. Mutinies such as the Bounty suffered, in which a ship was violently seized from her officers on the high seas, happened occasionally in merchantmen and privateers, but had hitherto been almost unknown in the Navy. Incidents frequently occurred which were styled "mutinies", but they fitted very closely into the established pattern of riots ashore. It has been said that "the study of the pre-industrial crowd suggests that it rioted for precise objects and rarely engaged in indiscriminate attacks on either properties or persons": this was how men behaved in the Navy. There were well-established and effective procedures for men to make known complaints, and they generally found senior officers willing to redress reasonable grievances, but sometimes things went wrong. If they had grievances which had not been attended to, the men would stage a noisy demonstration accompanied by a token refusal to obey some order, often to weigh anchor. Much noise would be generated, often the men went ashore in a body to speak to the port admiral, but the officers involved seldom seem to have felt themselves in any danger. Such "mutinies" invariably conformed to a series of unwritten rules:

1. No mutiny may take place at sea, or in the presence of the enemy.

2. No personal violence may be employed.

3. Mutinies may only be staged in pursuance of objects sanctioned by the traditions of the Service (such as the payment of overdue back pay or the ejection of intolerable officers).

Genuine lower-deck mutiny invariably conformed to these rules, and so long as it did, authority had been accustomed to regard it with a weary tolerance. The reaction was always to remove the grievance complained of and smooth over the business as quickly as possible; never to punish the mutineers. In this as in other matters, however, there was a tendency as the 18th century drew to its close for attitudes to harden, for authority to treat even the most moderate and traditional of mutinies as a threat to the established order, calling for harsh punishment as a deterrent to others. This process was enormously accelerated by the French Revolution, presenting a terrible example of the dangers of giving the lower orders their head, and destroying for ever the casual, even relaxed attitude towards mutiny held by officers 30 years before.

But attitudes towards mutinies which broke the unwritten rules had never been casual. Such mutinies, though rare, did occur, and when they did it invariably appeared that they had been openly led or covertly incited by officers.

The men always kept to the established principles of naval mutiny, but officers sometimes did not. Christian, of course, was an officer, and it seems most unlikely that the grievances of the Bounty's men, whatever they were, would have issued in mutiny on the high seas unless an officer had taken the lead. Only once before in that century had one of HM ships been seized by mutineers away from port, and in that case too it had been the First Lieutenant who had been responsible. The Chesterfield was at anchor off Cape Coast Castle on the coast of West Africa in 1748, her captain and most of his officers dining ashore with the governor, when Lieutenant Couchman took over the ship and put to sea, declaring his intention of turning pirate. A few days, later the ship's company, led by the Boatswain who was the only other officer left aboard, recaptured her and confined Couchman, who was later court-martialled and shot. Couchman can have had no rational hopes of a successful career in piracy in 1748; and it seems impossible to attribute his actions to anything except personal instability. He may have had real grievances, and he was certainly drunk the night of the mutiny, but like Christian he was undertaking something irrational to the point of being suicidal. The Bounty mutiny has sometimes been seen as belonging to the new Romantic era, even as the inspiration for Coleridge's "*Rime of the Ancient Mariner*", and it is true

Wordsworth was a friend of the Christians. Perhaps it is reasonable to see Christian as a Byronic figure, a Manfred tortured by his own sensibilities; some such instability would have been required to produce the extraordinary situation of mutiny on the high seas. Common seamen had more sense.

In the past, the social history of the Navy has very frequently been illustrated by reference to the Bounty mutiny, or to some imaginary version of it. In particular, it has often been said that simple brutality lay at the bottom of it, and that brutality was characteristic of relations between officers and men in the 18th century Navy. In fact, Bligh was a humane officer, perhaps weak but certainly not cruel. Nor was cruelty typical of the Navy. What seems, in the present state of our knowledge, to be true is that the old rough intimacy, the close personal bonds of shared service and mutual dependency which had held the Navy together 30 or 40 years before, were slowly yielding to a more modern and impersonal system, with a more powerful central authority, more rigid control over the life of the Service at every level, and a harsher discipline. With this development came the slow but steady rise of class sentiment which was gradually teaching officers and men to suspect and fear each other. How far these movements had gone by 1789 is at present hard to say; probably far less than they were to travel under the impetus given by the example of Revolutionary France. Perhaps they provide some partial explanation, or at least some context, for the tensions which gave rise to the Bounty mutiny, but they cannot possibly give us a complete reason for it. Only under the leadership of an officer could such a mutiny have occurred, and only perhaps an officer acting outside the bounds of rationality. There is nothing yet known in the ordinary social life of the Navy in 1789 which could fairly account for mutiny on the high seas.

Nicholas Rodger is an Assistant Keeper in the Public Record Office.

■ Luxborough Galley (1727). One of a series commissioned by Commander Boys in 1728 after it was lost by fire in the Atlantic. 23 survivors took to a launch but only seven survived – the others died through cannibalism. *National Maritime Museum.*

*'It is possible that it may not come, during our lives.
We shall not see the triumph.'*
'We shall have helped it,' returned madame.

A TALE OF TWO CITIES
Charles Dickens 1812-1870

The Financial Times
celebrates the first year of
simultaneous printing
in London and Roubaix

FINANCIAL TIMES
EUROPE'S BUSINESS NEWSPAPER

The Pacific: Great Unknown

Any European power with naval pretensions made for the Pacific in the 18th century. Glyn Williams follows the explorers and reveals some of the fascination the huge ocean held.

AS LATE as the middle of the 18th century Europe's knowledge of the Pacific basin, covering almost one-third of the earth's surface, was sketchy and incomplete. The situation was transformed in the last 40 years of the century, when a spectacular surge of seaborne exploration, associated above all with the voyages of James Cook, resulted in the discovery and mapping of the previously unknown areas of the great ocean. Left unqualified, this statement would give a misleading impression of the nature of that "discovery". Long before Magellan's ships entered the Pacific in 1520, its 25,000 or so islands had been subject to a steady process of exploration, migration, and settlement. To its own inhabitants the Pacific was known, and some indication of their knowledge is suggested by the map drawn for Cook in 1769 by Tupaia, a priest or *arii* from Raiatea (one of the Society Islands Taking its centre at Tahiti, the map showed 74 islands in all, scattered aross an area of ocean measuring about three thousand miles from east to west, and a thousand miles from north to south. Although some of the map is difficult to interpret now because of name changes, and an arrangement of islands in concentric circles based on sailing times rather than linear distances, it remains, in the words of one of Cook's scientists, "a monument of the ingenuity and geographical knowledge of the people of the Society Islands".

If we turn to a European map of the Pacific of the early 18th century, then it is clear that the uncertainties far outnumbered the certainties. Although from Magellan onwards Europeans of several nations – Spaniards, French, Dutch, English – had ventured into and sometimes across the great ocean, their explorations were for the most part inconclusive if not downright confusing. The immensity of the ocean, problems in ascertaining longitude, the threat of scurvy on the one hand, mutiny on the other, and the constraints of wind and current, posed formidable obstacles to methodical exploration. In the north Pacific stretched the one regular European trade route across the ocean, that of the annual galleon between Acapulco and Manila which touched at Guam in the Marianas. Japan was roughly charted, but the ocean to the north and east remained unexplored. The Pacific coast of America was known only as far north as California; what lay beyond was a matter of guesswork. How far east Asia stretched was equally problematical; and what lay in the colossal void, 5,000 thousand miles or more, between Kamchatka and California, was a mystery. The darkness might conceal ocean or land, islands or continent, a land-bridge between Asia and America, or the entrances to the North-west and North-east passages.

In the south Pacific, some knowledge had been obtained of the islands on the diagonal sailing course between the tip of South America and New Guinea – the Tuamotus, the Marquesas, Santa Cruz, the Solomons, Espiritu Santo – but their location shifted from voyage to voyage. "There are in the South-Sea many Islands, which may be called Wandering-Islands," an English geographer drily remarked in the l750s. The coastline of New Guinea, the western half of New Holland (Australia), and stretches of the shoreline of Van Diemen's land (Tasmania) and New Zealand were known from Dutch and Spanish explorations; but the relationship between these lands was far from clear. In particular it was not known whether any of them formed part of the hypothetical southern continent – *Terra Australis Incognita*. The concept of a southern continent was as old as geographical science, for Ptolemy in the second century AD had argued that there was a huge counter-balancing land mass in the southern hemisphere, and later advocates were not unduly depressed by the failure of the explorers of the 16th and 17th centuries to bring back conclusive evidence. Since the prevailing winds tended to push vessels onto a track which slanted away from high latitudes as they left Cape Horn or the Straits of Magellan map-makers merely had to shift the continent a degree or two farther south. Geographers found compensation for this limited retreat by hinting that the islands or cloud-banks sighted by explorers to the south were the capes or mountain tops of a continent lying just over the horizon.

In the European opening of the Pacific, the quest for knowledge for its own sake, though never entirely absent, was not a dominant force. The major powers of Europe were rivals overseas as they were nearer home. Exchanges of information were reluctant, and although total secrecy was an almost unattainable goal, it was still a lingering ideal. Europe's interest in the Pacific was practical and chauvinistic; so in the pages of Hakluyt and Purchas it was the circumnavigations of Drake and Cavendish, spectacular in intention but meagre in geographical information, which took the limelight. When English interest revived in the later 17th century the motives were the same as those which had prompted the Elizabethans: trade and plunder. The Pacific caught the English imagination not as a vast, trackless ocean but as the western rim of Spain's American empire. The "South Sea" which now began to exercize its fascination over distant enterprises was confined, in English eyes, to the waters

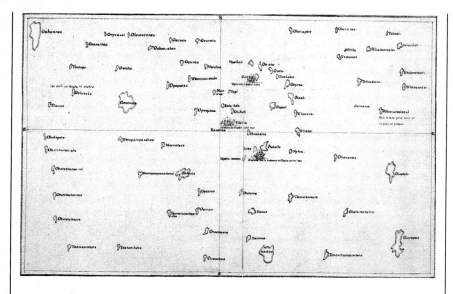

surpassed in exploration terms by the Dutch voyage of Roggeveen in 1722 which touched at Easter Island and Samoa.

More significant as a precursor of the Pacific expeditions of the second half of the 18th century were the voyages of Edmond Halley in the *Paramore* (1698-1701), concerned to prospect new navigational methods rather than new lands, and above all "to improve the knowledge of the Longitude and variations of the Compasse". They stand out in the history of English oceanic enterprise, not least in the burgeoning relationship they showed between the Admiralty and the Royal Society, a relationship which reached proper consummation in the Pacific voyages of George III's reign. Although there was originally some intention of reaching "the East Indies or South Seas", Halley's voyages took him no further than the South Atlantic, and the largest blank space on his magnificent world map of 1702 showing magnetic variation was the Pacific. As he explained: "I durst not presume to describe the like Curves in the South Sea wanting accounts thereof." Accounts or no accounts, the region was no longer quite *terra incognita*. The seas beyond Cape Horn were not simply the haunts of buccaneers and adventurers; they also provided the setting for some of the most popular imaginative fiction and satire of the period – from *Robinson Crusoe* to *Gulliver's Travels*. Interest and activity fell away after the collapse of overseas "bubble" projects in England and France in 1720. As Daniel Defoe complained it was "as if we had done our utmost, were fully satisfied with what we have, that the enterprising Genius was buried with the old Discoverers, and there was neither Room in the World nor Inclination in our People to look any further".

Revival of interest came with the heightening of international tension in the middle decades of the century, and in particular with Anson's voyage across the Pacific and around the world (1740-44), that melodramatic episode of wartime achievement and disaster which brought back memories of Drake and half forgotten feats of English arms

which lapped the shores of Chile, Peru, and Mexico; and attention was centred on the exploits of the buccaneers who pillaged and burnt along the Pacific shores of Spanish America. Among them were men with literary skills, notably William Dampier, a perceptive observer whose books became classics of travel and adventure. Although Spanish America and the East Indies saw most of him, he also ventured into areas on the very periphery of Europe's knowledge. He visited the western shores of Australia in 1688 and 1699, and just east of New Guinea discovered the islands of New Britain. In general, though, the voyages of Dampier and his privateer-successors such as Rogers and Shelvocke produced little in the way either of geographical or commercial benefit. They paled in importance before the altogether more numerous and expert French trading ventures to the Pacific coasts of Spanish America and across to China, and were

against the Spain of Philip II. The official narrative of the expedition became a bestseller. It was more than a tale of treasure-seeking on the high seas, though this no doubt was the prime reason for its popularity. At one level it was designed to encourage "the more important purposes of navigation, commerce and national interest", interpreted by another mercantile writer of the same period in terms of establishing a new empire in the Pacific, ranging from New Guinea in the west to Juan Fernandez in the east and, it was hoped, including the vast southern continent. At another it made an appeal to the imagination, with reminders of Crusoe's island and Rousseau's Nouvelle-Héloise. It strengthened the hold of tropical island fantasies on the European consciousness, a continuing fascination which was to last into the 19th century with Melville, Stevenson, and Gauguin.

As considerations of geography, politics, and trade combined in pointing to the Pacific as one of the most important global objectives left to Europeans, so in Paris in 1756 Charles de Brosses published the first collection of voyages devoted exclusively to the Pacific, – *Histoire des Navigations aux Terre Aus-*

■ Portrait of William Dampier by Thomas Murray (1697-8). *National Portrait Gallery.*

trales. Plagiarized a few years later by John Callander in an English edition, confidently retitled *Terra Australis Cognita*, this work contained accounts of the main Pacific expeditions from Magellan to Anson. The accounts printed in these volumes confirmed that the earlier voyages had produced as much confusion as enlightenment. Islands had been sighted and resighted, identified and then lost again; isolated volcanic peaks had been mistaken for continental ranges; straits had become bays and bays straits. The

map of the Pacific was scarred with squiggles of coastline which hinted at undiscovered lands of continental dimensions, and dotted with island groups whose names and locations changed with the whims of cartographical fashion. As the astronomer William Wales tersely remarked while on Cook's second voyage: "I firmly believe Islands have been greatly multiplied and much confusion has arisen in the Geography of these seas from a desire of being thought the first discoverers of any land that has been seen." If the geography of the Pacific was blurred, so was knowledge of its inhabitants. The observations of the explorers were usually hasty and superficial, often the result of a visit of only a few days, sometimes only a few hours. Encounters varied from violent to friendly, but misunderstanding was more common than comprehension, and all too often contact ended with the blast of cannon or musket on one side and a shower of stones and arrows on the other.

The Seven Years' War – ominously the first European conflict of truly global

■ Map of South Pacific mid 18th century by J N Bellin. *British Library.*

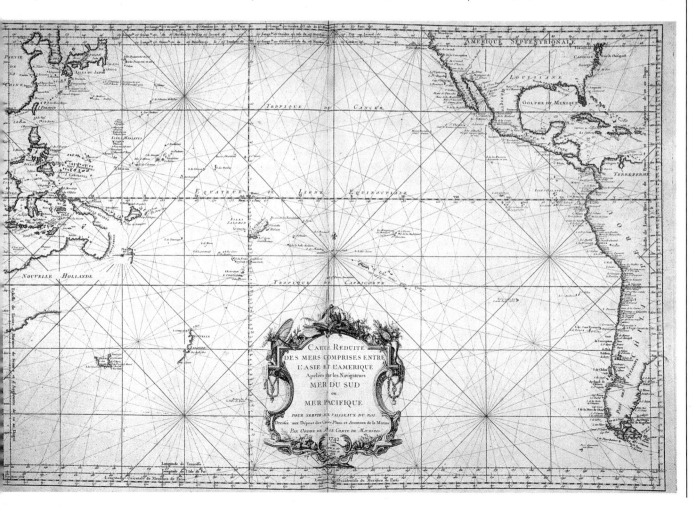

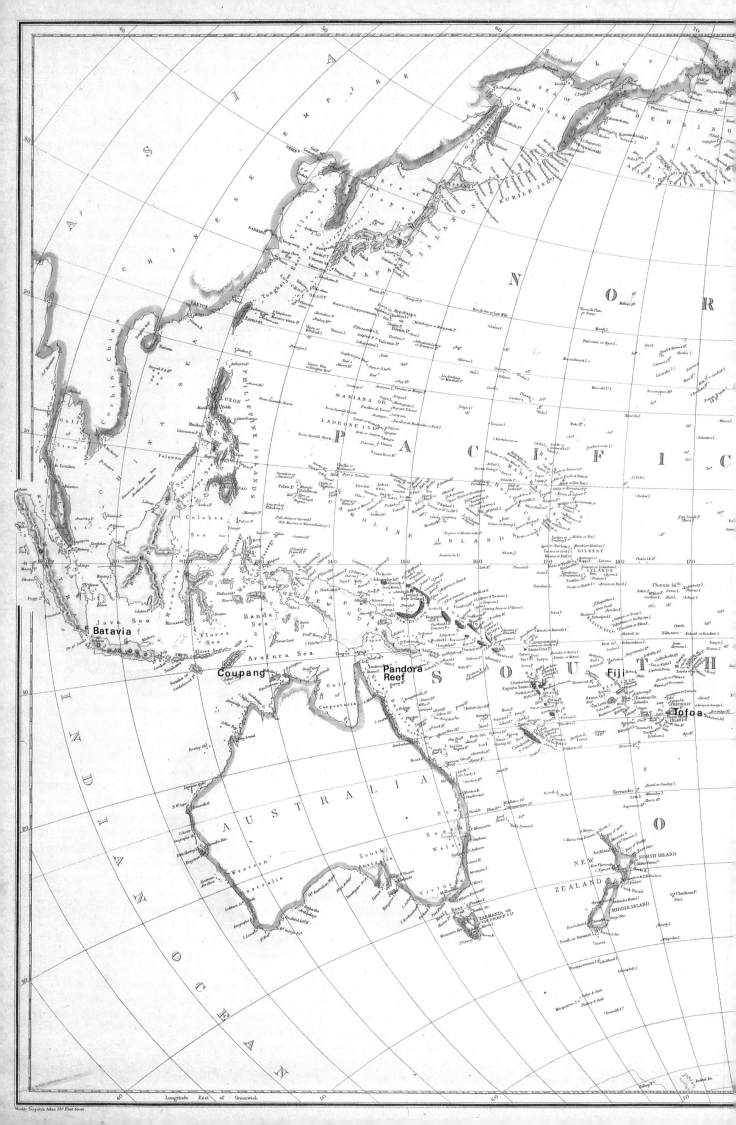

Capt. James Cook
of the Endeavour.

■ Captain James Cook by William Hodges c 1775. *National Maritime Museum.*

dimensions – put an end to talk of Pacific exploration. With the conclusion of peace in 1763 official discovery expeditions were mounted in Britain and France, though they took place in an atmosphere of continuing rivalry. The Pacific promised resources of such potential that its discovery and control might tip the commercial balance of power in Europe – for Britain confirm the overseas superiority brought by the wartime conquests, for France redress the humiliations of an unsuccessful war. The first venture in the new era of oceanic exploration was that of Commodore John Byron in 1764, a false start because despite his comprehensive instructions and his assurance to the Admiralty that he would cross the Pacific "by a new track", Byron followed the customary route west-north-west from the Strait of Magellan and made no discoveries of note. His rediscovery and annexation of the Falklands had a political rather than geographical significance, and that he completed his circumnavigation in less than two years showed his inability to distinguish between an explorer and a record-breaker.

Byron's voyage was followed by an increase in activity, for not only was the British Admiralty determined on a further Pacific expedition, but in France the bookish interest in the South Seas displayed by De Brosses had hardened into plans to forestall the English. In August 1766 Captain Samuel Wallis in the *Dolphin* and Lieutenant Philip Carteret in the *Swallow* left England for the South Seas. A few months later, the *Boudeuse* and the *Etoile* sailed from France under the command of one of the outstanding Frenchmen of the day, Louis Antoine de Bougainville, aristocrat, soldier, diplomat, bound for the Falklands and the Pacific. Carteret proved an enterprising commander and crossed the Pacific farther south than any other explorer had done, so making considerable inroads into the conjectural southern continent. He also rediscovered, though he did not identify, the Solomon Islands, almost two centuries after they had first been sighted by the Spaniards. Wallis, by contrast,

■ The Resolution at Nootka Sound 1778 by John Webber. *British Library.*

showed little initiative in his track across the Pacific, but his voyage was marked by a chance discovery whose emotional impact was out of all proportion to its geographical significance, for in June 1767 he sighted Tahiti. As the crew prepared for landing, the master of the *Dolphin* described his initial reactions – "the most Beautiful appearance its posable to Imagin ... a fine Leavel country that appears to be all laid out in plantations ... Great Numbers of Cocoa Nut Trees ... beautiful valeys between the Mountains ... tall Trees ... the most populoss country I ever saw, the whole shore side was lined with men women and children." It was one of those encounters between sailors and Polynesian women which was to stamp an erotic imprint upon Europe's image of the South Seas. To the breaking surf, the palm-fringed beaches, and the gentle climate were added sensuous overtones – of welcoming, garlanded women. When Bougainville's ships reached Tahiti the following year, reactions were even more effusive and extravagant. The island was named New Cythera by some of the French in memory of Aphrodite's island, and for long Tahiti was to remain a symbol of the romance of the Pacific islands

■ View from Point Venus, Tahiti by William Hodges. *National Maritime Museum.*

in defiance of those cautionary voices which pointed to the darker side of life there. A quarter of a century later, George Hamilton, surgeon of the *Pandora,* then hunting down the *Bounty* mutineers, wrote of Tahiti in terms reminiscent of those first European encounters: "The Cytheria of the southern hemisphere ... where the earth without tillage produces both food and cloathing, the trees loaded with the most odoriferous flowers, and the fair ones ever willing to fill your arms with love."

Despite these additions by British and French explorers to knowledge of the island groups of the south Pacific, little progress had been made towards solving the crucial issue of the southern continent. Although Bougainville had sailed westward from Tahiti to find that the Espiritu Santo of the earlier Spanish explorers was insular rather than continental the New Hebrides (or Vanuatu), the lands east of New Holland remained marked on the maps as they appeared after the Dutch discoveries of the previous century – in effect, swirling question marks. Yet within a few years there was no longer any doubt. The south Pacific took shape on the maps in much the same form as it does today, and the man responsible for this leap in knowledge, and for much else, was James Cook. His three voyages, following each other in

quick succession, revealed the Pacific to Europe in a way no previous explorations had done. As the books, maps, and views came off the presses – not only in England, but also in France, Holland, Germany and Italy – Cook became a figure of European renown. Other explorers were in the Pacific during the years that Cook's ships were out, but attention was focused on the methodical, comprehensive explorations of the remarkable Englishman.

Lieutenant Cook, as he was on his first voyage, had taken part in the surveying of the St Lawrence during Wolfe's campaign in Quebec, and in the first years of peace between 1763 and 1767 had made detailed charts of the intricate coastline of Newfoundland. He had studied, in practical fashion, mathematics and astronomy, and in contrast to some of his predecessors in the Pacific possessed the technical skills needed to make an effective explorer. The next few years were to show that in addition he was gifted with those less tangible qualities of leadership, determination, and judgment which were to make him the outstanding explorer of the 18th century. As he once wrote, it was his ambition not only to go "farther than any man has been before me, but as far as I think it possible for man to go". Supported by an Admiralty willing to allow detailed publication of the voy-

agers' findings, Cook and his officers were able to give a fuller picture than had emerged during the previous two centuries of sporadic, often secretive, exploration.

Cook's first voyage (1768-71) was a collaborative venture by the Admiralty and the Royal Society. The instructions for the voyage – more detailed than those of Byron or Wallis – were to report on all aspects of new lands discovered and to bring back specimens, drawings, and surveys. With him went the young and wealthy botanist, Joseph Banks, who fol-

lowed the example set by the French (Bougainville had on board the naturalist Commerson and the astronomer Véron) and took on the voyage a small retinue of assistants – the Swedish naturalist, Solander, secretary and draughtsman, Spöring, and the artists, Buchan and Parkinson. Though the scientific equipment seems primitive by modern standards, the ships used on the Pacific voyages were in 18th century terms floating laboratories, while the Admiralty put on board a range of experimental equipment and food, ranging from a device for dis-

tilling sea water to a supply of, it was hoped, anti-scorbutic carrot marmalade. Even Dr Johnson had called for voyagers with a scientific turn of mind, intent on "ever object of curiosity, and at leisure for the most minute remarks".

Shortly before the expedition sailed, the President of the Royal Society, Lord Morton, appealed to Cook and Banks for "the utmost patience and forbearance with respect to the natives of the several lands where the ship may touch", and encouraged them "to observe the genius, temper, disposition, and number of the

natives". Predictably, Cook felt more at ease describing the geography of the Pacific than the culture of its peoples. However difficult to follow a shoreline might be, it could be traced, surveyed, pinned down on a chart in exact outline. Investigation of the human population had no such firm and recognized basis on which to proceed. Not only was there among the peoples of the three great divisions of the Pacific – Polynesia, Melanesia, and Micronesia – no fundamental similarity of language and custom, but there was no accepted method of categorization and classification. Europeans were entering a region where after successive migrations, and a seeping of culture influences from one island group to another, societies were organized in a series of baffling, overlapping layers; and the tools the explorers possessed to probe these tesselated areas of humanity were crude and poorly adapted to the task. Problems of comprehension were made more difficult because of the strained nature of the contact. The Pacific navigators of the period were for the most part moderate and humane, by earlier standards remarkably so. Even so, the Europeans were intruders, emerging by the score from their great vessel anchored in some island bay, *atua* or "men from the sky", appearing and disappearing without warning, often violating sacred sites. Over the encounters between voyagers and islanders hung an inescapable tension, sometimes dissi-

■ The Bark 'Earl of Pembroke' – later Endeavour – leaving Whitby Harbour by Thomas Luny. *National Library of Australia.*

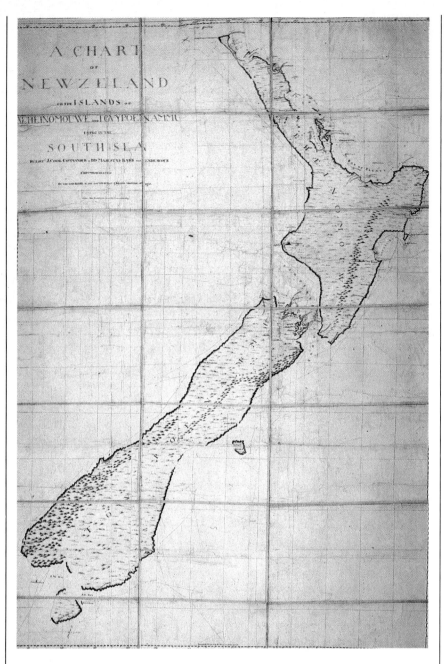

A CHART
of
NEW ZEELAND
or the ISLANDS of
AEHEINOMOUWE and TOVYPOENAMMU
lying in the
SOUTH SEA

pated by individual contacts and trade which offered benefits to both sides, but on other occasions erupting into violence. In the longer term, the introduction of venereal disease, alcohol, and firearms brought a depressing and familiar train of circumstances – sickness, demoralization, depopulation.

This was all in the future when Cook, still unknown outside a narrow circle of naval men, left England in 1768 in the *Endeavour* for his first Pacific voyage. His vessel was not the usual neat naval sloop or frigate, but a bluff-bowed Whitby collier chosen for her strength, shallow draught and storage capacity. Although Cook's ship was to change, the type was not. The *Resolution* of the second and third voyages was of the same build and even came from the same ship-

■ Cook's Chart of New Zealand 1770. *National Maritime Museum.*

yard as the *Endeavour*, of which vessel Cook wrote: "It was to these Properties in her those on board owe their Preservation. Hence I was able to prosecute Discoveries in those Seas so much longer than any other Man ever did or could do." He sailed first to Tahiti to carry out those astronomical observations for the Royal Society which were the ostensible reason for the voyage before he turned south where, his secret instructions told him, "there is reason to imagine that a Continent or Land of great extent, may be found". But he reached latitude 40°S without sighting land, and he noted that the long rolling swell coming from the south argued against the existence of any

land-mass in that direction. He then turned west to New Zealand whose coasts he mapped in a little over six months by means of a superb running survey from the sea which showed, among much else, that the two islands were not part of any continent. From there Cook pointed the *Endeavour* towards that region of mystery, the unexplored eastern parts of New Holland. Cook reached Australian shores just north of Van Diemen's Land, and coasted northwards, stopping at Botany Bay, and then at Endeavour River after the vessel was almost wrecked on the Great Barrier Reef. From there he sailed through Torres Strait, and so settled the uncertainty whether New Holland and New Guinea were separated. He had carried out his instructions, and more – as he later told a French inquirer, an explorer who simply followed orders would never accomplish great things. With only one ship, and without the loss of a single man from scurvy he had put more than 5,000 miles of previously unknown coastline on the map. The twin islands of New Zealand, the east coast of Australia, and Torres Strait, had at last emerged from the mists of uncertainty. On the significance of his voyage as far as it related to the great southern continent, Cook was emphatic and sceptical: "I do not believe that any such thing exists unless in a high latitude ... hanging Clowds and a thick horizon are certainly no known Signs of a Continent."

This feat of detailed exploration had been accomplished without the loss of a single man from scurvy, that terrible scourge of the sea caused, we know now, by vitamin C deficiency. Cook's achievements would not have been possible without healthy crews, and his record in this respect was an impressive one. There were no deaths from scurvy on his second and third voyages, and very few from natural causes generally. Yet, in the 1740s, Anson's expedition around the world had lost three-quarters of its men. Four had died from enemy action, more than 1,300 from disease, mostly from scurvy. Much research had gone into scurvy since Anson's voyage, notably by James Lind at the Haslar Naval Hospital. He had "cracked" the problem with his discovery, or rather rediscovery, of the anti-scorbutic properties of lemon juice. The work of specialists has corrected the popular view that it was Cook who discovered and applied the cure for scurvy on long sea voyages. Paradoxically,

■ Ice Islands on Cook's Second Voyage by William Hodges.

Cook's success in keeping his crews alive delayed the acceptance of the remedy for scurvy, for although he used lemon juice he attributed no particular importance to it, and preferred sauerkraut and malt wort (which contain no vitamin C). What was unusual about Cook was the thoroughness with which he carried out a whole range of anti-scorbutic measures. His crews were given only a small ration of salt meat. Instead, sauerkraut, vinegar, orange, and lemon juice, malt wort, and (whenever they could be found) fresh meat and vegetables were substituted. Cook had men flogged for refusing to follow their prescribed diet; he used subterfuges to persuade them to eat sauerkraut and walrus meat. Exacting standards of cleanliness were enforced; dry clothing and bedding were provided; lower decks were kept dry by stove. Uncertain of the causes of scurvy, Cook combined all suggested remedies in a

■ Map of the supposed new discoveries in the North Pacific, by Philippe Buache (1752). *British Library*.

way described by the medical historian, Sir James Watt, as "the blunderbuss approach which confused the issue by failing to differentiate true anti-scorbutics from the empirical remedies of long-standing tradition". Even so, as the contributor to a medical journal claimed in 1799, Cook had "proved to the world the possibility of carrying a ship's crew through a variety of climates, for the, space of near four years, without losing one man by disease; a circumstance which added more to his fame, and is supposed to have given a more useful

lesson to maritime nations, than all the discoveries he ever made".

The public saw the first voyage through the eyes of John Hawkesworth, who fused the separate journals of Cook and Banks into a single narrative to make the *Endeavour* expedition the resounding climax to his three-volume *Voyages* of 1773, which also took in the accounts of Byron, Wallis, and Carteret. An editor of literary rather than nautical expertize, Hawkesworth inserted reflective and philosophical passages, switched locations and opinions, and made frequent and sometimes substantive changes to the journals. Publication led to dispute and controversy in which Hawkesworth was attacked by John Wesley among others for the work's frank description of Polynesian sexual customs, for scepticism about the "particular interposition of Providence", and for technical inaccuracies. Doubts about the handling of the text were summed up by Boswell when he remarked to Cook that Hawkesworth "has used your narrative as a London tavern keeper does wine. He has *brewed* it." The stir which all this caused no doubt helped Cook and his successors to keep publication of their later journals

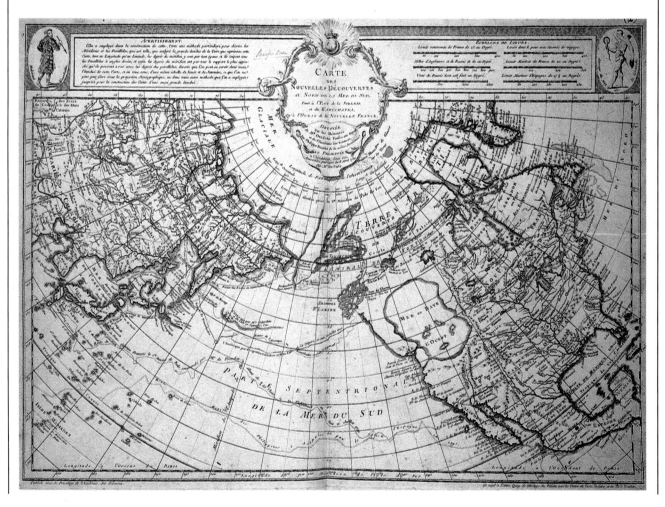

■ Resolution and Discovery in ice. August 1778. *The Peabody Museum of Salem.*

out of the clutches of literary gentlemen, but there can no doubting the impact of Hawkesworth' s *Voyages.* As one newspaper remarked: "It may be called a real authentic Account of a new world, such as no European could have figured in his own Imagination."

Cook was to read and be irritated by Hawkesworth's *Voyages*, but not for two years after publication, for by 1773 he was in the Pacific again. On his first voyage Cook had lopped a considerable slice off the supposed continent of the south, but there remained vast unexplored stretches in the high latitudes of the Atlantic, Pacific, and Indian oceans where land might yet be found. Pressure in Britain for another voyage grew as reports came in that the French were again sending expeditions to the Pacific: four in fact visited the southern seas between 1770 and 1773, hunting for islands and continents, but accomplished little in the way of coherent exploration. The Spaniards were also stirred into activity in these years, and the Viceroy of Peru sent ships to investigate Easter Island and Tahiti. Their report led to further visits to Tahiti, and even the establishment there in 1775 of a short-lived Franciscan mission. So in 1772, Cook left England to search once more for the great southern continent. There was no Banks with him this time, but instead that learned if prickly man of science, Johann Reinhold Forster, and his son George, as well as the painter William Hodges, whose luminous landscapes evoked the South Seas as no artist had

done before. Cook also had on board chronometers, one of which was Kendall's copy of John Harrison's masterpiece, his fourth marine timekeeper. The instrument proved itself by keeping accurate time through the buffeting of the long voyage, and one of the most persistent problems of oceanic navigation had been overcome.

Cook's second Pacific expedition (1772-75) was arguably the greatest, most perfect, of seaborne voyages of discovery. In his three years away he disposed of the imagined southern continent, reached closer to the South Pole than any man before him, and touched on a multitude of lands – New Zealand and Tahiti again, and for the first time Easter Island, the Marquesas, Tonga, New Caledonia, the New Hebrides, and South Georgia. In doing so he confirmed, located, and connected many of the uncertain discoveries of earlier explorers which had brought so much confusion to the map of the Pacific. In high latitudes, he crossed and recrossed the Antarctic Circle in a series of long, methodical sweeps. At his farthest south he reached latitude 71°S before being stopped by the ice barrier which encircles the immense continent of the south. This was not the fertile land of the theorists' dreams, but the frozen Antarctic – in Cook's words, "a Country doomed by Nature never once to feel the warmth of the Suns rays, but to lie for ever buried under everlasting snow and ice". There was, Cook judged, little more to do in the south Pacific. He thought "the Southern Hemi-

■ Resolution and Discovery in Ice, by John Webber c 1770. *National Maritime Museum.*

sphere sufficiently explored and a final end put to the searching after a Southern Continent, which has at times ingrossed the attention of some of the Maritime Powers for near two Centuries past and the Geographers of all ages". From the safety of his Strawberry Hill study, Horace Walpole was even more dismissive – "they fetched blood of a great whale called Terra Australis *incognita*, but saw nothing but its tail". It would be wrong to think of Cook's achievement as a negative one. In his first two voyages he had established the framework of the modern map of the south Pacific, Polynesia, and southern Melanesia; New Zealand and New South Wales; Torres

Strait and the southern extremities of the great ocean.

Cook's third and final voyage (1776-80) had its own logic in that it took him to the north Pacific in an effort to solve that, other long-standing geographical mystery – the existence of a North-west Passage. Given the contemporary obsession with South Sea islands, it is easy to overlook the fact that the first great increase in Europe's knowledge of the Pacific in the 18th century had come from Russia, where Bering in the 1740s followed by other navigators sailing east from Kamchatka had thrown a flickering light on the geography of the north Pacific. Although there were scientists with

Bering, the failure to publish the working charts of the Russian explorers, and the eagerness of speculative geographers to fill the spaces with their own eccentric creations, brought mystification rather than illumination to the scene. The Spaniards, too, sailed north from Lower California in the 1760s and 1770s and touched Alaska; but again little was known of these voyages at the time. Cook, who by now in effect wrote his own instructions, intended to head for latitude 65°N on the north-west coast of America where the maps suggested the existence of an ice-free passage through to the Atlantic. He sailed once more in the *Resolution*, with the *Discovery* as his

consort. On board the two vessels were a dozen future captains – among them the master of the *Resolution*, William Bligh, at 22 years unusually young for so responsible a position.

Once again, as on his previous voyages, Cook called at Tahiti, and for a second time at Tonga, before heading northwest and into the unknown. At Tahiti the grim centrepiece of Cook's visit was his presence at a ceremony of human sacrifice; his surgeon counted at least 50 skulls at the *marai*, and suspected that "the practice is extended all over the islands of these seas". In taking the unfrequented route from the Society Islands to the north-west coast of Ameri-

ca, Cook made the big, and for himself fatal, discovery of the Sandwich (Hawaiian) Islands, before turning to the main task. The summer of 1778 he spent in hazardous exploration along the coast from Nootka Sound to Bering Strait, searching in vain for the way through to the open Arctic Ocean shown on the maps of the theoretical geographers. No such passage was found before Bering Strait was reached, and after only a week's sailing through that narrow opening Cook found his way blocked by ice grinding down upon his ships. He had been imposed upon to the world's advantage, his biographer John Beaglehole has written; and the results of this single season of exploration were indeed impressive. Although unaware of the insular nature of much of the coastline along which he was sailing, Cook charted the main outline of America's shores from Mount St Elias to Bering Strait, determined the shape of the Alaskan peninsula, and touched on the coast of modern British Columbia. He closed the gap between the Russian and Spanish probes, and for the first time the region takes recognisable form on the maps.

On the return track, Cook was killed at Hawaii in February 1779, news which overshadowed all other reports from the voyage when it reached England. The Earl of Sandwich, First Lord of the Admiralty, wrote to Banks: "What is uppermost in our minds always must come out first, poor captain Cooke is no more." Cook's death brought into sharper focus the conflict of attitudes about the peoples of the Pacific which had developed both among the discovery crews and in Europe. To those who had seen the islands, Tahiti and its neighbours might be nearer to an earthy paradise than any other region known to man, but they now realized that there was shade as well as light – there was war, infanticide, distinctions of rank, and property. The killing of Cook, following as it did the massacre of one of his boat crews in New Zealand in 1773, and the killing of the French navigator Marion de Fresne and two dozen of his men not far away a year earlier, was proof to many of an innately treacherous and murderous disposition. There were others who saw in the islands traces of the golden age of man's past, and feared that it was European influences which were corrupting and contaminating. More dispassionate observers were influenced by the fashionable insistence in European philosophical circles on measuring human societies by their capacity and desire for improvement. And whether the discoverers and the readers of their accounts looked at the incurious Aborigines or the boisterous Tahitians, they found few Pacific peoples who conformed to western ideals of progress and development.

To see the importance of Cook's voyages in terms only of maps and mapping would be to underestimate their broader significance. There was more to the achievement than the accumulation of geographical knowledge; there was, if it is not too grand a term, a new methodology. It was European rather than narrowly English in scope, but its clearest manifestation in this period came by way of Cook's voyages. Boswell hinted at it when he observed of the explorer that he had "a ballance in his mind for truth as nice as scales for weighing a guinea". It was the insistent determination to show things as they were, to dispel myths and illusions by way of empirical observation, and prompt publication. This is the keynote of the journals of Cook and his successors – and the indignation which greeted Hawkesworth's free adaptations revealed something of this, of the "dispassionate investigation of the truth", as

■ Human Sacrifice at Tahiti by John Webber. *British Library.*

George Vancouver termed it. Ice-free north-west passages, fertile southern continents, fabulous islands of silver and gold, had no place in this approach. Scholars might carp at the amateurish nature of some of the observations, but there was more precision and less fiction about the accounts now. As Sparrman, who was with Cook on his second voyage, wrote: "Men with one foot, indeed, Cyclops, Syrens, Troglodytes, and such like imaginary beings, have almost entirely disappeared."

The observations made by Cook and his associates played an important role in hydrography, oceanography, meteorology, and astronomy – and much else. In the realm of natural history, the voyages were among the great collecting expeditions of any era. The specimens, sketches, data brought back were overwhelming in their profusion. The amount of material simply could not be assimilated by the older encyclopædic science; the polymaths – the Banks and the Forsters – were to be superseded by the specialists. Above all there was the human dimension. Neither Cook nor his scientific companions had any training in anthropological investigation because there was none to be had. It was their voyages which helped to give birth in the next century to the new disciplines of ethnology and anthropology; for the earnest inquiry by the explorers into the exotic life styles which confronted them, and their careful if uninformed collection of data, brought a new urgency to the need for a more systematic study of man. As the younger Forster noted: "What Cook has added to the mass of our knowledge is such that it will strike deep roots and will long have the most decisive influence on the activity of men."

On his three voyages, Cook had established the salient features of the Pacific. Much remained to be done, but mainly in the way of defining detail rather than in solving important geographical problems. There were further voyages of exploration to the Pacific before the end of the century: the tragic expedition of La Pérouse, Vancouver's painstaking survey of the north-west American coast which corrected and completed Cook's charts; the Spanish venture under Malaspina – the most elaborate of them all – and D'Entrecasteaux's search expedition for La Pérouse. Cook's men dominated the British voyages to the Pacific, whether for exploration or

trade: Bligh, Dixon, Portlock, Colnett, Riou, Hergest, Vancouver, had graduated in the most demanding of training schools. As William Windham remarked to James Burney on hearing of Bligh's open-boat voyage after the mutiny: "But what officers you are! you men of Captain Cook; you rise upon us in every trial." It was Bligh who had helped to bring the ships home in 1780 after the death both of Cook and then, a few months later, of Charles Clerke, captain of the *Discovery*. His surveys, charts, and views formed an important part of the published account of the voyage, and brought him one-eighth of the profits from the publication of 1784, if not proper acknowledgment of his efforts.

The editor of the Journals of the third voyage, John Douglas, pointed the way forward to the next stage of Pacific enterprise when he wrote in his introduction that, "every nation that sends a ship to sea will partake of the benefit [of the published accounts]; but Great Britain herself, whose commerce is boundless, must take the lead in reaping the full advantage of her own discoveries". By the end of the century, there were British settlements in New South Wales; Nootka had taken on a new significance – no longer Cook's watering place on the north-west coast of America but a centre of international dispute; the first missionaries had reached Tahiti, Tonga, and the Marquesas; and everywhere the traders and the whalers were beginning to follow the explorers' tracks.

Prominent in these ventures was Joseph Banks. The young naturalist of

Sea Otter by John Webber. 1784. *National Maritime Museum.*

Cook's first voyage was now one of the most influential men in England: President of the Royal Society, virtual 'Director' of Kew Gardens, friend of ministers and leading merchants, and the patron of scientific enterprises in all parts of the world. The new Pacific voyages were more practical and commercial than scientific, but Banks seemed to be involved at almost every turn. In the north Pacific, trading vessels arrived on the northwest American coast from 1785 onwards in search of the lustrous sea-otter furs reported by Cook's men. By 1790, international competition was so intense that Britain and Spain came close to war over the possession of Nootka Sound. A government minister summed up the issues at stake when he told the House of Commons: "We are not contending for a few miles, but a large world."

The south Pacific after Cook was reached simultaneously by settlers and whalers. Cook's report on New South Wales was enhanced by Banks's recollection in 1785 that the land there was "sufficiently fertile to support a considerable number of Europeans", and this may have been sufficient to prompt the government to choose Botany Bay as its new place of transportation for convicts who would previously have been sent to the American colonies. Less publicized reasons may also have played a part: the possibility of developing Botany Bay as a base strategically situated on the south or "blind" side of the Dutch East Indies; the hope of pro-

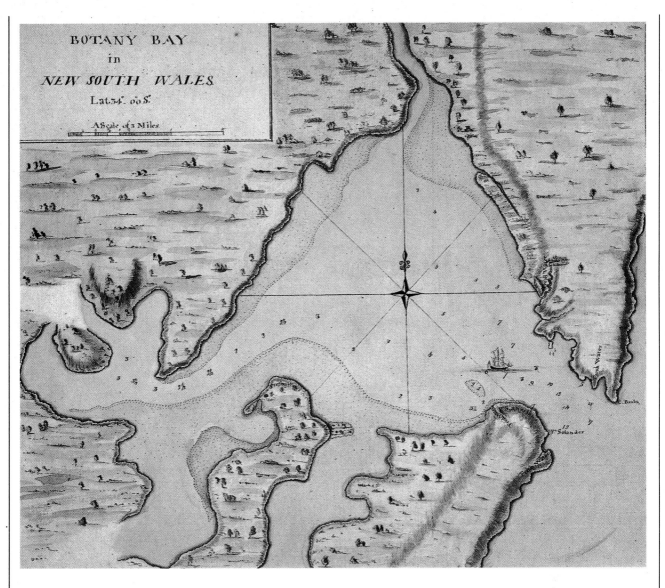

BOTANY BAY
in
NEW SOUTH WALES
Lat.34°.00 S.

A Scale of 3 Miles

ducing naval stores in the form of timber and flax; the necessity of a preventive move to stifle French initiatives in the region. Among the transports of the First Fleet which arrived at Botany Bay in January 1788, and of subsequent convict fleets, were whalers. Once released from their transportation duties, they turned to the quest for the great sperm whales of the southern seas, whose oil was more highly valued than that of the "right" whales of the traditional Greenland fishery. Soon whalers were sailing direct from Europe and the United States to the whaling grounds, and were also hunting the fur seals whose locations – from South Georgia in the south Atlantic to Dusky Sound in New Zealand – had been pinpointed by Cook on his second voyage.

At one stage during the preparation of the First Fleet there were plans to use one of its vessels to put into effect a favoured scheme of Banks: the shipping of breadfruit plants from Tahiti to the British West Indies where their cultiva-

tion would provide cheap food for the slave population. During his stay in Tahiti in 1769, Banks had been entranced by the islanders' easy reliance on breadfruit: "Scarcely can it be said that they earn their bread with the sweat of their brows when their chiefest substance, Breadfruit, is procur'd with no more trouble than that of climbing a tree and pulling it down." Plans to transfer breadfruit plants from the Pacific to the West Indies were halted by the War of American Independence, but revived with the coming of peace in 1783. Added incentives came from the realization that now American shipping was excluded from the West Indian trade food supplies for the plantations would be more expensive, and from the news that the French were already transplanting breadfruit from Mauritius to their West Indian possessions. Banks's initial suggestion was to use one of the First Fleet transports for the task after it had offloaded its human cargo at Botany Bay. In March 1787, he decided that it would

◼ Chart of Botany Bay. 1770.
British Library.

be better to send a vessel from England direct to Tahiti, properly adapted to take the plants, and with a captain appointed for this specific voyage. In May, a suitable merchant vessel, approved by Banks, was purchased by the Navy Board. In August, a half-pay naval lieutenant employed in the West India trade returned from Jamaica to hear, as he wrote to Banks, "the flattering news of your great goodness to me, intending to honour me with the command of the vessel which you propose to go to the South Seas". By the late summer of 1787, the chosen vessel, renamed, and the chosen commander, had come together: the vessel was the *Bounty*, its commander William Bligh.

Glyn Williams is Professor of History at Queen Mary College, University of London

Bligh and the Mutiny

The central figure of this great naval yarn has been pilloried or praised, feted or cursed. Stephen Walters tries to set the record straight

"BREADFRUIT BLIGH...", "That Bounty Bastard...", Bully Bligh...", "who came up through the hawse hole"..., or "Beloved, respected and lamented". Bligh who would "oft come to Fleet Street with his many salt water friends". Throughout his adult life Bligh resolutely maintained the fondest association with the Right Hon. Sir Joseph Banks Bart PC GCB FSA, President of the Royal Society and confidant of King George III of England.

What is the truth about this man who has so exercized the public interest across the world this last 200 years? What were his achievements and failings as hindsight now permits us to see, and why has his association with his peers been so coloured by that relatively minor incident in world and British naval terms, the mutiny on board His Majesty's armed vessel, the Bounty, on the 28 April 1789. To answer these questions we must go back beyond his birth in Cornwall in 1754.

His family, related to the Earls of Darnley, long established in the Manor of Tinten, near St Tudy by Bodmin, had farmed and lived the life of good yeomen for hundreds of years as the parish records show. His father obtained a senior post in HM customs office at Plymouth and, on his marriage to Jane Pearce, they moved to the naval city where William their only child, was baptized at St Andrews church. The history of Bligh's early years is uncertain, but the display of a good mathematical sense and an inquiring mind show throughout his life not least in his superb navigational skill.

His first formal encounter with the Navy would have been later than his entry, aged 7, as captain's servant on board HMS Monmouth, though the earliest possible listing helped to ensure a true served record in later promotion and also provided added income for the ship's captain by way of an allowance from the Admiralty. At 15 he was entered as able seaman on HMS Hunter and was well advanced in his academic studies for 14 months later he was rated midshipman (5 February 1771).

He was discharged on 14 September that year and moved to HMS Crescent a week later, remaining on board until 23 August 1774. He was again paid off, but in his zeal for work signed on as AB volunteer aboard HMS Ranger on 2 September 1774. A year later, he was rerated to midshipman while the Ranger was employed in offshore blockade work. She sailed out of Douglas in the Isle of Man. The British government was concerned to prohibit illicit supply

Elizabeth Bligh by John Webber 1782. *Private collection.*

or trade out of Liverpool and White-haven, Cumberland, with the colonists of North America who were on the point of rebellion. The social life of a young naval officer was then as now an entice-ment to travel and no doubt his familiar-ity with HM customs brought him to the Manx home of the Betham family also of Trinity Grange in Westmorland. Richard Betham was collector of cus-toms at Douglas. His daughter Elizabeth left a lasting impression on William Bligh. They were later to meet again and to be married for 31 years.

On the 17 March 1776, Bligh received orders to join James Cook's ship Resolution as sailing master, having recently passed his master's certificate – a tribute to his skills as navigator, hydro-grapher and, as his work shows, author. So at 22 years of age he had been direct-ed to work alongside the finest seamen, explorers, artists, and scientists that 18th century England could muster. Why he was chosen we can only surmize but cer-tainly by this time Bligh was in contact with Sir Joseph Banks and his potential must have impressed the organisers of the voyage. Cook had intended to retire to a shore-based job at Greenwich Hospi-tal before being pressed to sail, in ill-health, to the Pacific again – where he met his death at the hands of the Hawai-ians on 14 February 1779.

From this terrible event and all that led to it, Bligh as a keen observer and capable seaman had added responsibility thrust upon him for when the ship left Hawaii both the senior officers, Lieu-tenants Clark and King were out of action due to illness. Bligh was forced to assume responsibility for HM ships Res-olution and Discovery.

Bligh had learned well from Cook: he maintained health and hygiene aboard ship, knew how to deal with the native peoples they encountered, and how to get the best from the crew on a three year voyage in cramped conditions through uncharted waters. He also began to form a lasting affection for the Polynesians and their culture which fascinated him to his dying day. In the Admiralty Library, Bligh's personal copy of the printed account of the voyage has illuminating manuscript additions by him which sup-port his claim to be the major contributor to the production of charts of the new

discoveries made despite the public attri-bution to others, including Cook and Lieutenant Henry Roberts. These notes also show his expressive and often vitri-olic temperament. On their return to England the crew found their country at war with her American colonies, France, Spain, and Holland.

On February 4 1781, Bligh married Elizabeth Betham in the Isle of Man, 11 years after their first meeting in Douglas. There was to be no long honeymoon, for on 1 February he was in the North Sea fleet serving as master of a captured French frigate Belle Poule at Sir Hyde Parker's action off the Dogger Bank. Hostilities in Europe ended in 1782 and Bligh, like so many naval officers, was ashore on half pay. To keep himself and his young wife in their new London home at 3 Durham Place, he obtained work with Elizabeth's uncle Duncan Campbell in command of several of Campbell's ships plying to and from the West Indies. It was here that he first worked with Fletcher Christian who had been recommended to him by another Manxman, Captain Taubman.

On at least two occasions they

sailed together in Campbell's ship, the Britannia, with Bligh as commander and teacher and Fletcher the eager pupil. Lawrence Lebogue, a sailmaker, and Edward Lamb, a butcher, also aboard Britannia later sailed with them to the Pacific in the Bounty.

In 1772, Valentine Morris, Captain General of St Vincent, West Indies, wrote to Sir Joseph Banks about the pos-sibility of introducing the breadfruit to the British Caribbean colonies on a sug-gestion by William Dampier, the early 18th century adventurer who had first written about it on his return to England from his cruise aboard a privateer in the Pacific. James Cook and others had com-mented on its ease of cultivation and pleasant taste. The West India merchants and sugar planters seconded the sugges-tion as breadfruit would be far less sus-ceptible to hurricanes than the banana, while the West Indies were in roughly corresponding latitudes to Tahiti. The prospect appealed to the business com-munity in the West Indies as a cheaper form of food for their slave workers on the sugar estates.

No one took up the challenge even

though the Society of Arts offered a gold medal to anyone who succeeded in completing the voyage with healthy plants for propagation. The plantation committees in St Vincent and Jamaica added weight to the project by offering a reward of 2,000 guineas, no small amount then. On 5 May 1787 King George III responded to a personal plea by Banks and instructed the Admiralty to find and fit out a suitable ship. Several vessels were inspected but as the Navy Board did not wish to get involved in great expenditure they minimized the scale of the expedition. Eventually, they chose a small north-east coastal cutter, Bethia purchased from her owners, Wellbank Sharp and Brown, for £1,950 then moved her to the Admiralty yard at Deptford on the Thames to spend a further £4,456 fitting her out.

Bligh was not yet formally involved, but was clearly up for consideration as expedition commander. He was a highly skilled navigator, was adept at ship handling, had experience with Cook in Pacific waters, knew the islands and islanders of Tahiti, had sailed to the West Indies and had met the people of influence there, among whom was his uncle-in-law Campbell, who would profit by the cheaper operation of the plantation.

Bligh's appointment was confirmed on 16 August 1787 and he immediately set about ordering further changes to the Bethia. The after section of the ship

below decks had been ripped apart and a huge floating greenhouse was installed to hold more than 1,000 breadfruit saplings. The great cabin floor was leaded and fitted with water runways to conserve spillage and channel it below into reusable kegs. Consequently, the officers' accommodation as well as crew quarters were compressed into a smaller area than usual for so neat a bluff-bowed vessel, now renamed The Bounty in honour of George III's patronage. Bligh was concerned about the Admiralty's increased sail area which was not suitable to the heavy swells of the deep Pacific. He therefore had the top mast shortened. Her shallow draught and flat bottom enabled her to travel in shoal waters. To protect her bottom against the ravages of the teredo worm which regularly destroyed ships' hulls immersed in the warmer waters of the tropics. She was sheathed with copper – some of which has survived. She was armed with four short 4lb cannons and 10 half-pound swivel guns to protect her from hostile boarders.

Bligh's concern for his crew was no less than that for his ship. His complement of 45 men caused much concern, for although he chose many personally from those he knew or who had been recommended to him, their relative inexperience was marked. Furthermore, he had not, despite pleas to the Admiralty, from Sir Joseph Banks, been promoted above

HMS St Albans floated out at Deptford by John Cleveley the elder. *National Maritime Museum.*

the rank of Lieutenant, and because of this under naval regulations a ship commanded by a lieutenant could only carry non-commissioned officers without a marine backup. The Admiralty was trying to save money. During this preparation men were appointed to all the posts but many deserted or were not to Bligh's liking and by the time he sailed down the Thames and out into the Channel he was still unhappy about his situation.

The ship's boats – the Bounty carried three – were to be taken on board after leaving Deptford. Those promised at Long Reach were below standard and in part destroyed by the atrocious weather Bounty ran into on the voyage to Portsmouth. The sailing orders took a long time coming and Bligh was only able to sail on 24 November. Three times they broke out into the Channel, twice being beaten back by fierce storms, and they finally departed on 23 December 1787. The delays and poor weather enabled Bligh to take stock of his ship and his men under extreme conditions. By departure 16 had deserted and three were transferred. All were replaced as were the ships boats, a gig, a launch, and a cutter. The standard issue launch of 21ft was exchanged for a new 23 ft vessel by Whites of Gosport, lately moved to

Watercolour of the Bounty prior to departure on 23 December 1787, by Geoffrey Hubbard. *Private collection.*

Cowes, using their new diagonal construction which gave it enormous strength. A windlass was fitted across the middle section to haul anchors or tow ropes aboard. This added stability and weight and kept the sides well spread. Little did Bligh and his companions realize just how important this was to be in enabling their safe return to England. While awaiting orders Bligh paid a final visit to his young family for now he had four daughters, Harriet, Mary, Elizabeth, and Anne, one of whom had smallpox. Apart from the official account of the voyage at the Public Record Office, we are fortunate because Bligh kept a private rough copy log and a notebook of the launch voyage, both of which are now in Australia.

Among the crew, John Fryer, the master, and Bosun's mate James Morri-

son also wrote up detailed accounts of the voyage from notes taken at the time. These too are preserved. Journals were kept by young midshipman Peter Heywood – a family friend of the Bethams and a Manxman. No doubt Fletcher Christian also recorded his experiences for he is known to have disposed of his possessions shortly before the mutiny. None has survived. Letters "home" were sent on the way out until they reached the Cape of Good Hope and on the return by the loyal crew members and mutineers alike from the Dutch East Indies. We can therefore piece together the story of the next two years.

The "shakedown cruise" to the Canary Islands proved uneventful and Bligh wrote home that he was "well pleased with his little ship". As yet he had not discovered the ship's surgeon's drinking habits, but in an effort to con-

Peter Heywood RN by unknown artist. *Manx Museum, Isle of Man.*

serve the health of his crew he ordered the creation of a third watch thereby giving the men longer rest periods between the four-hour turns of duty. He put Fletcher Christian in charge and 11 weeks later made him acting 2nd Lieutenant.

A week later AB Matthew Quintal and John Fryer had a heated argument, and Bligh ordered punishment of the "insolent and mutinous" seamen: 24 lashes with the cat o'nine tails as proscribed by the Articles of War.

At Tenerife, Bligh recorded his dissatisfaction with the surgeon for his drunkenness and bought supplies including pumpkin before setting out for Cape Horn. By now he had already antagonized his master Fryer by the promotion of Christian, made an enemy of Quintal, taken on the doctor's responsibilities in all but name, and introduced a regime of healthy eating, dancing for exercize, and airing of the tween decks by fumigating and lighting fires below. The seamen

found this strange. Naval ceremonies were observed as they crossed the Equator, though Bligh would not allow ducking as he believed it "inhuman" and they battled on to Cape Horn.

For 31 days they fought against the elements and unbeknown to them passed the Cape three times but eventually on 22 April 1788 with huge seas, little daylight, and rare clear skies to take observations for their position, Bligh ordered the ship about and made for the Cape of Good Hope. He must have cursed the Admiralty for the delays in receipt of their sailing orders which brought them to the southern latitudes in early winter and all the bed weather. He must have cursed the surgeon by now permanently drunk and incapable in his cabin. But he praised his crew and called them together to thank them for their efforts. On 22 May they anchored in False Bay under Table Mountain, staying to repair the ship before setting out on the long leg to Tasmania, Van Diemens Land, where again

HMS Bounty bearing down the English Channel in January 1788, by Geoffrey Hubbard. *Private collection.*

they stopped to take on water. Here they also cut wood for repairs and firewood. The carpenter, Purcell, refused to work and Bligh publicly castigated him: another enemy created.

From Adventure bay to Tahiti was a wonderful sail across and into the deep Pacific. Due to the surgeon's incapability Able Seaman Valentine, wrongly diagnosed, was bled and died: Bligh's first casualty. The Bounty dropped anchor at Matavai Bay, Tahiti, on 26 October 1788, having travelled half way around the world. The warmth of their reception and the generosity of the people overcame the crew who could not believe their good fortune. The Europeans' light skins and the size, and the might of the ship combined to create a strong belief among the Tahitians that one of their gods and his retinue had come to visit. Naturally,

■ Peter Heywood's first letter home to his mother after the Mutiny. A copy in his sister Nessy's hand.

all they possessed had to be made available. The climate, the place, its beauty and allure along with that of the women and the free expression of their favours soon contrasted with the cramped conditions on board ship and the fading memories of Georgian England. Although the breadfruit cuttings bed been transplanted within six weeks of their arrival, Bligh became engrossed in the ways of the islanders and oblivious to the action, or rather inaction, of his crew.

Between October 1788 and April 1789, 23 weeks passed, friendships were cemented, and discipline disintegrated. When at last Bounty sailed from Tahiti on 5 April she left a buried surgeon and the buried dreams of all the crew.

The rigour of shipboard discipline, the foetid, cramped conditions created by the 1115 breadfruit plants on board, the humid atmosphere combined to create tension everywhere. Tempers frayed as had the rigging and sails which were not attended to by Fryer, Christian and their subordinates.

Bligh was beside himself – his favoured protégé had let him down – had destroyed his trust. Worse still Bligh had made a personal misjudgment and he could not forgive himself. His only reaction was to take it out on the crew and in particular on Christian. The hotbed of resentment within the seamen fuelled by the desertion of Charles Churchill the ship's corporal, John Williams AB and William Muspratt before their departure from Tahiti, the resentment of Quintal still smouldering. The crew knew that Fryer and Bligh were not on speaking terms. Christian was unhappy after all the brow beating by Bligh.

The mutiny came with a dispute over a trivial matter. Bligh publicly accused Christian of stealing coconuts from the ship's store while on night watch. Although Bligh usually forgave and forgot after his eruptions, on this occasion he did not. Christian refused an invitation to dinner and instead planned escape on a makeshift raft to one of the nearby islands. While disposing of his possessions to his closest shipboard friends, Midshipman Stewart hinted that "… the men are ripe for anything …"

"That is it. I have been in hell for weeks past", screamed a demented

■ The first of two anonymously issued works purporting to be Fletcher Christian's own account and justification for the mutiny and subsequent activities, published in 1796. *Private collection.*

Christian to Bligh on the following morning – April 28 1789. Bligh had been dragged up on deck and bound by Churchill to meet Christian, bayonet in hand, surrounded by mutineers.

"But you have dandled my children on your knee …" Bligh pleaded – forgive and forget, but they were too far gone.

Fryer was already forced into the launch, by now lowered over the side after pleas had been made that the cutter was rotten. Bob Byrne the blind fiddler had in his haste been bundled into the gig on the other side of the ship and thereby remained on board as did a number of loyalists, for the launch was overloaded with 19 men and all they were allowed to carry.

As Andrew David relates elsewhere in this book the epic launch voyage began by chance out of chaos and was successful, with only one man dead – John Norton the Quartermaster, killed by natives at Tofua, the first island they called at within sight of the ship. Bligh and his companions finally reached England on 14 March 1790.

Bligh was enraptured by his two new twin daughters, Jane and Frances, born in his absence. He was presented to the King by Sir Joseph Banks and promoted commander of the sloop Falcon.

He then set about writing his account of the mutiny for publication. The book was on the streets of London by July. He was then promoted full captain, well on the way to a long and successful career.

The Admiralty naturally wanted to set an example and seek out the mutineers and bring them back to justice. Captain Edward Edwards was appointed to search them out in HMS Pandora.

Bligh was on half pay again until appointed on 16 April 1791 to command the second breadfruit voyage in HMS Providence. This time no expense was spared. A tender HMS Assistant with full complement under Lieutenant Portlock was to accompany them.

The voyage was a great success. Bligh returned via the West Indies to England in 1793 and was voted the 2,000 guineas by the West India Committee at Kingston and St Vincent. He was also presented with a silver salver to commemorate his success. During the voyage he was able to confirm his discoveries,

■ Captain Bligh transplanting the breadfruit trees collected from Otaheite. With him is King Pomare I. Mezzotint engraved by Thomas Gosse (1796).

■ Bligh's Heron, a notable example of his talent as a fine watercolour artist incorporated with his love of nature. *Mitchell Library*.

made in the launch, of the main islands in the Fiji group. But what saddened him was to see the decline that had set in among the islanders of Tahiti.

The Providence voyage added weight – if any were needed – to Bligh's qualities as well as frailties. He was able to repay his uncle Frank Bond for his help in his own early days in the Navy by taking his nephew Francis Godolphin Bond aboard as Lieutenant and second in command of the Providence. Bond was to write to a colleague of Bligh's ill health, his fits of temper and inability to realize the hurt he caused his subordinates.

The mutineers and their shipmates aboard Bounty had by this time returned to Tahiti after their unsatisfactory attempt to found a colony on Tubuai in the Aus-

tral Islands. Having then moved on Christian and his hard core group ultimately found and settled on Pitcairn as recounted by Glyn Christian and Brian Scott in their articles on Fletcher's life and that of John Adams the sole surviving mutineer.

In Bligh's absence in the Providence those mutineers returned in captivity by Edwards were brought to trial amid great publicity which damaged Bligh's image.

Edward Christian, a lawyer, defended his brother and the war of words continued for four years after Bligh's return from the Pacific in the Providence. Despite the success of the voyage, Bligh was never to sway public opinion back in his favour.

In 1795 Betsey gave birth to two sons, William and Henry, but they died within 24 hours. Bligh was able to bury himself in work and while on HMS Calcutta helped to restore order after the mutiny on HMS Defiance at Leith.

On 7 January 1796 he was appointed to command HMS Director, a 74 gunner. Early in 1797, the fleet mutinies at Spithead and the Nore took place and Bligh helped to put them down. By mid June, Admiral Duncan was at last able to put to sea with his North Sea fleet. Bligh's involvement in the action at Camperdown has been a matter of speculation but he did play a role in the dismasting of the Dutch Admiral de Winter's flagship Vrijheid and its subsequent surrender. He commissioned three paintings by Samuel Owen to depict the action, later shown at the Royal Academy, and proudly displayed his Camperdown medal. He kept a significant trophy – the canton to the Dutch Admiral's flag and when later in Australia named a port after the action.

Bligh left the Director on 2 July 1800 and went on to commissioned survey work, one of the most notable being

■ Top Watercolour of Bounty Bay, Pitcairn, by Beechey while on the Blossom voyage in 1826. *Private collection (Rolph du Rietz).*

■ Centre West side of Port Morant Jamaica, 1793, painted by George Tobin on HMS Providence, 2nd Breadfruit Voyage. *Mitchell Library.*

■ Left The Providence off Point Venus, steel engraving late 18th century. *Private collection.*

Battle of Camperdown 11 October 1797. Three watercolours by Samuel Owen RA.

Top The Director coming up and engaging the Vrijheid.

Above The Director raking the Vrijheid.

Right The Director and the Vrijheid at the conclusion of Camperdown. *Private collection*.

Hunter River by Bligh, the seaward view from the land behind Newcastle New South Wales. *Private collection.*

his work for the Dublin Harbour commissioners. Other work is still in use. With the threat of more war against Napoleonic France, Bligh was recalled to active service and given command of HMS Glatton on 13 March 1801. On 2 April Admiral Sir Hyde Parker and his fleet were in action off the Trekroner Forts guarding the entrance to Copenhagen. It was here that Nelson put his telescope to his blind eye and said, "Damn the signal ..." to withdraw.

The Danish ships began to strike their colours as Bligh's Glatton and Foley's Elephant continued to pound the Dannebrog until she too surrendered, "blazing furiously" before drifting back into the Danish fleet where she blew up.

Nelson called Bligh to his ship and publicly thanked him for his support. Glatton had lost 17 men with 34 wounded of her complement of 309. Her foremast was shot to pieces, and her rigging and sails were in tatters. On 2 May he was elected a Fellow of the Royal Society.

Over the next four years Bligh moved from ship to ship, but in 1804, while captain of HMS Warrior, his 2nd Lieutenant, John Frazier, brought a court martial against him for ill treatment and abuse. On three occasions Bligh refused Frazier's requests for sick leave from watch duty. This led to a stormy scene on deck which was dredged up in detail in front of the court who found in favour of Frazier and admonished Bligh for his use of words probably the stronger with his increasing age.

In 1805 his loyal supporter and friend Sir Joseph Banks recommended

him to the position of Governor of the infant penal colony in New South Wales. An offer was made at a salary of £2,000 a year which after much heart searching Bligh accepted. Betsey his wife was now ill and could not accompany him so he took his newly married daughter Mary to act as hostess at official functions. Bligh nominated her new husband Lieutenant Charles Portland as his ADC.

They left England in the transport Lady Madeleine Sinclair in company with three convict ships and HMS Porpoise under captain Joseph Short. Portland was ordered to serve on the Porpoise which split the family. Bligh disapproved of Short's shiphandling. Short had ordered a shot to be put across the bow of the Lady Sinclair when Bligh changed course without notice. On arrival at Sydney, Bligh held a court of inquiry and posted Short back to England to face a court-martial at which he was acquitted. Bligh's impetuosity and temper had let him down again and those waiting in the wings in Australia and at home took full advantage of the situation.

His first year as governor passed well and the colony began to settle down but its inherent problem which he was sent to cure – the illicit trade in rum – had yet to be tackled. John Macarthur, a local entrepreneur, and others had begun to con-

ABOVE RIGHT Blighton Farm drawn by George William Evans (1810). *Private collection.*
RIGHT The Hawksbury River, unsigned but inscription is in Bligh's hand, as is the style of painting. *Private collection.*
LEFT Bligh's watercolour of Table Bay, painted on his return to England (1790). *Private collection.*

Bligh Arrested. The famous cartoon scurrilously issued to blacken Bligh's character in New South Wales during the Rum Rebellion. *Mitchell Library.*

trol the colony's economy by using rum as a commodity currency rather than trading for cash. Those who did not comply were kept under, those who did prospered.

On 26 January 1808 the local militia commander, Major George Johnston, ordered the release of Macarthur from gaol where Bligh had him incarcerated after failing to meet a shipowner's bond. Macarthur was accused of aiding the escape of a convict in one of his ships. The release order was signed by Johnston as Lieutenant Governor. Johnston moved on Government House in Sydney and placed Bligh under arrest. Bligh escaped in the Porpoise. Governor Collins in Hobart, Tasmania was unable to help him and Bligh was unable to get news back to England until 1809.

A new Governor, Lachlan Macquarrie, was appointed and sent out to relieve Bligh. On Macquarrie's arrival in New South Wales in December 1809, he found that Johnston and Macarthur had left for England. Bligh returned home in 1811 leaving his daughter Mary behind.

Her husband had died and while Bligh was away seeking assistance in Tasmania, she had met "Lieut Colonel O'Connel commander of the 73rd Regiment (who) had unknown to me won her affections", as Bligh wrote to his wife.

Johnston was court-martialled at the Royal Hospital, Chelsea on 7 May 1811. He was found guilty and cashiered. Bligh's actions had been totally vindicated and his long awaited promotion to Rear Admiral of the Blue was backdated to his return.

Macarthur – a big fish in a small pond in New South Wales – found in England that though he had the ears of important people he could not sway state opinion against Bligh and rather than – as he had hoped – spending only a few months in England it became eight years before he could return to New South Wales to pursue his business interests in relative obscurity. Nevertheless he founded the now huge Merino sheep industry of which Australia is justly proud.

Bligh's wife Elizabeth was by now ill and she died in 1814 leaving her husband to care for their 4 surviving daughters, one of whom, Alice suffered badly from epilepsy and had to be lodged in a

home near Bath to see out her last days. With a pension for his services as Governor he quit his long time family home at Durham Place, Lambeth, and took a lease on Farningham House, Kent, a beautiful country manor.

Occasionally he would travel back to London to see friends, discuss business, and old times at sea. On one of these visits, in December 1817, he collapsed in Baker Street and died at Durham Place later of cancer, but not before he had been promoted twice more to end as Vice Admiral of the Blue.

Perhaps the best summary of the man by those who knew him is found in a letter sent by one of his earlier junior officers in Providence, George Tobin to Bligh's nephew Francis Bond in which he writes on hearing of Bligh's death:

"So poor Bligh, for with all his infirmities you and I cannot but think (well) of him, has followed Portlock. He has had a busy and turbulent journey of it – no one more so, and since the unfortunate mutiny on the Bounty has been rather in the shade. Yet perhaps he was not altogether understood. I am sure my dear friend that in the Providence there was no settled system of tyranny exercized by him likely to produce dissatisfaction. It was in those violent tornadoes of temper when he lost himself, yet when all in his opinion went right, when could a man be more placid and interesting? For myself I feel that I am indebted to him. It was the first ship in which I ever sailed as an officer – I joined full of apprehension – I soon thought he was not dissatisfied with me – it gave me encouragement and on the whole we journeyed smoothly on. Once or twice indeed I felt the unbridled licence of his power of speech, yet never without soon receiving something like an emolient plaster to heal the wound. Let our old Captain's frailties be forgotten and view him as a man of science and excellent practical seaman. He has suffered much and ever by labour and perseverence extricated himself. But his great quality was foresight. In this I think Bond, you will accord me. I have seen many men in his profession with more resources but never one with so much precaution – I mean chiefly as a navigator."

Bligh was buried in St Mary's church, Lambeth where his unique coadstone tomb survives. "Beloved, respected and lamented."

Mutineer who made History

Hero or pirate?
Glynn Christian
discusses a distant
relation and uncovers
the personality of
Fletcher Christian

◼ FLETCHER CHRISTIAN and William Bligh had more in common than friendship, mutual career patronage and family neighbourliness on the Isle of Man where they lived. They were both driven by a distinct and unshakeable expectation of their place in the future and a profound belief in their inherent right to rule other men. Christian's was based on birthright and confidence in the extraordinary pattern of his family's service to others through the administration of justice for more than three centuries. Bligh's was based on the authority and marble-like sense of righteousness he believed he donned with his naval uniform. They were classic, immovable objects, fuelled by the same irresistible force.

Bounty's muster shows Fletcher Christian to have been 21 when he signed on as Master's mate, but this is not true. He was 22 and would be 23 weeks later, on 25 September 1787. In contrast to Bligh's startling porcelain-white skin, Fletcher Christian was brown-skinned and darkhaired. He was 5ft 10 inches, and his body was muscular; throughout his recorded life, other men told of his physical strength and his delight in it – he could make a standing jump from one gun barrel directly in to another and would hold a heavy musket at arm's length so that it might be measured how straight it was. His appearance was marred only by a slight outward bending of his knees, which the breeches of his midshipman's uniform would emphasize into the appearance of being positively bow-legged. Perhaps symptomatic of a nervous propensity, he was subject to violent sweats, particularly in the palms of his hands. Bligh, who was the only one to comment on this, said that unless he constantly carried handkerchiefs he would sully anything he touched.

For all his fame we do not know what Fletcher Christian looked like. There are images about, but these are as likely to be accurate as the features of Marlon Brando or David Essex who have portrayed him. The nearest we might get is the picture of Christian watching Bligh in the long boat in Dodd's famous oil painting and subsequent prints. Bligh approved the original after his epic return and is thought to have helped to correct the likeness of the men portrayed. There is a wicked contemporary irony in the picture, little understood these days, but as barbed as a modern Private Eye cartoon. Christian is standing precisely where in reality Bligh's private lavatory would have been cantilevered over the stern …

Fletcher Christian was born in 1764 at Moorland Close, tucked just below the brow of a hill which slopes eventually to Cockermouth on the edge of Cumbria's Lake District. He was christened the same day in the tradition of his maternal grandmother's influential family, in Brigham church. His first school was here, too, in Eller Cottage which may still be seen. Next he went on, by piebald pony we are told, to the Cockermouth Free Grammar School. He was there at the same time as William Wordsworth, but stories of their friendship are silly. Christian was six years older and schoolboys rarely fraternize over such a wide age gap; even brothers do not. In fact, a brother, Edward Christian, later taught Wordsworth English and later acted for William and his sister Dorothy, winning for them their celebrated case against Clive of India.

Fletcher then followed his brothers to St Bees School, close to Whitehaven, a venerable institution then and now founded by charter of Elizabeth I in 1583 and closely linked to Queen's College Oxford, which now owns Moorland Close. The Catechism, Latin, Greek, Mathematics and Navigation were the ingredients of a young gentleman's education and Fletcher was a good scholar. Brother Edward, when he was later defending him, pointed out that Fletcher Christian had stayed at school far longer than most young men who joined the Navy. This is true, but it is unlikely that the sea had any place in Fletcher's plans until the greed of his older brothers and his mother's financial disabilities cruelly and abruptly ended his education. Instead of continuing to Cambridge, following a centuries-old family tradition, he had nothing presently or for the future.

His mother Ann Christian, widowed when Fletcher was four, was bankrupted when he was 16, owing more than £6,000 (probably £¼ million today). Moorland Close and the income its land produced was no more. His father's family, the Christians of Milntown on the Isle of Man and Ewanrigg (above Maryport), had already done more than their share by previously bailing out Ann and her fatherless brood and by lending constantly to her older sons to finance their fine educations and law practices in London and Cockermouth. In future, Fletcher had only himself to rely upon.

Fletcher's direct Christian ancestors had been recorded since 1380, beyond which few records are reliable anyway. The long line of grandfathers had numerical suffixes, to ease the confusion

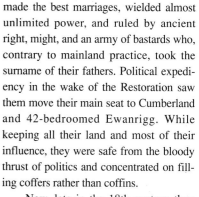

■ Moorland Close, birthplace of Fletcher Christian. *Glynn Christian*.

caused by the constant use of Ewan, William and John as first names. We know much about them, for by unwritten hereditary right the Christians of Milntown, close to Ramsey in the north of the Isle of Man, were First Deemsters, judiciary heads responsible for the administration of the unwritten laws of the island. For generations they had acted as interpreters and buffers between the

■ The Free Grammar in Cockermouth, where Fletcher was a contemporary of William Wordsworth.

uncrowned kings of Man (such English aristocrats as the Earls of Derby) and the people of Man, and were specially respected for the trouble they took to be fair and to avoid the imposition of the death penalty. It was the family's defence of the island which made it the last area to capitulate to Cromwell, for which the Christians became the only family to suffer after the Restoration of Charles II in 1660 – not from the King of Great Britain, but from a piqued Earl of Derby who felt that his own kingship of Man could overrule the general pardon by the British King to all but regicides.

For more centuries than one can be sure, the Christians owned the best lands,

made the best marriages, wielded almost unlimited power, and ruled by ancient right, might, and an army of bastards who, contrary to mainland practice, took the surname of their fathers. Political expediency in the wake of the Restoration saw them move their main seat to Cumberland and 42-bedroomed Ewanrigg. While keeping all their land and most of their influence, they were safe from the bloody thrust of politics and concentrated on filling coffers rather than coffins.

Now, late in the 18th century they were almost at their zenith. The sons being prepared to inherit, Fletcher's brothers and first cousins were destined to become memorable men in the corridors of Westminster and the Inns of Court, in the Cabinet, the peerage, the Palaces of the Church, the government and commerce of India the East and West Indies, the highest ranks of the Navy and universities and, most unforgettably, the newly discovered islands of the South Pacific. John XVII, the young head of the family was as revolutionary and experimental as his ancestors, delivering England's first free milk, experimenting with winter animal feed, founding the first agricultural shows, and evolving for his mining employees friendly societies which were acknowledged in the 20th century as the pattern for the Welfare system.

Most families proudly point to men of power or wealth or influence in one generation or another; some even trace these attributes in several generations. But there are few, royalty and aristocracy included, who can claim the combination in an unbroken father-to-son line since the mid-14th century. The Christians could and it had a marked relevance to anyone born into the family. It would have been impossible for Fletcher Christian not to be influenced by the heritage and the expectation. In Georgian society he could now only beg, marry an heiress, or join the Navy That he did the latter and was later often called ambitious meant something quite different in the 1780s than it does two centuries later. Ambition, the changing of the position into which you are born, was rare and thus it was commented on: you generally did more or less well in a position over which you had little control and less choice. The one acceptable way to change your social status was success in the Navy. Unlike the army, into or out of which your bought your way, the Navy promoted on ability – indeed you could

■ Ewanrigg, Cumberland; the seat of the Christian family largely destroyed in 1904.

be dismissed if you were found unfit for the responsibility of command in what was then Britain's most important and expensive means of defence. It was perfectly acceptable for men of common trade or agricultural background to be raised high in the Navy, and such success would give Christian back the status and role he was born to expect, and some income to go with it. Bligh had never wanted for income, but he too looked to the Navy for status and respect.

Frustrated love and marriage plans are likely further to have strengthened Fletcher's resolve. Considering that he later called his Tahitian wife Isabella, and that his name has many times been linked romantically with his relative, Isabella Curwen, it is perhaps poignant that in April 1783, six months after

Isabella married his cousin John XVII (to whom she was even more closely related), he signed on as a midshipman aboard HMS Eurydice; there is no evidence to support the claim that in 1782/3 he served aboard HMS Cambridge when Bligh was this ship's sixth lieutenant – he was a boarder at St Bees, in the Isle of Man with his mother and sister, or both. Isabella Curwen was prodigiously rich and beautiful and the sole heiress to one of the country's 10 oldest family names, a mining, shipping and agricultural fortune which neatly dovetailed into that of the Christians, and heiress to Workington Hall. Her trustees jumped to most of her whims, including the purchase of an amusing round house in an island in Lake Windemere; it was renamed Belle Isle for her and is still in the family. John XVII had regularly returned from his Grand Tour to court her and finally they eloped to Scotland. Marriage to Isabella Curwen would have been a sensible

dynastic and financial step for Fletcher to have taken. But Isabella and he were both the same age. His older and incredibly richer cousin married her instead.

HMS Eurydice, Captain George Courtney, was a 6th rater, the last British naval ship to be manoeuvred by oars. In October she sailed for India via the Cape of Good Hope, and in Madras Christian's naval career took a signal step upwards. Courtney made him an acting lieutenant and gave him charge of a watch during the return voyage. Fletcher was described on the voyage as strict, but someone who "ruled in a superior pleasant manner". To his brother Edward he said of his experiences on returning in June 1785: "It was very easy to make oneself beloved and respected aboard a ship; one had only to be always ready to obey one's superior officers, and to be kind to the common men, unless there was occasion for severity, and if you are when there is just occasion they will not like you the less for it."

Fletcher now decided he had enough experience to look for a better paid job in the merchant navy and sought a mate's posting on a West Indiaman. He was using family and friends' influence well enough to be treating with a merchant in the City when a relative arrived in London from the Isle of Man. Captain Taubman, who had been married to Fletcher's first cousin Dorothy Christian, said he would write to William Bligh, who had married the daughter of the Collector of Customs in the island, and who owed him some favours. Christian would certainly have met Bligh or his wife in Douglas, or at least knew of him, for his mother was often at the Nunnery, Taubman's mansion, and could hardly have avoided knowing Betsy Bligh in the small town. Bligh politely told Christian by letter that he had a full complement on the ship on which he was trading in the West Indies. Edward says that by return Fletcher wrote that "wages were no object, he only wished to learn his profession and if Captain Bligh would permit him to mess with the gentlemen he would readily enter the ship as a foremast man until there was a vacancy amongst the officers … We midshipmen are gentlemen. We never pull at a rope; I should even be glad to go one voyage in

■ Dorothy Wilson, Fletcher's great-great grandmother, wife of Edward XII. *Ewan Christian.*

that situation for there may be occasions when officers are called upon to do the duties of a common man." Bligh agreed, but it was to be 15 months before they traded in the West Indies aboard Britannia. It was a mutually good arrangement in contemporary terms. Christian was learning from a man respected for his navigational skills; Bligh had done a favour for a member of the Christian clan and that was no bad thing. I think there was another reason for the strength of friendship and dependence which immediately sprang up between the two men. Although only 10 years older than Christian, Bligh seems to have been seen as the father Christian lost when he was four. Christian was the son Bligh did not, and would never, have.

It is not easy to discover exact details of the two men's trips aboard Britannia, except that when they returned to Britain at the end of the second one in August 1787 Bligh learned he was to lead an expedition to the South Seas. On their first voyage Christian had sailed as an ordinary seaman, but dined with the officers and middies (midshipmen). He told his family that Bligh had furthered his knowledge of navigation and that although a very passionate man he prided himself on knowing how to humour him. Of their second voyage, Edward Lamb, who is the only man ever to have criticized Christian for not doing his duty, wrote that Bligh was " blind to (Christian's) faults and had him to dine and sup every other day in the cabin, and treated him like a brother in giving him every information". Lamb also described

Christian as "then one of the most foolish young men I ever knew in regard to (women)". His shipmate Lebogue who also sailed aboard Bounty is the one who later remembered Fletcher always having a girl with him in Tahiti.

Only one thing is certain about Britannia's voyages. Bligh and Christian were firm friends, teacher and pupil, and pleased enough with one another for Bligh to recommend and request the appointment of Christian to Bounty. When the ship returned, Christian was certain to become a lieutenant years before Bligh had reached the same rank. Christian had thus been sought out for special responsibility and attention aboard Eurydice and Britannia and was well on the way to a laudable recovery from the family misfortunes. There was just one more sensational experience to add to the makeup of the young man who was about to sail from Britain forever.

The twin problems of bad weather and a dilatory Admiralty which so delayed the departure of Bounty proved a boon and a turning point for Fletcher Christian. It gave him an unexpected chance to meet his brother Charles, surgeon aboard the East Indiaman Middlesex (Captain Rogers), which was returning from India. Fletcher was so anxious to see his brother that he took a small boat out to meet Middlesex before she had anchored and the two men spent the evening together. Charles' unpublished biography is part of the Christian Family Archive recently placed on permanent loan at the Douglas Library and Museum. Charles remembers Fletcher's great physical strength and says he was " full

■ Humphrey Christian, Fletcher's uncle. *Major H M Hare.*

■ Fletcher's great-grandfather, Ewan XIII. *Ewan Christian.*

of professional Ambition and Hope. He said: 'I delight to set the Men an Example. I not only can do every part of a common Sailor's Duty, but am on a par with a principal part of the Officers'".

Fletcher brought his brother up to date with family news – their sister was dead, and so was Uncle Edmund Law, Bishop of Carlisle. For his part, Charles had something to tell which few others knew and thus could not consider when dissecting the mutiny which was to follow. Incredible as it may seem, there had been a mutiny aboard Middlesex and Charles was one of the officers involved. He was not in chains, for mutiny in the East India Company was not a crime against the King. But the last conversations Fletcher had in England were about the proper duty of officers to their men, and the actions that could be taken against captains who were cruel or thoughtless, as Rogers had been. (Subsequently, Rogers was punished as heavily as the officers who mutinied against him).

Bounty's voyage to the South Seas stretched everyone to the limit. Christian was sent as emissary to the Marques de Brancheforte, Spanish Governor of Tenerife, representing Bligh. Once Bounty sailed from here, Bligh announced officially their destination for the first time and finalized the introduction of his revolutionary plans for the health of his crew, with new styles of diet, compulsory daily dancing, and, most humanely, the introduction of a three watch system which gave men four days on and eight hours off. The new watch needed an officer in charge and once again Fletcher Christian found himself promoted to act-

ing lieutenant, a hat trick of promotion and preference aboard three ships. This time he was second in command. It is often written that this was unfair to Fryer, an insult in fact. But Fryer knew, as modern men do not, that masters were never promoted at sea, and there were other reasons for the tensions between him and Bligh. Indeed, Christian was probably promoted as a buffer between the two.

The story of Bounty's failure to round Cape Horn and subsequent uncomfortable trek to Cape Town, dogged by discomfort as the wind direction meant the galley fires belched smoke throughout the living quarters, is more remarkable to me for the fact that Bligh had not lost a single man through ill health, whereas other ships arriving directly from Europe came with stories of scurvy and death.

There has long been a persistent thread of gossip that Cape Town was where Bligh and Christian first fell out. Adams, the sole male survivor of the settlement of Pitcairn, said that he believed Christian to be under some obligation to Bligh and that their original quarrel happened there and was kept up until the time of the mutiny. Certainly Christian was under obligation to Bligh for his posting to Bounty and for his promotion, but Bligh gives flesh to the bones of another rumour which later came from Christian's descendants, that of financial dependence. In his own correspondence in the Mitchell Library, Australia, Bligh writes to Edward Christian, reminding him that Fletcher had money whenever he wanted. Nothing comes between friends as easily as money and Bligh's famous ability to wound with words rather than action would have enjoyed nagging at something like this. The voyage eastwards to Tahiti was unremarkable for Christian. Midshipman Peter Heywood, another with Manx connections, said that Christian spent time helping him complete his education, with lessons in mathematics and classical languages.

In Tahiti, Christian's position aboard Bounty was strong enough to earn him the plum job, as commander of the shore party first collecting then guarding the breadfruit plants which were the object of the voyage. The spread of varieties of breadfruit tree means that one at least is in season all year round, and as they do not reproduce by seed but by suckers and shoots Boun-

Isabella Curwen, by Romney. It is likely that Fletcher named his Tahitian wife after her. *Private collection.*

ty's gardener Nelson was able to organize collection parties on 7 November 1788, and by the 15th they had 774, almost all they needed. Within a fortnight of arriving, the task was all but completed, and allowing for repairs and some certainty that the young shoots were healthy and growing, Bounty could have set sail in a month or so. Instead she stayed 20 weeks: Bounty was the first British ship to spend the summer's rainy season in Tahiti. The season still brings hurricanes and even today small ships prefer not be exposed in the Pacific. It was too dangerous for Bligh to follow his orders and set sail, for even if he crossed the Pacific safely westward the prevailing winds at that time would have prevented him from entering the Endeavour Straits, north of Australia. For Christian, it was another unexpected watershed.

While Bounty swayed in the pleasant breezes of Matavai Bay, Tahiti, and most of her men sweated and pined for life ashore, Christian had little to do but enjoy life in the breadfruit camp. He learned some Tahitian and went through the considerable pain and danger of tattoing. Most of all he was close to living the life he might have expected – as the benevolent master of land, its produce, and people. He may have been foolish

about women, but that was acceptable here, provided you kept within the very detailed rules, stuck to your own equivalent class, and were prepared to accept some of the less savoury views of sex and its inevitable results – children. In Tahiti, a great proportion of female children was smothered at birth, as were children born to couples of mixed class, or who were members of the anoi secret society. Bligh had to deal with problems of deserters in Tahiti, but there is nothing to indicate tension between Bligh and Christian. That was to happen at sea, for in Tahiti, Fletcher Christian had finally grown into a man, independent, sexually experienced, and with a heightened sense of position and capability. He now wanted and expected something different from life; Bligh wanted exactly what he had enjoyed before. The suggestion that they were homosexual lovers is yet another theory based on the shifting sands of fashion and opportunistic publishing sensationalism. If there had been the slightest suspicion or evidence of this the Bounty mutineers could tellingly have used it against Bligh at their trial The penalty was death and Bligh, above all people, was too great a respecter of the law to break it in the pursuit of pleasure. He did not, remember, share the temptations of Tahiti, but remained faithful to his wife Betsy and his family.

Although Bligh publicly wrote that he and Christian never fell out over anything until immediately before the mutiny, his private papers tell a different story, corroborated by others aboard Bounty. Fryer says that after leaving Tahiti they "had some words when Mr Christian told Mr Bligh – 'Sir your abuse is so bad I cannot do my duty with any pleasure. I have been in hell for weeks with you'; several other disagreeable words passed which had been frequently the case."

The most public of these happened ashore at Nomuka, in the Friendly Islands. Christian was in charge of an armed watering party that was threatened by armed Polynesians – the first time this had happened. When Christian told Bligh that his party were unable to do their duty because of this, Bligh is said to have damned him for a cowardly rascal, asking if he were afraid of a "set of Naked Savages while he had Arms?" Christian replied: "The Arms are of no use while your orders prevent them from being used."

The later loss of a grapnel anchor angered Bligh so much that he kidnapped some of the islanders and sailed with them aboard, creating awful scenes of blood-letting and anguish in the small boats which followed until his prisoners were released.

It was irrational overreaction which amazed Bounty's men, and for those in the firing line worse was to come. The "coconut incident" is astonishing for many reasons, but mostly because Bligh's published accounts do not mention it, whereas everyone else gives it great importance. In essence, Bligh publicly accused Fletcher Christian of theft: "Damn your blood you have stolen my coconuts." Christian replied that as he was dry and that he thought it of no consequence to have taken one while on watch. "You lie, you scoundrel, you have stolen one half." Christian demanded to know why he was being treated like this; he had free access to Bligh's spirit supply simply, by asking for the key – why should he bother to steal coconuts which had been bought at 20 for an iron nail! Bligh would not answer, clearly enjoying the hurt he was inflicting. And what hurt it was. Bligh was famous for his invective, knowing it was far more painful than sticks and stones. To accuse a gentleman, and his second in command, of so paltry a theft, and one which may have been imagined, was well beyond the boundaries of disciplinary requirements. No wonder Fletcher's brother Charles wrote: "What scurrilous abuse! What provoking insult…base, mean-minded wretch…"

It was more than that; it was breaking point.

Later that day Purcell the carpenter

The Fort George site. Built by the mutineers on Fletcher Christian's orders in July 1789. *Glynn Christian.*

learned that there had been more abuse. Christian had run forward with tears welling and when asked what happened said: "Can you ask me and hear the treatment I receive?" When Purcell said that they all felt the same way, Christian reminded him that as a warrant officer he could not be flogged ; "but if I should speak to him as you do he would probably break me, turn me before the mast, and perhaps flog me, and if he did it would be the death of us both, for I am sure I should take him in my arms and jump overboard with him." Even though an acting lieutenant, Christian was in fact still Master's Mate, a superior sort of midshipman, and could have been flogged as he said. Bligh's famous bullying knew how to stretch a man, but only to a point where he was thought not in danger of any back lash.

"I would rather die ten thousand deaths than bear this treatment. I always do my duty as an officer and a man ought to do, yet I receive this scandalous usage. Flesh and blood cannot bear this treatment," Christian wept. It was the first time men on board had seen him crying. "He was no milksop;" said one. Bligh knew that Christian's background made it unlikely that he would descend to battle with a superior officer or entertain any dereliction of duty. Instead, Christian decided that the only gentlemanly thing to do was to leave the ship, not a cowardly act, but by contemporary terms an honourable one. Late in the afternoon, Christian gave away his Polynesian curios, tore up his letters and papers, and threw them overboard. If he had planned to mutiny well in advance, there was no need to do this. Helping an officer desert his duty was a serious offence, but such was the sympathy aboard Bounty that Christian was collecting nails and other barter items from Purcell; with wood and bindings he was going to construct a raft and slip overboard to a new life.

In modern terms Christian may simply have been "doing something" to attract attention and to dissipate his frustrations. Christian was certainly a good enough navigator, linguist, and farmer to survive, and a single man was likely easily to have been assimilated. It is important to remember also that among the men who were aboard Bounty, Bligh was the only one who ever suggested that it was Tahiti or women which had inflamed Christian. Christian lashed two masts to his raft and hid some pork and breadfruit. His preparations were well observed, but he used the flimsy excuse to stay on board that there were too many men on deck at night to leave in secrecy.

What happened next has been the subject of much argument, and this is not the place to rehearse even one of the theories. Suffice to say that at some time during the night, when he slept for only one hour, or in the early minutes of his watch which began at 4am, Christian decided that it was not he who should leave the ship but Bligh. There was no well-conceived plan to take the ship, but simply a desire to rid the ship of Bligh

Buttock tattoo typical of the time.

A plan of Fort George c 1980.

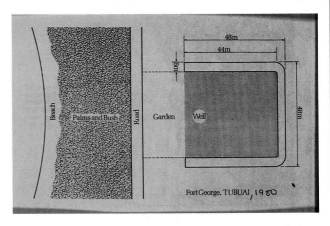

Fort George, TUBUAI 1980

and the worst of his gang. But Bounty was no ordinary ship. Her complement was the first all-volunteer crew to sail a naval vessel. They were free men who had chosen adventure and in return had tasted the pleasures of Tahiti and the South Pacific. Whatever had driven Fletcher to mutiny was not what suddenly ignited others to join him. The reported raging and pleading of Bligh with Christian – "you have dannled my children on your knees" – exposed for all to see the depth of their previous friendship and Christian's despair His wild eyes and temperament have been used to suggest, among many theories, that he was suffering from syphillis; I expect most of us in the throes of leading a mutiny after one hour's sleep and weeks of torment would look something less than composed and in good health.

The largely unpublished life of Fletcher Christian after the mutiny gives the clearest views of his aspirations and beliefs. He may not have planned to

■ Pitcairn Island. *Glynn Christian.*

mutiny, but like all those second in command he clearly had thought about what he might do as commander. He now embarked on a series of radical changes aboard Bounty which made him a true revolutionary. Months before the storming of the Bastille in Paris in the interests of liberty, equality, and fraternity, something of which he would have had no inkling, Fletcher Christian introduced democratic decision making aboard the ship. Leaders were elected, often from among those who had resisted Christian's actions; but men at sea are more sensible of their safety than to give authority only to those they liked. Far more telling than democracy was Christian's decision that everyone on board should have a uniform. In the 18th century, only the officers and gentlemen wore uniforms, but Christian believed that uniformity of dress created a sense of fraternity and would also present a more powerful image to others as he searched now for a safe haven. Thus jackets were stitched from sail cloth and edged with the blue of his own uniform. When later confronted

by belligerent Polynesians, the uniforms appeared to have the desired effect, but the unity was barely skin deep. Bounty remained a ship of suspicion, sailed by Christian's suppporters and those who would have gone with Bligh.

After returning to Tahiti to collect livestock, and gathering also Tahitian men and women, Christian attempted to settle on Tubuai. It is a credit to his administrative ability that this motley and partly unwilling group was persuaded in the sickly subtropical heat to build a huge fortress of earth surrounded by a deep moat. But a political error meant the siting of the loyally-named Fort George had upset the mightiest chief in the island. War followed and Christian sailed his unhappy charges back to Tahiti. The future was put to the vote once more; Christian wanted only Bounty but found himself with eight followers as well. The rest, mutineers and Bligh loyalists alike, chose to stay in Tahiti.

In a decision which remains one of his most puzzling, Christian cut the anchor cable without warning early in

■ Bounty Bay. *Glynn Christian.*

the morning of 23 September 1789 and Bounty slipped through the reef. By daylight there had been a sort out and the ship headed back to Moorea, releasing six "rather ancient" women who had been among those trapped, but who had not found the companion or other reason to stay. On board was Mauatua who was to bear Christian's three children, but there is no evidence that they had previously been lovers, and he was never said to have had a single attachment. She may have been older than he for she remembered the visits of Captain Cook and many years later said that she had left children in Tahiti. Also aboard was a baby girl, who was eventually to marry Charles, the second son she bore to Fletcher: all his grandchildren were more Tahitian than English. Christian called his companion Isabella and others called her Mainmast for her upright bearing; this later became Maimiti in the Pitcairn dialogue and this is the name generally used in film and stage depictions.

It was only in the 1950s that Professor Maude of Canberra finally pieced together the long trek Bounty now made with eight European men, six Tahitian men, and 14 females, including the baby. Far from the usual indication that she sailed southwards to Pitcairn, Bounty sailed west as far as the Fijian islands. On the way she discovered Rarotonga, and probably introduced the orange, now a mainstay of that economy. In the Fijians, it became finally clear that populated islands would never offer safety. Chris-

tian's constant studying of the charts left in Bligh's cabin focused on Pitcairn's Island. Remote, uninhabited, and difficult to land at – it was perfect, but it was almost 2,000 miles and a month's sailing back the way they had come. To me, the fact that Bounty, seriously undermanned by a group of men and women who spoke little of each other's language and knew less of each other's culture, could now choose to sail with Christian deep in to the colder southern waters of the Pacific is wonderful. That there was eventually some discussion about returning to Tahiti if Pitcairn had not been found seems perfectly reasonable: to suggest that Fletcher had no qualities of leadership is puerile. The voyage took two chill and dispiriting months.

When Bounty finally reached the position Pitcairn was supposed to occupy there was only sea. It had been charted incorrectly and Christian now knew his decision was right. If he could find Pitcairn no one in the world was likely to guess where they were or to find them. He zig zagged carefully, using all navigational skills and eventually found it on the evening of 15 January 1790. Only a mile by a mile by a mile and a half, it is remoteness itself, and the community was not discovered until 1808. The new society founded as a result of Christian's single, precipitate decision had no help from precedent. The Tahitians had to break down further the taboos that shipboard life prevented anyway – back home women were not allowed to touch much of the food men ate, for instance. The Europeans saw themselves as landed gentry and quickly turned the Tahitian men into servants and slaves, aping positions in society they could never have

aspired to at home. The end was inevitable. More mutiny, this time by black men against white. In October 1793, on the day his third child Mary was born, Christian was shot and clubbed as he worked in his garden. There he undoubtedly died. The two-century-old industry in Bounty/Bligh/Christian surmize has largely been fanned by the possibility that Christian escaped Pitcairn and returned to Britain. It is indeed possible. But assiduous checking of each of the 11 conflicting stories of his death, including visiting Pitcairn Island itself, proved to me that none had credibility.

As with so many heroes of protest and escapism, it seems that the public did not and does not want Christian to have died ignominiously with his broken head blackening in the red soil of Pitcairn; Christian was given the 18th and 19th century treatment that tabloids give to Elvis Presley and James Dean today, though abetted by the dissembling of Adams and the misunderstanding of early visitors who were dissuaded from speaking to the surviving Tahitian women. To those who understand such things, Fletcher Christian is one of the finest navigators of his time, a shining pupil of Bligh, who in return reflected the brilliance of Cook. With the help of Larcum's newly perfected chronometer, Christian was safely to sail the undermanned ship 8000 miles in search of a home and founded a brave new world of his own.

Christian was a law-breaker, a mutineer, a pirate, a blackbirder, and probably a fool. He was also an important, but unheralded explorer, the founding father

■ The Pool; Fletcher Christian's alleged murder spot. *Glynn Christian.*

of a unique people, and like so many of his powerful family a courageous social pioneer. What Rousseau dreamed, Christian did. His descendants became the most God-fearing community on earth and thus it is through the Victorian Church, which adapted the Bounty story as a modern parable, that the 19th century was fed a constant flow of Pitcairn and Bounty fable. But there was no myth about the legacy of fairness and justice that Fletcher left his island, for Pitcairn was the first community in the world to give women a full franchise.

There never was a mutiny of the Bounty. Rather was there a revolt by one man against another, Christian against Bligh. Logically, that clash can only be understood if the passions and perversities of both men are understood. In the bibliography of more than 2,500 books and articles there remains only one biography of Fletcher Christian, proof indeed that this is a story which touches some seminal core: the truth about Fletcher Christian is less important to many people than what he has come to represent, or how he can be manipulated to enhance the reputation of other heroes. When I first began to research my ancestor, I expected to whiten Bligh and blacken Christian, but the contemporary facts do not allow this. Now I look forward to the day when there is no longer the urge to cast Bligh or Christian as black or white, but simply to remember them as they were. Blame does not matter today. They are men who are remembered. Few men who are remembered for as long and as thrillingly as they can have been wholly black or white.

Glynn Christian is known as a television personality and author.

■ Pitcairn cousins. *Glynn Christian.*

The Victoria and Albert Museum

It's been described as a Treasure House, an Aladdin's cave, even "the nation's attic", but there are very few tags which really do justice to London's Victoria and Albert Museum.

Founded in 1852 from the profits of the Great Exhibition, the V & A, as it is popularly known, started its life as a Museum of Manufactures to stimulate students of design. Since then it has grown into one of the world's greatest museums, including everything from Indian sculpture to contemporary jewellery.

The statistics alone are breathtaking. Seven miles of galleries, covering over 30 acres of ground and containing something like five million precious objects large and small. Not surprisingly it's the kind of museum you can visit for years and still find something new to look at.

"It's the best place to get lost in London" runs a recent comment in the V & A's visitors' book. Fortunately the museum is blessed with some of the most charming information staff you'll find in any tourist attraction in London.

So what are the highlights?

For sheer exhilaration it's difficult to beat the famous Victorian Cast Courts – the V & A's most spectacular monument to Victorian style. Here you will find full size plaster replicas of sculpture and architecture from all over Europe, dominated by a towering cast of Trajan's column in Rome. Then, in distinct contrast, there's the V & A's other big popular attraction, the Dress Collection - recently voted the museum s biggest draw – which includes everything from tricorns and bustles to the latest creations of the 1980s.

A few steps away, you will find the Raphael Cartoons, the most important examples of large-scale Renaissance art in Britain. These are Raphael's original designs for tapestries in the Sistine Chapel in Rome.

On a smaller scale you shouldn't miss the Museum's extraordinary jewellery collection, housed in its own top-security gallery and including dazzling pieces dating right back to Ancient Egypt.

And there's much much more ... the national collection of furniture that includes the famous Great Bed of Ware, the sixteenth century prodigy mentioned in Shakespeare's Twelfth Night, breathtaking Italian Renaissance sculpture, Britain's largest collection of the paintings of John Constable, the national collections of silver, ceramics, glass, not to mention extraordinary displays of Chinese and Japanese Art and the single largest collection of Indian art outside the subcontinent.

If all that isn't enough the V & A is well worth a visit just for its buildings. The museum was conceived as an "an exhibit in itself" - a place where the great Victorian and Edwardian craftsmen and designers could display their skills. The result is a monument to the enormous industry and ingenuity of the late nineteenth century ... and the story goes that the ghost of Sir Henry Cole, the museum's founder, still paces the galleries at dead of night admiring his handiwork.

Since Cole's day the Museum has undergone many changes and it now faces an exacting programme of redevelopment, which includes the creation of new galleries and a major series of temporary exhibitions, on everything from photography to architecture. If you would like to know more about the V & A, it's well worth joining the new V & A Club. Membership costs £16 a year and brings you regular mailings about the museum's activities, courses and exhibitions. For more details, give the Club secretary a ring on 01-938 8365.

The epic open boat voyage

Bligh's brilliant navigational skills have long been overshadowed by the mutiny. Andrew David sets out to redress the balance

■ WILLIAM BLIGH served his apprenticeship as a hydrographic surveyor and explorer as the master of HMS Resolution during Captain Cook's third voyage to the Pacific. As a ship's master, Bligh was in theory solely responsible to the captain for the navigation, in addition to other duties. A ship's master was also expected to carry out any minor surveys that might be required. However, on board the Resolution, Bligh's position was unusual since an astronomer was aboard to take astronomical observations to fix the ship's position at sea and Cook was a surveyor of vast experience, who would clearly take charge of all important surveys. Nevertheless, it is clear that Bligh was responsible for much of the navigation during the voyage and was closely involved in most of the survey work, particularly after Cook's death in Hawaii.

After Cook's third voyage, Bligh had little scope for carrying out further surveys until he was appointed in command of HM Armed Vessel Bounty in 1787 to transport breadfruit plants from Tahiti to the West Indies. For this voyage Bligh was well equipped, having on board a very early chronometer made by Kendall, known as K2, which enabled him to fix his longitude accurately. He was also supplied with three brass sextants, which Bligh considered to be "exceedingly perfect", namely a 10-inch and a 14-inch sextant made by Ramsden, and a 12-inch sextant made by Troughton. There was at least one "old quadrant" on board, probably a Hadley's quadrant, which despite being made mainly of wood, was still reasonably accurate. This instrument was, in fact, an octant and as such was only capable of measuring angles up to 90°, while the sextants were able to measure angles up to 120°. Bligh was also supplied with two azimuth compasses made by Adams, principally for taking bearings of shore objects to fix the ship's position, but also for taking bearings of the sun to determine magnetic variation. The importance of good instruments, particularly the need to carry sextants rather than octants for taking astronomical observations at sea, is stressed in the Tables Requisite to be used with the Nautical Ephemeris for finding the Latitude and Longitude at Sea, published by the Commisioners of Longitude:

> The observer must be furnished with a good Hadley's quadrant, and a watch that can be depended upon for keeping time within a minute for six hours. But it will be more convenient if the instrument be made a sextant, in which case it will measure 120°, for the sake of observing the moon's distance from the sun, for two or three days after the first and before the last quarter. The instrument will be still more fit for the purpose, if it is furnished with a screw to move the index gradually in measuring the moon's distance from the sun or star; an additional dark glass, lighter than the common ones, to take off the glare of the moon's light in observing her distance from a fixed star, and a small telescope, magnifying three or four times, to render the contact of the star with the moon's limb more discernible. A magnifying glass of 1 1/2 or two inches focus will assist the observer to read off his observation with greater ease and certainty.

There were at least five navigational manuals on board the Bounty, which Bligh consulted at various stages in the voyage. Of these, the *Tables Requisite* (second edition, 1781), Hamilton Moore's *The Practical Navigator* (probably the eighth edition, 1784) and John Robertson's *The Elements of Navigation* (probably the fifth edition, 1786) proved particularly useful, since these manuals contained tables giving the latitudes and longitudes of various places around the world. Bligh was also issued with copies of *The Nautical Almanac and Astronomical Ephemeris* for the years he was expected to be absent from England.

Bligh must have carried many charts for his voyage, but those covering the Pacific would have been unreliable unless they had been brought up to date since Cook's three voyages. However, the only charts that Bligh refers to in his journal are those contained in the accounts of Cook's voyages. In particular, he refers several times to the world chart, drawn by Henry Roberts under Cook's personal supervision, which is contained in the atlas published with Cook's third voyage. Bligh also had on board accounts of other voyages, providing useful navigational information, including Hawkesworth's *Voyages,* containing accounts of Cook's first voyage and the voyages of Byron, Wallis, and Carteret, the *Voyages* of Dampier, Anson, and Bougainville, and Dalrymple's *Voyages,* containing accounts of all the principal Spanish and Dutch voyages in the Pacific before 1764. Bligh also took with him all his surveys, drawings, and remarks made during the previous 15 years, which he consulted from time to time.

During the Bounty's voyage, Bligh employed two methods of finding longi-

■ TOP LEFT Captain James Cook. Wedgwood Portrait Medallion, made for the bicentenary of first voyage.
TOP RIGHT A 10" Ramsden Sextant, contemporary with 1789.
BOTTOM LEFT Title Page, Tables Requisite,1781, 2nd Edition.
BOTTOM RIGHT Title Page, Hamilton Moore's, The Practical Navigator, 1784, 8th Edition.
ALL FOUR ITEMS:
National Maritime Museum.

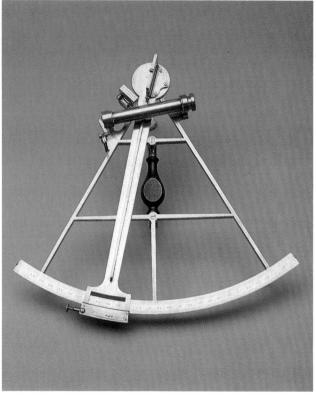

T A B L E S

John   *Sutton*

REQUISITE TO BE USED WITH THE

March 1st 1786

NAUTICAL EPHEMERIS

FOR FINDING THE

LATITUDE AND LONGITUDE AT SEA.

PUBLISHED BY ORDER OF THE

COMMISSIONERS OF LONGITUDE.

THE SECOND EDITION,

CORRECTED AND IMPROVED.

LONDON:

PRINTED BY WILLIAM RICHARDSON IN THE STRAND;

AND SOLD BY

C. NOURSE in the STRAND, and Meff. MOUNT and PAGE
on TOWER-HILL,
BOOKSELLERS to the faid COMMISSIONERS.

MDCCLXXXI.

THE

PRACTICAL NAVIGATOR,

AND

SEAMAN's NEW DAILY ASSISTANT.

BEING

A complete SYSTEM of PRACTICAL NAVIGATION,
Improved, and rendered eafy to any common Capacity.

THE WHOLE EXEMPLIFIED IN

A JOURNAL kept from LONDON to MADEIRA

WHEREIN IS SHEWN,

How to allow for Lee way, Variation, Heave of the Sea, Set of the Currents, &c. and to correct the dead Reckoning by an Obfervation, in all Cafes.
The Method of Mooring, Unmooring, and Working a Ship in all difficult Cafes at Sea, on a Lee-fhore, or coming into Harbour.
The Manner of Managing the great

Guns; of Forming the Line; of an Engagement at Sea; and of Surveying Coafts and Harbours; with an Explanation of the Sea Terms.
The New Method of finding the Latitude by two Altitudes of the Sun; and of finding the Longitude by the Moon's Diftance from the Sun or a fixed Star.

To which are added,

The Tables of Difference of Latitude and Departure to 300 Miles Diftance;
New Solar Tables; the Table of Natural Sines; a new Table of the
Latitude and Longitude of Places, according to the lateft Obfervations;
a Table, fhewing the Times of the rifing and fetting of the Sun, Moon,
fixed Stars, and Planets; and all other Tables ufeful at Sea.

CONSTRUCTED UPON A NEW PLAN.

By JOHN HAMILTON MOORE,
Teacher of Navigation, &c. No. 104 in the Minories, Tower-Hill, London.

The EIGHTH EDITION.
Carefully corrected, and greatly enlarged by the AUTHOR.

In this Edition are added the Method of finding the LATITUDE by the MOON
and PLANETS; and two COPPER PLATES; one fhewing the SOLAR
SYSTEM the other the TERMS of GEOGRAPHY at one View.

LONDON:

Printed for and Sold by B. LAW, in Ave-Maria-Lane; G. ROBINSON,
Pater-nofter-Row; and the Author, at No. 104, in the Minories, near
Tower-Hill.

M,DCC,LXXXIV.

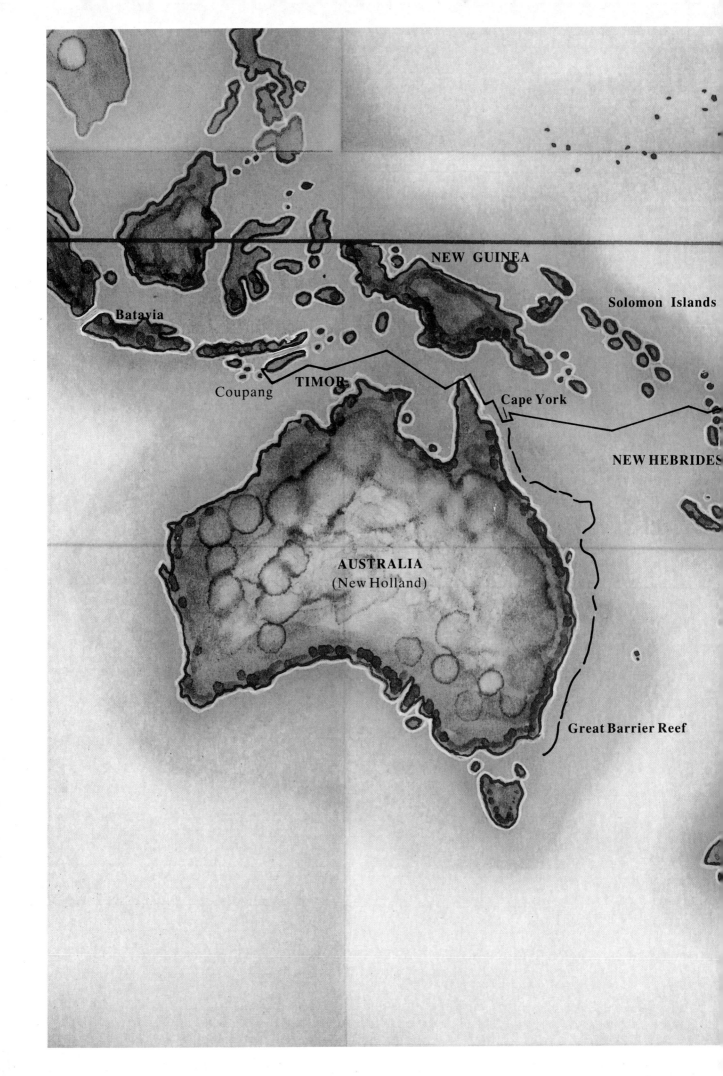

NEW GUINEA

Solomon Islands

Batavia

Coupang

TIMOR

Cape York

NEW HEBRIDES

AUSTRALIA
(New Holland)

Great Barrier Reef

Bounty's Launch voyage from Tofoa to Timor

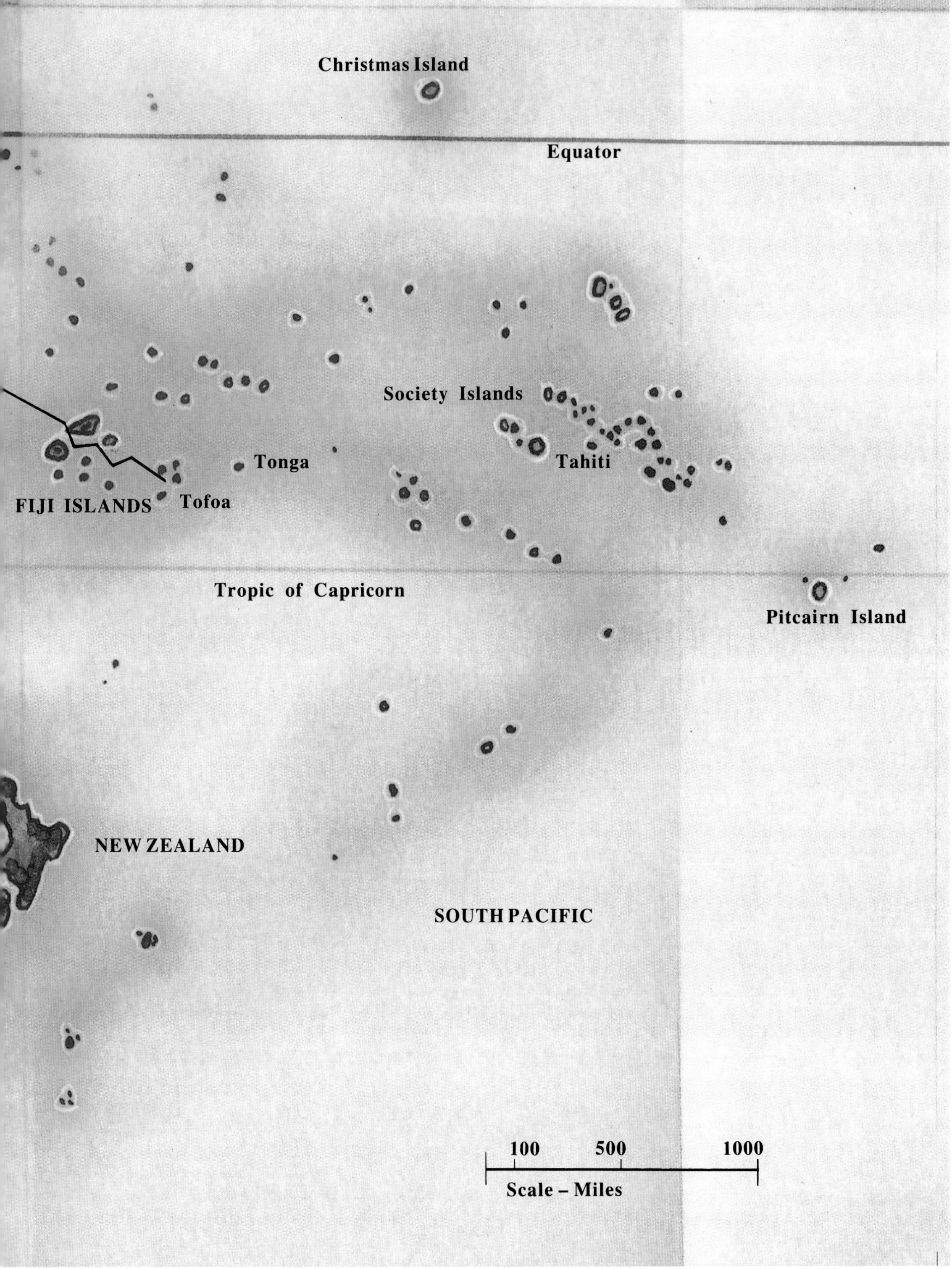

Christmas Island

Equator

Society Islands

Tonga

Tahiti

FIJI ISLANDS Tofoa

Tropic of Capricorn

Pitcairn Island

NEW ZEALAND

SOUTH PACIFIC

100   500   1000

Scale – Miles

tude at sea. The first method, known as lunar distances, had been perfected by the time of Cook's first voyage. This method was based on the fact that the moon in its motion through the heavens˜ can be used as a clock. To put it simply, by measuring the angle between the moon and the sun, or between the moon and one of nine selected stars and comparing the angle obtained with values tabulated in the *Nautical Almanac* it was possible to obtain the Greenwich time of the observation. The procedure was in fact a little more complicated and required two additional observers to observe simultaneously the altitudes of the moon and the sun or one of the selected stars, while a fourth observer noted the precise time of the observation by deck watch, which he recorded together with all three observations. Next the local time of the observation had to be obtained, either directly from the deck watch, if its rate had been checked earlier in the day, or from the observation of the sun or star. The angles then had to be cleared of the effects of lunar parallax and refraction to obtain their true values. The *Nautical Almanac* was then consulted and by interpolation the Greenwich time of the observation obtained. Finally, the difference between the local and Greenwich times of the observation was the ship's longitude, expressed in hours and minutes east or west of Greenwich. The calculation was a tedious affair, taking several hours, and an accuracy of less than about 30 minutes of longitude was rarely achieved by this means.

The second method employed by Bligh for finding longitude at sea was by using his chronometer to obtain a direct reading of Greenwich time, which was then compared with local time, as for lunar distances, to obtain longitude. The accuracy of this method, which had been tested successfully by Cook during his second voyage, depended on the time keeping qualities of the chronometer. First, it was necessary to establish the error of the chronometer on Greenwich time and the rate it was gaining or losing each day at the start of the voyage. For the Bounty's chronometer these values were initially obtained at the observatory in Portsmouth dockyard before leaving England. Thereafter, Bligh was able to obtain new rates for the chronometer, whenever it was possible to take two sets of observations on shore of the sun crossing the meridian, spaced about seven days apart.

It was, however, an easy matter for Bligh to obtain his latitude at sea. The usual method he adopted was to observe the sun's altitude as it crossed the meridian at noon. The calculation of latitude was then a simple matter, taking only a few minutes. First, he had to convert the observed altitude of the sun to its true value by applying corrections for the index error of his sextant, refraction, which varies with altitude, his height of eye above sea level, and an allowance for the sun's semi-diameter if he observed the sun's lower limb. He then subtracted the sun's true altitude from 90° to obtain the sun's zenith distance and finally applied the declination of the sun north or south of the Equator, taken from the *Nautical Almanac*, to obtain his latitude. Thus on every day that the sun was visible at noon, Bligh was able to obtain an accurate value for latitude. Bligh also took observations, whenever possible, to obtain magnetic variation, which differs quite considerably over the earth's surface, so that he could calculate the true courses steered by the magnetic compass and also convert magnetic bearings to true bearings.

Bligh sailed from Portsmouth on 23 December 1787. After calling briefly at Tenerife to take on supplies, he attempted to reach Tahiti by rounding Cape Horn, in accordance with his instructions. However, he encountered such rough weather off the cape that he was able to make little progress, with conditions so bad on some occasions that he had to be lashed to the mast when taking his astronomical observations. After fighting for 30 days against the bitterly cold westerly gales, Bligh was eventually forced to come about and run for the Cape of Good Hope. During his passage across the South Atlantic, he unsuccessfully searched for Tristan da Cunha, whose position he was keen to fix since his navigational manuals and Cook's world chart gave widely differing values for its longitude. Bligh broke off his search when he was only about 14 miles west of Nightingale Island, situated 17 miles SSW of the main island of Tristan da Cunha, without sighting either, probably passed close to the former island during the night, while continuing his voyage to the Cape of Good Hope.

Bligh anchored in Simon's Bay on 24 May, after having been at sea continuously for 134 days since leaving Tenerife. His crew were in excellent health

despite the hardships suffered off Cape Horn. This was in marked contrast to a Dutch East Indiaman, which had arrived shortly before the Bounty with a great many on board sick, though having made a quicker passage from Europe. This was undoubtedly due to the care taken by Bligh over his crew's health. It is worth noting that Bligh's small library on board the Bounty contained three classic accounts about the health of seamen by Dr James Lind, a naval surgeon who has been aptly described as "the father of nautical medicine". The books were *An Essay on the most effectual means of Preserving the Health of Seamen, An Essay on Diseases incidental to Europeans in Hot Climates,* and *A Treatise of the Scurvy*. It was Lind who carried out the first controlled experiment which proved that lemons or oranges were the best available cure for scurvy.

Soon after arriving at the cape, Bligh called on Governor van de Graaff, taking the opportunity to make arrangements for fresh meat and greens to be supplied to the Bounty so that these could be issued daily, an important factor in building up resistance to scurvy and disease for the long voyage ahead. He next landed with his chronometer to obtain a fresh value for its rate. Since the *Requisite Tables* contained an accurate longitude for False Bay, Bligh was able to obtain the chronometer's error on Greenwich time. Bligh also had time to make a plan of the bay, which has not survived and to obtain a more accurate value for the latitude of Cape Point, the southern extremity of the Cape of Good Hope.

From Simon's Bay Bligh set a course for Van Diemen's land (Tasmania), where he intended to wood and water, selecting a course which he hoped would prove useful to merchant ships in the winter months, bound for the proposed convict settlement at Botany Bay. During his passage across the South Indian Ocean, Bligh decided to make for St Paul Island, situated some 1,500 miles west of Cape Leeuwin, the SW extremity of Australia, to fix its position with his chronometer. He therefore consulted his navigational manuals and Cook's world chart and found that not only did they give widely different values for its latitude, but some of these authorities even transposed the island's name with that of Amsterdam Island, some 60 miles to the north. Bligh decided that if he ran down

■ Bounty Islands. 19th century steel engraving. *Private collection.*

the latitude of 38°40'S there was a good chance of sighting at least one of these two islands. This plan was successful and on 28 July an island was sighted, which Bligh correctly identified as St Paul, enabling him to fix its position accurately. He had hoped to investigate a reported anchorage to the east of the island, but a gale blew up before he could do so, and he bore away for Van Diemen's land without stopping.

As Bligh approached Van Diemen's land, another gale blew up, bringing with it thick weather. Relying on his chronometer, Bligh set a course for the Mewstone, a bold rocky islet, off the island's southern coast. Soon after, land was sighted at 2pm on 20 August, the wind dropped, and it was not until 5.15am the following morning that he anchored in Adventure Bay, on the SE side of the island. Bligh landed with his chronometer on several occasions to obtain its rate, erecting a tent to act as an observatory. He also obtained the longitude of Penguin Island at the southern end of Adventure Bay by 19 sets of lunar distances, but he did not carry out a detailed survey of the bay, confining his efforts to improving his survey made during Cook's third voyage, commenting that his plan:

has met with little or no improvement from the State I formed it in when I was here with Capt[n]. Cook; for unless a Person is immediately on the business of Surveying, little can be done with great exactness or certainty, altho sufficient for the general Management of a Ship: however I believe few places are better determined either as to Latitude or Longitude, and the General direction of all the Coast may be relied on.

Nevertheless, Bligh did discover "a remarkable high flat Top'd Mountain", the first recorded reference to Mount Wellington, which today overlooks the city of Hobart.

On sailing from Adventure Bay on 4 September, Bligh passed well south of New Zealand, before altering course ENE towards Tahiti, to establish a new track to the Society Islands. On 19 September, a group of small rocky islands was discovered some 400 miles east of the southern tip of New Zealand, which Bligh named Bounty Islands after his ship. From here Bligh made for a position about 1,000 miles SE of Tahiti so that he could approach the island with the SE trade wind blowing in his favour,

anchoring in Matavai Bay on the north side of Tahiti on 26 October after an uneventful passage.

Bligh remained in Matavai Bay until 25 December, when he found it necessary to move to a more sheltered anchorage in Oparre Harbour, about 2 1/2 miles WSW, with the onset of bad weather. For reasons which are not entirely clear, possibly concerned with establishing the breadfruit plants in their pots or the likelihood of encountering contrary winds in Torres Strait, Bligh remained in Tahiti for more than five months. This enabled him to carry out a

Portrait of John Fryer, Master of The Bounty. *Mitchell Library, Sydney.*

survey of Matavai Bay and Oparre Harbours with the assistance of Mr Fryer, master of the Bounty, which he described as "a most correct Survey" in his journal, in which he also gave some details of the methods he employed during the survey:

> I employed myself to-day principally in completing my Survey, which will however take me a few days more, as to be exact requires absolute measurement, the Angles on the Coast not being sufficient with few determined Bases to establish the whole with certainty. This Survey, that it may be usefull to those who may come after me, I shall complete between point Venus and the West point of Taowne Harbour

This survey was lost with the Bounty, but Bligh reconstructed it from memory, based on the anchor bearings he took in Matavai Bay and Oparre Harbour, which he had recorded in his journal.

On sailing from Tahiti on 5 April 1789, Bligh set a course for the Friendly Islands (Tonga), following closely the tracks of Cook and his predecessors. He was surprised to discover, on 12 April, an unknown island of moderate height. Bligh remained off this island for three days to examine the cays off its SSE side and a reef extending a considerable distance westward from it, which he felt could constitute a danger to future navigators. Some natives came on board and from them Bligh learnt that their name for the island was Whytootackee; it is one of the southern Cook Islands and is now known as Aitutaki. Cook's Savage Island (Niue) was sighted on 18 April, enabling Bligh to confirm the position he and Cook had obtained for it in 1777. On 24 April, Bligh anchored off the island of Nomuka, in the Friendly Islands, to obtain wood and water and any provisions that could be procured, before sailing again three days later for Torres Strait.

On 28 April, Fletcher Christian, Bligh's second in command, led the successful mutiny on board the Bounty off the island of Tofua, casting Bligh and 18 companions adrift in the ship's 23-foot long launch. There then followed one of the most remarkable open boat voyages on record. In 47 days, Bligh navigated the unprotected and grossly overcrowded launch some 3,600 miles, measured in a straight line by his own calculation, from Tofua to the Dutch settlement of Coupang in Timor without the aid of a chart and without any means of obtaining his longitude. Christian deliberately retained the chronometer on board the Bounty and he also expressly forbad Bligh being given a copy of the *Nautical Almanac*. But Bligh was not devoid of means of navigating the launch, since Christian allowed him to take a sextant, recently identified as the 10-inch brass sextant by Ramsden, which was on board the Bounty, and Bligh somehow managed to obtain a copy of a "daily assistant", a clear reference to Hamilton Moore's *Practical Navigator*. In addition, Bligh had a compass and there was also an old quadrant in the launch, proba-

■ Matthew Flinders RN, who sailed with Bligh on The Providence and who later charted the coast of Australia. *National Maritime Museum.*

bly one of Hadley's quadrants. Midshipman Hallet brought with him a copy of the *Tables Requisite* and Midshipman Hayward a notebook, which Bligh appropriated to record his navigational remarks, while Mr Peckover, the gunner, brought with him his watch, which Bligh made use of for navigational purposes. Christian would not allow Bligh any firearms, but four cutlasses were thrown into the launch shortly before it was cast adrift. The launch was well provisioned for a short voyage since there was on board 150 pounds of bread (ie ship's biscuits), 16 pieces of salt pork, 6 quarts of rum, 6 bottles of wine, and 28 gallons of water.

After getting clear of the Bounty, Bligh set a course for Tofua to obtain additional water and provisions, with the intention of then returning to Nomuka. However, at Tofua, after some water and provisions had been obtained, the natives attacked the launch once they realized that Bligh lacked firearms. Although Bligh succeeded in getting the launch clear, John Norton, one of the seamen, was stoned to death while attempting to let go the rope attaching the launch's stern to the beach. The loss of Norton, who was reputed to be the stoutest man in the ship, may well have been a blessing in disguise since with his death the launch's dangerously low freeboard was thereby increased by a small but perhaps significant amount.

After this narrow escape, Bligh realized, it would be folly to return to Nomuka, where, without firearms, he would once again be at risk of attack by the natives. He, therefore, decided to make for the nearest known European settlement, which was that of the Dutch at Coupang in Timor, since he had no way of knowing whether the British settlement in Botany Bay had been started. Bligh then consulted the two navigational manuals in the launch, and finding in the *Tables Requisite* the geographical position of the SW tip of Timor, he was able to calculate the straight line distance from Tofua to Timor by means of the traverse tables in the *Practical Navigator*, as "full 1,200 leagues", that is 3,600 sea miles. However the actual distance that Bligh covered, allowing for various alterations of course to clear islands and reefs en route, was probably in the region of 3,900 miles. It was clear to Bligh that the quantities of provisions and fresh water in the launch were clearly inadequate for a voyage of this length and that these would have to be severely rationed if they were to last as far as Timor. All hands were acquainted of these facts and having obtained their agreement to live on an ounce of bread and a quarter of a pint of water a day, Bligh bore away for Timor before a strong easterly wind.

At first, Bligh ran before the prevailing easterly wind, under a reefed foresail, while deciding what course to steer, since without a chart, he had no easy way of knowing what islands or dangers might lie ahead. However, he soon set a course "to the WNW that I may see a Group of Islands called Fidgee if they lie in that *Continued on page 97*

Continued on page 97

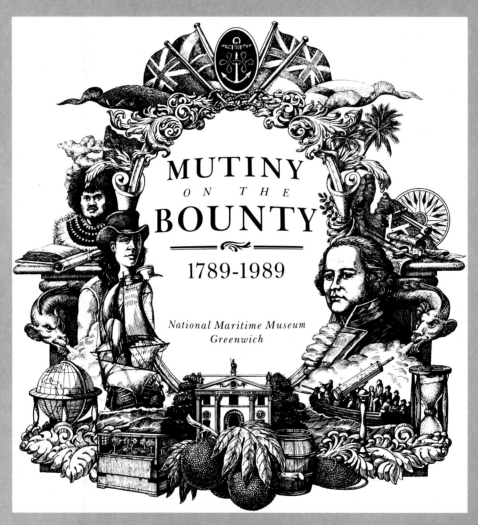

MUTINY
ON THE
BOUNTY
1789-1989

National Maritime Museum
Greenwich

Guide to the Exhibition

by Rina Prentice

"Just before Sun Rise the People Mutinied, seized me while asleep in my Cabbin tied my Hands behind my back – carried me on Deck in my Shirt – Put 18 of the Crew into the Launch and me after them and set us adrift."

LIEUTENANT WILLIAM BLIGH RN,

28TH APRIL 1789.

1. HIS MAJESTY's NAVY AND COMMERCE IN THE 1780s.

"Leaving Billingsgate we were rowed along the mid-channel bounded on each side by vast fleets of all nations and sizes, as high as six hundred tons, disposed, I may say, in squadrons with small intervals between them."
Thomas Pennant, 1787.

London in 1787 was the centre of an expanding commercial empire. Shipping congested the Thames, the shipbuilding yards were busy, and Britain's maritime pre-eminence was undoubted. James Cook's explorations and his untimely death were still much in people's minds, and there had grown up a close relationship between the naval voyages of exploration and scientific research, colonization, and the commercial exploitation of the new discoveries.

At this time a career at sea could easily span both the Royal Navy and the merchant service, as Cook's had done. In 1787 William Bligh, Master of HMS Resolution on Cook's 3rd Voyage, and later in action at the Dogger Bank and Gibraltar, had just spent four years in the West Indies trade.

It was fitting that with such a background, Bligh should have been chosen to carry out the government's latest venture, an expedition to Tahiti to collect breadfruit plants and transplant them to the West Indies, where it was hoped they would provide a cheap food supply for slaves on the sugar plantations. Cook had already pointed out the economic value of the plant, but merchant captains had shown no interest in the scheme, despite the offer of a Premium from the Society for the encouragement of the Arts, Manufacturers and Commerce. Sir Joseph Banks, however, who had himself sailed with Cook, used his influence with King George III to make the expedition a naval enterprise, and the scene was set for the Bounty's fateful voyage.

1. SHIPPING IN THE POOL OF LONDON. Oil painting by Robert Dodd (1748-1815).

2. SHIPBUILDING ON THE THAMES AT ROTHERHITHE. Oil painting by Thomas Whitcombe, 1792.

3. CARGO HANDLING EQUIPMENT. *Museum of London.*

4. WILLIAM BLIGH (1754-1817). Oil painting attributed to John Webber, circa 1776. Said to show Bligh as a young midshipman, before his departure on James Cook's 3rd Voyage. *Private Collection.*

5. ELIZABETH BLIGH (1752-1812). Oil painting by John Webber, 1782. *Private Collection.*

6. CAPTAIN JAMES COOK RN (1728-79). Marble bust by Lucien le Vieux. *National Portrait Gallery.*

7. CHART OF TAHITI. By Lieutenant James Cook, 1769. Tahiti came to public prominence with Cook's visit to observe the Transit of Venus in 1769.

8. RESOLUTION's TRACK THROUGH THE PACIFIC AND SOUTHERN OCEAN, 1772-5 by Joseph Gilbert, circa 1776. Gilbert, Master of the Resolution during Cook's 2nd Voyage enjoyed Cook's confidence as an excellent hydrographic surveyor. This chart is drawn on a circumpolar projection to emphasise the thoroughness of Cook's search for the "southern continent."

10. CHART OF THE DISCOVERIES OF HMS RESOLUTION AND DISCOVERY ON THE COAST OF ASIA AND AMERICA. By William Bligh, Master of HMS Resolution, 1778-9. Unsigned chart of the North Pacific in Bligh's hand, showing the track of James Cook's 3rd Voyage, and high quality land profiles. *Hydrographic Department, MOD.*

12. RESOLUTION AND DISCOVERY OFF THE COAST OF TAHITI. Watercolour by Samuel Atkins (flourished 1787-1808). As the artist did not sail on Cook's 3rd Voyage, the painting must be a later commission.

13. CHART OF LUCEA HARBOUR, JAMAICA. Surveyed by Lieut. William Bligh RN, circa 1783. The chart shows the cluster of settlements at the coast, linked with the sugar export. Between 1783 and 1787 Bligh commanded the merchant ships of Duncan Campbell, his wife's uncle, trading to Jamaica. *Hydrographic Dept., MOD.*

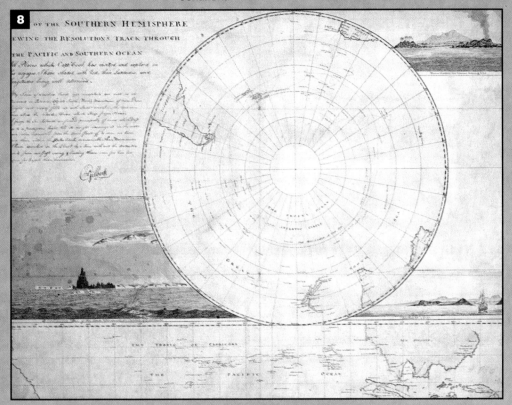

14. MAP OF BARBADOS. By William Mayo, 1722. This map illustrates the sugar plantations of Barbados. Insets show Codrington College with its sugar mill, curing house and boiling house, and a plantation being surveyed.

9. RESOLUTION IN THE MARQUESAS. Pen and wash drawing by William Hodges, 1774. HMS Resolution is shown at anchor in Vaitahu Bay during Cook's 2nd Voyage.

11. A VOYAGE TO THE PACIFIC OCEAN (COOK's THIRD VOYAGE) by James Cook and James King, 3 Vol., 1784. Bligh annotated the three volumes with angry remarks on the lack of acknowledgement for his own charts and surveys, and alleged inaccuracies in Lieut. James King's account of Cook's death. *MOD Naval Library Collection.*

15. MAP OF JAMAICA. By Thomas Craskell and James Simpson, 1763. This map was compiled to show the island's parishes at the instance of Henry Moore, Lieut.Governor of Jamaica, 1756-61. It shows the range of crops grown for which slave labour was used: sugar, cotton, coffee and pimentoes.

16. SHIPPING SUGAR. Aquatint by unknown artist, 1823. A plantation in Antigua, West Indies.

17. A VIEW OF THE TOWN OF ST GEORGE IN THE ISLAND OF GRENADA. Aquatint by W Daniell, 1819.

12

15

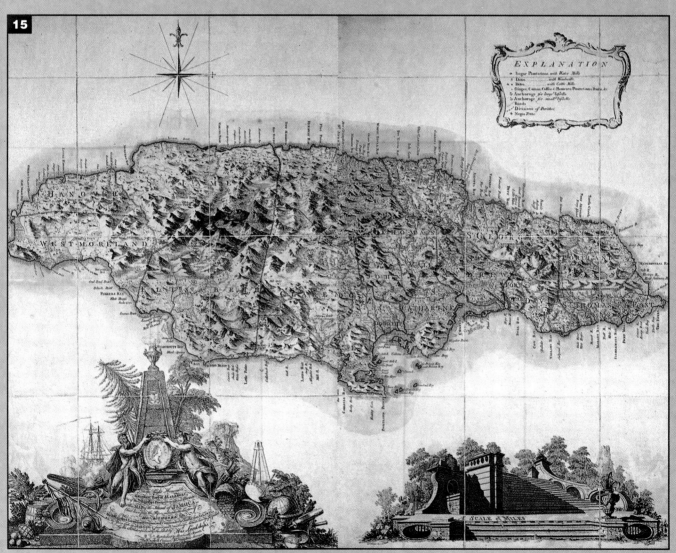

18. BRANCH OF BREAD-FRUIT TREE AND FRUIT. Engraved by J Miller. "They bake it in an oven, which scorcheth the rind and makes it black; but they scrape off the outside black crust, and there remains a tender thin crust; and the inside is soft, tender, and white like the crumb of a penny loaf." Dampier, 1688.

19. BREADFRUIT SPECI-MENS. Dried plant specimens of the breadfruit (artocarpus communis) collected on Cook's 1st Voyage to Tahiti in 1769, and from Fiji in 1860. *Trustees of the British Museum (Natural History).*

20. SIR JOSEPH BANKS (1743-1820). Marble bust by Peter Turnerelli, 1814. Banks, President of the Royal Society, wrote to Lord Hawkesbury, President of the Board of Trade, on March 30th 1787: "It is full my opinion that the plan for sending out a vessel from England for the sole purpose of bringing the breadfruit to the West Indies is much more likely to be successful than that of despatching transports from Botany Bay."

21. GREAT ROOM OF THE SOCIETY FOR THE ENCOURAGEMENT OF ARTS, MANUFACTURES AND COMMERCE. Engraving after A Pugin and T Rowlandson, 1809. *Royal Society of Arts.*

22. TRANSACTIONS OF THE SOCIETY OF ARTS 1776-7. Anonymous letter dated January 24th 1776 suggesting that the cultivation of breadfruit be introduced to Jamaica and Barbados. *Royal Society of Arts.*

23. PREMIUM OF THE SOCIETY OF ARTS. Offer of a Premium for bringing into the Port of London living breadfruit plants, dated January 22nd 1777. *Royal Society of Arts.*

24. A DESCRIPTION OF THE MANGOSTAN AND THE BREADFRUIT. By John Ellis, London 1775. Illustrated pamphlet, "To which are added directions for bringing over these and other Vegetable Productions, which would be extremely beneficial to the inhabitants of the West Indian Islands." *Royal Society of Arts.*

25. ABSTRACT OF THE PRE-MIUMS OFFERED BY THE SOCIETY OF ARTS. Offer of the Society's Gold Medal for conveying six living breadfruit plants from the South Sea to the West Indies, May 1789. *Royal Society of Arts.*

26. KING GEORGE III (1738-1820). Oil painting by Sir Thomas Lawrence, 1792. Painted in the robes of the Order of the Garter. Herbert Art Gallery and Museum, Coventry.

27. TERRESTRIAL AND CELESTIAL GLOBES. Made by George Adams (Snr) circa 1760 at the sign of Tycho Brahe's Head, Fleet Street. This pair of globes formed part of King George III's personal collection of instruments, probably kept with his maps and charts in the Royal Library, and are rather similar to globes which Adams supplied for use on Cook's 2nd Voyage. *Science Museum.*

2. FITTING OUT FOR A VOYAGE TO THE SOUTH SEAS.

The Board of Admiralty ordered a vessel to be purchased and converted for the voyage at Deptford Yard. The choice of the Bethia, a small merchant vessel of 220 tons and 91ft length, renamed as Bounty, demonstrated the

the command of Lieutenant William Bligh RN was made up of volunteers, and some men had previously sailed with him. There were, however, some unfortunate choices among the warrant officers, including the Surgeon, who proved to be a drunkard. Fletcher Christian, one of those who had sailed before with Bligh, joined as Master's

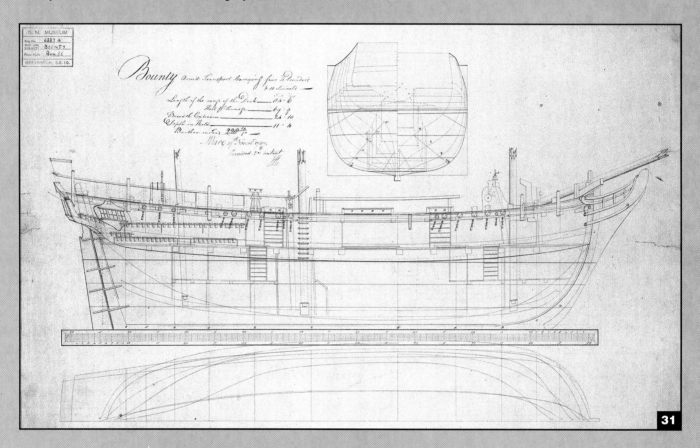

Admiralty's low assessment of the enterprise. Her small size and inadequate manning was a potential danger, for Bligh as a Lieutenant in command lacked the support of any other commissioned officer, and there were no marines on board, an obvious risk on a voyage far from civilization.

This section of the exhibition looks at the conversion and equipping of HM Armed Transport Bounty for her specialised task in the Pacific, and illustrates some of the typical navigational and other equipment necessary for a long voyage.

The ship's company, under

Mate, but was soon promoted to acting Lieutenant. Bligh thereby risked the resentment of the other two watchkeeping officers, the Master John Fryer, and the Gunner William Peckover.

28. MODEL OF HM ARMED TRANSPORT BOUNTY. Made to a scale of 1/4 in to l ft by M Wilson and K Britten, 1989. The Bounty, previously a merchant ship named Bethia, was a small vessel of 220 tons and 91ft length. She was purchased for £1950 and after conversion for the voyage she carried a light armament of four 4pdr guns and ten swivel guns. The Bounty's decorative details are not known and can only be conjecture, but Bligh describes the figurehead as a woman in a riding habit.

29. SHEER DRAUGHT OF BOUNTY, LATE BETHIA OF LONDON, June 25th 1787.

30. DECK PLAN, June 25th 1787.

31. SHEER DRAUGHT, November 19th 1787.

33. PLAN AND PROFILE OF AFTER PART OF LOWER DECK, 1790. These five plans demonstrate the conversion of Bounty from a merchant vessel to a naval transport. She was copper-sheathed at Deptford Yard to protect against marine worm. The plans show the detailed arrangements made for the breadfruit pots. Sir Joseph Banks wrote: "The master and crew must not think it a grievance to give up the best of her accommodation for that purpose."

32. DECK PLAN, November 20th 1787.

37. EQUIPMENT OF AN 18th CENTURY SHIP. Ship's equipment and personal items recovered from the wreck of HMS Royal George lost at Spithead in 1782.

38. 18th CENTURY SEA CHEST. This chest went round the world with Midshipman James Ward on Captain Cook's 3rd Voyage.

40. MODEL OF A SHIP's FIREHEARTH. Stove patented in 1780 by Alexander Brodie, and manufactured by his apprentice George Cawthorn of Rotherhithe. A Brodie firehearth was ordered for the Bounty when she was converted for the voyage, and provided all the cooking facilities for the ship's company.

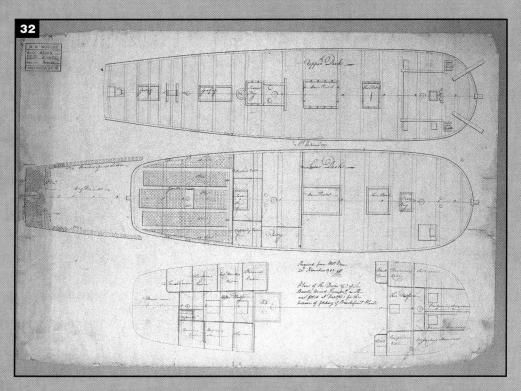

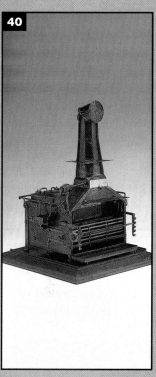

34. HM ARMED TRANSPORT BOUNTY. 20th-century watercolour by G Robinson.

35. HIS MAJESTY's DOCKYARD AT DEPTFORD. A Geometrical Plan and North East elevation. Engraved by P C Canot after Thomas Milton, 1753.

36. VIEW OF THE ROYAL DOCKYARD AT DEPTFORD. Engraved by W Woollett after Richard Paton, 1773.

39. BLIGH PERSONALIA. Silver corkscrew, clay pipe and hinged reading glass reputed to have been personal possessions of William Bligh.

41. PORTABLE SOUP. Block of soup stamped with a broad arrow, from Capt. Cook's stores. Recommended as an anti-scorbutic in the 1750s by Dr James Lind, portable soup was among the provisions issued to the Bounty, which also included sauerkraut, essence of malt, barley and wheat.

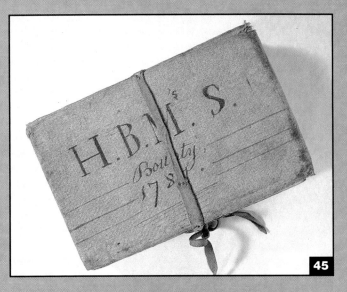

45

45. DOMESTIC MEDICINE by William Buchan MD, London, 1799. Inscribed "His Britannic Majesty's Ship Bounty Spithead 23 December 1787." Canvas-covered medical book used by the Bounty's Surgeon Thomas Huggan and later by Fletcher Christian in Pitcairn Island.

46. SHIP's MEDICINE CHEST OF THE 18th CENTURY.

47. SHIP's BELL, UNKNOWN SHIP OF 1787.

34

42. SHIP's BISCUITS. Original biscuit of 1784 and two modern copies.

43. NAVAL SPEAKING TRUMPET, 1799.

44. SAILOR's NECKER-CHIEF.

48

48. HMS BOUNTY's CHRONOMETER. By Larcum Kendall, London, 1771. Ordered by the Board of Longitude in 1769, this marine timekeeper is a simplified version of the £20,000 prize-winning chronometer made by John Harrison. It was issued to Lieutenant Bligh in 1787 and retained by the mutineers, one of whom later sold it to Captain Folger of the American whaler Topaz. After a chequered history of theft and other adventures, it was returned to London in 1843.

49. STEERING COMPASS. By George Adams, London, 1766. Illustrated below with items 50, 51 and a telescope of the period.

50. AZIMUTH COMPASS. By Rust and Eyre, London, circa 1785.

51. OCTANT. By Benjamin Cole, London, 1761. (*Owned by Lt Philip Carteret*)

NAVIGATIONAL EQUIPMENT OF THE 18TH CENTURY. Instruments and manuals similar to those issued to HMS Bounty.

52. SEXTANT. By Jesse Ramsden, London, circa 1785.

56. PRACTICAL NAVIGATOR AND SEAMAN's DAILY ASSISTANT. By John Hamilton Moore, London, 1784.

57. TABLES REQUISITE TO BE USED WITH THE NAUTICAL EPHEMERIS. By Nevil Maskeline, London 1781. It is known that a sextant, an old octant, and a steering compass by Adams from the Bounty's binnacle were given to Bligh when he was cast adrift in the launch following the mutiny, together with navigation manuals, but no chronometer.

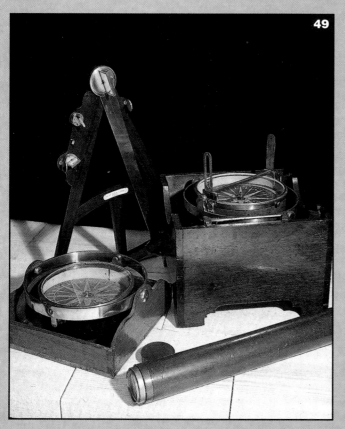

49

53. TELESCOPE. By T Harris & Son, London, circa 1800. (Inscribed: John Fryer, Master 1787.)

54. HALF-HOUR SAND-GLASS, circa 1770.

55. NAUTICAL ALMANAC AND ASTRONOMICAL EPHEMERIS FOR THE YEAR 1789.

3. FIRST BREAD-FRUIT VOYAGE 1787-9.

The third section of the exhibition follows the Bounty on her voyage to Tahiti on what should have been a relatively straightforward low-risk mission.

With Bligh in command the Bounty sailed from Spithead in December 1787. Delays in her departure got the expedition off to a bad start, and following Admiralty orders, Bligh wasted valuable time vainly attempting to round Cape Horn at far too late a season. He was obliged to give up eventually, and altered course for the Cape of Good Hope. It was 26th October 1788 by the time the Bounty was finally anchored off Tahiti.

The breadfruit plants were to take five months of preparation, but the men welcomed the opportunity to relax in the idyllic and friendly island, delighting in the beautiful women, unfamiliar native customs and delicious food. This area of the exhibition attempts to convey something of this exotic atmosphere by displaying some of the "curiosities" collected on

Cook's visits to the island, and the paintings by artists who sailed with him. Bligh had no such artists on board, but he has left vivid descriptions of the island and its customs in the manuscript and published accounts shown here.

Events during the early part of the voyage and the period in Tahiti had already demonstrated some of the clashes of personality and discipline problems which were to contribute to the eventual disastrous outcome of the voyage. Although Bligh had shown humanity and care for his crew by introducing improvements in the ship's routine, to enable his men to keep clean, dry, healthy and adequately rested, he had also revealed his hot temper, refusal to compromise and tactlessness.

58. MANUSCRIPT LOG OF HMS BOUNTY. First volume of Bligh's private copy, December 1787-October 1788. This volume covers the departure, the attempt to round Cape Horn, and up to the arrival in Tahiti. This private copy of the log contains some details excluded from the official copy which Bligh deposited with the Admiralty. *Mitchell Library, State Library of New South Wales, Sydney.*

59. POEDOOA, DAUGHTER OF ORIO, CHIEF OF ULIETA IN THE SOCIETY ISLANDS. Oil painting by John Webber, 1777. The young princess painted during Cook's 3rd Voyage was no longer alive by the time Bounty arrived at Tahiti. *Admiralty House Collection.*

59

60. NATIVE CRAFT OFF OPAREE, TAHITI. Oil painting by William Hodges, 1773. Painted during Cook's 2nd Voyage. *Admiralty House Collection.*

62. VIEW OF PART OF THE ISLAND OF ULIETA. Oil painting by William Hodges, 1774. *Admiralty house Collection.*

61

61. TAHITI, BEARING SOUTH-EAST. Oil painting by William Hodges, 1773. Painted during Cook's 2nd Voyage. *Admiralty House Collection.*

63. TAHITIAN PLANTS. Eight watercolour drawings by Sydney Parkinson, 1769. Parkinson, a young man taken in Sir Joseph Banks' party as a botanical draughtsman on Cook's Ist Voyage to the Pacific 1768-71 died at Tahiti in 1771. 63a Breadfruit plant 63b Cordia sebestina. *Trustees of the British Museum (Natural History).*

64. A VOYAGE TO THE SOUTH SEA … IN HIS MAJESTY's SHIP BOUNTY. By William Bligh, London 1792. The 2nd edition of Bligh's Narrative included an account of the early part of the voyage and the period spent in Tahiti, with descriptions of Tahitian customs.

65. A VOYAGE TO THE SOUTH SEA. By William Bligh, 1792. As above, leather-bound with a miniature of Bligh after Russell set into the cover. *Mitchell Library, State Library of New South Wales, Sydney.*

66. ENGRAVINGS OF TAHITIAN LIFE by John Webber. TATTOOING INSTRUMENTS. FLY FLAP.
66a A YOUNG WOMAN OF OTAHEITE.
TAHITIAN IMPLEMENTS.
66b SAILING CANOE OF TAHITI. A YOUNG WOMAN OF OTAHEITE DANCING.

67. THE FLEET OF OTAHEITE ASSEMBLED AT OPAREE. Engraved by W Woollet after W Hodges, 1777.

68. OTOO, KING OF TAHITI. Engraved by Hall after Hodges, for Atlas to Cook's Voyages.

69. TAHITIAN MOURNING DRESS. This mourner's ceremonial dress, made of bark cloth, mother-of-pearl shell, wood, coconut shell and feathers, was collected on Cook's 2nd Voyage, 1772-4. Shortly before Bounty's departure from Tahiti, Bligh was presented with two such costumes as a gift of friendship for George III. *Pitt Rivers Museum, Oxford.*

72. TATTOOING INSTRUMENTS. Bligh records that many of his men were tattooed while in Tahiti with stars, hearts, names and other decorations on legs, arms, breast and buttocks. These specimens were collected on Cook's Voyages. *Trustees of the British Museum (Ethnography).*

69

4. THE MUTINY.

With the breadfruit plants eventually stowed aboard, Bounty sailed from Tahiti on 4th April 1789, many of the crew only leaving with the greatest reluctance. The following period was to be the real test of Bligh's ability to lead men and restore naval discipline and essential routine to the ship. During the morning watch of 28th April off Tofoa in the Friendly Islands Fletcher Christian made his decision.

In this section of the exhibition the visitor is invited to eavesdrop on the events of the mutiny as they take place, from a position below deck where the voices of the mutineers can be heard through the deck gratings as they prepare to cast adrift in one of the ship's boats Bligh and those loyal to him.

To Bligh the mutiny was totally unexpected and he regarded with disbelief the ingratitude shown by men like Fletcher Christian and Peter Heywood, whom he had believed to be indebted to him. We have only the various biased accounts to judge from, but piecing together the versions, there seems little in the way of specific grievances or convincing charges of tyranny to be made against Bligh. His irascible temper, pettiness and inflexibility must clearly have added to the already existing tensions on board, which Fletcher Christian with his own particular temperament eventually found to be intolerable. The actual act of mutiny was certainly a confused and disorganised affair, and Christian appears to have been acting on impulse, following initial desperate thoughts of jumping ship, when he realised there were others who would support him.

70. CEREMONIAL DRUM. Made in the Austral Islands, but very similar to drums depicted in Webber's engravings of Tahiti in Cook's time. *Trustees of the British Museum (Ethnography).*

71. TAHITIAN POI. Food pounder collected on Cook's 3rd Voyage.

73

73. TAHITIAN CURIOSITIES. Gorget, fly flap and other equipment and adornment collected on Cook's and Vancouver's Voyages. *Trustees of the British Museum (Ethnography).*

5. THE OPEN BOAT VOYAGE.

The tableau in this section features a dramatic full-sized reconstruction of the 23ft launch in which Bligh and his 18 companions were set adrift and made their epic voyage of 3618 nautical miles from Tofoa to Timor.

Without charts or chronometer, and with meagre provisions, barely adequate to support life, Bligh led his men to the safety of the Dutch East Indies in 41 days. Only one man was lost, the victim of a native attack when Bligh landed at Tofoa to try to supplement his food supply.

"Thus happily ended, his really spectacular achievement was that of survival. Fryer, the Master, was later to criticise Bligh's part in the boat voyage, but it was Bligh who had husbanded the resources, maintained morale in the overloaded boat, and commanded his starving crew through appalling weather conditions to safety.

From the tableau area the visitor passes through a lobby displaying engravings of Bligh's landfall and reception in Timor, and enters a display featuring the manuscripts and books which form the heart of the exhibition. Here is displayed the waterstained Notebook which Bligh wrote up regularly during the boat voyage. Not only did he record the outstanding events such as the mutiny, the death of Norton, and the landfall at Timor, but he maintained a regular navigational log, and even more remarkably, found the energy to make sketch charts of unknown islands and other features along the route.

in order to take passage for England. By 14th March 1790 Bligh had reached home, and in accordance with naval regulations, in October he was subjected to courtmartial to enquire into the loss of HMS Bounty. Having been honourably acquitted of responsibility, he became something of a celebrity, and was promoted first to Commander and a month later to Post Captain.

75

74. 23-FOOT SHIP's BOAT. Full-sized reconstruction of the launch in which Bligh and 18 of his men were cast adrift. Built for the 1984 film The Bounty. *Exeter Maritime Museum.*

75. THE MUTINEERS TURNING BLIGH AND PART OF THE OFFICERS AND CREW ADRIFT FROM HIS MAJESTY's SHIP THE BOUNTY. Hand coloured aquatint after the painting by Robert Dodd, Publ. Oct. 1790. The mutineers are seen throwing down cutlasses to the men in the boat, but they refused them firearms, which would have protected them from hostile natives and prevented the death of John Norton at Tofoa. *National Library of Australia, Canberra.*

through the assistance of Divine Providence, without accident, a voyage of the most extraordinary nature that ever happened in the world, let it be taken either in its extent, duration, or so much want of the necessaries of life." William Bligh, writing from Coupang in Timor, August 18th 1789.

While the succesful completion of the passage itself was evidence of Bligh's navigational and seamanship skill,

At Coupang in Timor, a schooner was purchased, and after recovering their strength, the party sailed on to Batavia

76. LIEUT. BLIGH & HIS CREW OF THE SHIP BOUNTY HOSPITABLY RECEIVED BY THE GOVERNOR OF TIMOR. Wash drawing by Charles Benezach, 1791. This drawing, later engraved by Bromley, shows Bligh's party arriving at the Dutch Fortress of Coupang in Timor on June 14th 1789 after the launch voyage. *National Library of Australia, Canberra.*

77. VIEW OF COUPANG IN TIMOR, 1801. Engraved after a drawing by Lesueur.

78. PLAN OF BATAVIA IN 1733. An earlier engraving of the town. Bligh purchased a small schooner in Timor which he named Resource and sailed on with his men to Batavia to find ships bound for England.

79. VIEW OF BATAVIA. Engraved by J Wells after Drummond, 1796. The Indonesian settlements were notoriously unhealthy, and three men died at Batavia, following the death of Nelson the Gardener at Timor. Only twelve of the original nineteen returned to England.

80. VIEW OF CAPE OF GOOD HOPE AND TABLE BAY. Pen and ink drawing with wash by William Bligh, December 1789. From Batavia Bligh sailed in the Dutch packet Vlydte via the Cape of Good Hope with his clerk and servant, arriving in England on March 14th 1790. *Private Collection.*

81. MANUSCRIPT NOTE-BOOK IN WILLIAM BLIGH's HAND. Leatherbound Notebook, taken into the boat by Midshipman Thomas Haywood, which was used by Bligh to record navigational observations and calculations, and to make rough notes of daily events during the boat voyage. The entries start as a narrative on April 28th 1789, the day of the mutiny, but after May 7th are entered in columns as in a conventional log. *National Library of Australia, Canberra.*

83. MANUSCRIPT LOG OF HMS BOUNTY. Second volume of Bligh's private copy, April 1789-March 1790. This volume covers the boat journey and takes up the account from the time of the mutiny until Bligh's return to England. Bligh transposed entries from his Notebook "into my fair Journal every day when the weather would admit." *Mitchell Library, State Library of New South Wales, Sydney.*

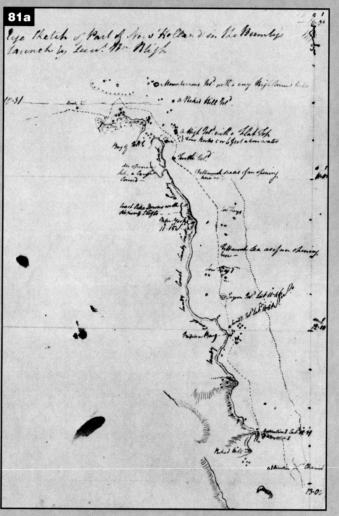

81a

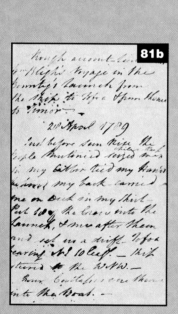

81b

85

85. MODEL OF BOUNTY's LAUNCH. Made to a scale of 1/4 in. to I ft. by R A Lightley, 1988. This modern model reconstructs the rig described in Bligh's Log. It also shows the windlass and anchor davit which were thrown overboard to make more room in the 23ft boat.

82. DESCRIPTIONS OF THE MUTINEERS IN WILLIAM BLIGH's HAND. Associated with the manuscript Notebook kept by Bligh during the open boat voyage is a list of men who stayed with Bounty. It includes notes on their physical appearance and tattoo marks.

84. THE MUTINEERS TURNING LIEUT. BLIGH AND PART OF THE OFFICERS AND CREW ADRIFT. Oil painting by Robert Dodd. The original of the well-known aquatint engraving. *Private Collection.*

90. BLIGH's READING GLASS. Said to have been taken in the boat. On May 29th 1789 Bligh records that, landing at Restoration Island, they cooked a meal, and he had:" Great trouble in getting a fire – my readg. glass did it."

91. JOHN FRYER. Oil painting by Gaetano Calleyo. Fryer, Master of the Bounty, survived the open boat voyage and continued his naval career on returning to England. He served at the Battle of Copenhagen in 1801, and died in 1817. The portrait shows him in a Master's uniform of 1807 pattern. *Mitchell Library, State Library of New South Wales. Sydney.*

86. AN ACCOUNT OF THE MUTINOUS SEIZURE OF THE BOUNTY, WITH THE SUCCEEDING HARDSHIPS OF THE CREW. London, no date. The frontispiece is a rare engraving of the mutineers seizing Bligh in his cabin. *Private Collection.*

87. GERMAN EDITION OF BLIGH's VOYAGE TO THE SOUTH SEAS. Published Berlin, 1793. The track chart shows the route of the launch from Tofoa to Timor, and the subsequent voyage of the schooner Resource to Batavia.

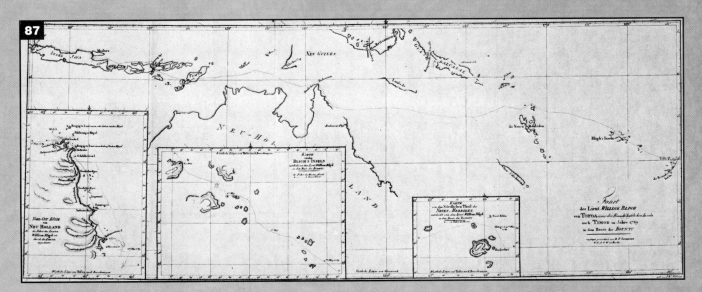

88. HORN MUG, GOURD, AND BULLETWEIGHT FROM THE LAUNCH. Bligh was provided with 150lbs of ship's biscuit, 32 lbs of pork, 6 quarts of rum, 28 gallons of water, and six bottles of wine. On the 11th day he made a pair of scales to weigh out the daily ration for each man of 2 oz of bread and 3/4 pt of water. *Private Collection.*

89. PITCAIRN: THE ISLAND, THE PEOPLE AND THE PASTOR, WITH A SHORT ACCOUNT OF THE MUTINY OF THE BOUNTY. By Revd. Thomas Boyles Murray, 1853. Engraving of the horn mug, gourd and bulletweight with the Notebook Journal.

92. NARRATIVE OF THE MUTINY AND LAUNCH VOYAGE. By John Fryer, Master of the Bounty, copied by his sister. Fryer had already quarrelled with Bligh earlier in the voyage, and his account of the boat voyage attempts to lessen Bligh's achievement by revealing errors, claiming that Bligh had better navigational equipment than he had admitted to, and asserting his own ability to perform the same navigational feat.

93. THE MARINER's MAR-VELLOUS MAGAZINE: STATEMENTS OF THE LOSS OF HIS MAJESTY's NEW SHIP THE BOUNTY. Published by Thomas Tegg, London, 1808. One of the many popular publications inspired by the story, with a version of the launch engraving.

95. A NARRATIVE OF THE MUTINY ON BOARD HIS MAJESTY's SHIP BOUNTY AND THE SUBSEQUENT VOYAGE OF PART OF THE CREW IN THE SHIP's BOAT. By William Bligh, London, 1790. This first edition of the Narrative (a fuller version followed in 1792) was published a few months after Bligh's return to England, in order to publicise his version of the Mutiny and its cause, for which he denied any responsibility.

97. COURT MARTIAL OF WILLIAM PURCELL. Bligh's written report of October 7th 1790 on Purcell, Carpenter of the Bounty, who had clashed with him both in Tahiti and during the voyage. Purcell was reprimanded after the six charges against him had been partly proven. *Public Record Office.*

6. HMS PANDORA IN PURSUIT OF THE MUTINEERS.

Bligh arrived in England in March 1790 with news of the mutiny, and five months later the Admiralty sent a 24 gun frigate, HMS Pandora, under the command of Captain Edward Edwards to apprehend the mutineers. Captain Edwards returned to Tahiti, where 16 of the Bounty's men had chosen to remain. The 14 who were still alive were arrested and confined on board in a cramped round-house, which inevitably became known as Pandora's Box. Edwards continued the search among the islands for Fletcher Christian and the ringleaders who had sailed Bounty off in search of a new home.

On 28th August 1791 Pandora struck and foundered on the Great Barrier Reef, with the loss of many of her crew and four of the prisoners. The survivors sailed to Timor in the ship's four open boats, repeating part of Bligh's journey, and eventually made their way back to England. The ten surviving prisoners were transferred to HMS Hector to await trial for mutiny.

This area of the exhibition features some of the recently-found artifacts from the wreck of HMS Pandora, which was rediscovered in 1977 and is currently being excavated by Australian marine archaeologists.

93

94. DUTCH EDITION OF BLIGH's NARRATIVE OF THE MUTINY. Published Rotterdam, 1790. The frontispiece engraving by E Sansom of Rotterdam shows the launch under sail in a storm. *Private Collection.*

96. COURT MARTIAL OF WILLIAM BLIGH. On return to England in March 1790, Bligh had to face court martial for the loss of his ship, a normal naval procedure. The Court which assembled on board HMS Royal William at Spithead on October 22nd 1790 found that the Bounty had been "violently and forceably taken from the said Lieutenant William Bligh by the said Fletcher Christian and certain other mutineers" and Bligh was honourably aquitted. *Public Record Office.*

98. COPY OF BLIGH's OFFICIAL REPORT OF THE MUTINY. After arriving at the Cape of Good Hope on his way back to England, Bligh wrote to the Admiralty on December 16th 1789 reporting on the mutiny and boat voyage. *Public Record Office.*

99. CAPTAIN WILLIAM BLIGH RN, 1791. Coloured engraving by J Conde after the pastel by John Russell, also shown in the exhibition. After he was acquitted of responsibility for the loss of the Bounty in October 1790, Bligh was promoted to Commander, and a month later to Post-Captain.

100. MODEL OF HMS PANDORA, FRIGATE OF 24 GUNS. Early 19th-century "sailor's model" of the vessel sent by the Admiralty to the Pacific to apprehend the mutineers. With fourteen prisoners on board, who had been arrested at Tahiti, the Pandora foundered on the Great Barrier Reef on August 28th 1791. Her wreck site is now being excavated by archaeologists from Queensland Museum. *Private Collection.*

104. ENQUIRY INTO THE LOSS OF HMS PANDORA. As the Pandora was sinking, George Hamilton signed a statement on the back of a blank stores list to confirm the opinion that nothing could be done to save the ship. The paper was produced at the Court Martial enquiring into the loss on September 10th 1792. *Public Record Office.*

106. MANUSCRIPT JOURNAL OF JAMES MORRISON (1761-1807). Evidently composed as a narrative after the event by the Boatswain's Mate of the Bounty, the manuscript claims to be a journal of Morrison's experiences during the breadfruit voyage, including the mutiny, and his arrest and confinement aboard Pandora, as well as the shipwreck. At his court martial Morrison was sentenced to death, but with Peter Heywood was pardoned. The journal, probably written at that time, is heavily biased and highly critical of Bligh, but it also includes much interesting and detailed information on parts of the story not otherwise covered. Its use as a source by Sir John Barrow and Lady Belcher in the 19th-century has given wide circulation to the opinions and inspired many myths. *Mitchell Library, State Library of New South Wales, Sydney*

107. SINKING OF HMS PANDORA 1791. Watercolour, attributed to William Joy. *Private Collection*

101. ADMIRALTY INSTRUCTIONS TO CAPTAIN EDWARD EDWARDS. Dated October 25th 1790. Before HMS Pandora departed for the Pacific, Captain Edwards was given specific directions where to search for the Bounty. On March 24th 1791 Pandora arrived at Tahiti, where it seemed most likely that Fletcher Christian and the mutineers would have chosen to return. *MOD Naval Library Collection.*

102. CAPTAIN EDWARD EDWARDS' MEMORANDUM MADE AT TAHITI. Captain Edwards made a rough record of the names of men from the Bounty who were arrested at Tahiti, particularly noting which surrendered and came on board of their own accord, and which had to be pursued. *MOD Naval Library Collection.*

103. CAPTAIN EDWARDS' SWORD. Spadroon with ivory and gilt hilt and George III cipher. *Borough of Poole Museum Service.*

105. CHART OF THE TRACK AND DISCOVERIES OF HM LATE SHIP PANDORA IN THE SOUTH PACIFIC OCEAN. By Thomas Hayward, 1791, 3rd Lieutenant of Pandora. The chart shows Pandora's search for the mutineers, her track from Easter Island to the Great Barrier Reef, where she was lost, and the subsequent voyage of the four ship's boats via Torres Strait to Timor. Her discoveries are shown in light yellow. *Hydrographic Department, MOD.*

108. SINKING OF PANDORA 1791. Wash drawing by George Reynolds, Midshipman and Master's Mate of Pandora. The sandy quay nearby enabled the survivors to prepare the ship's boats for their voyage to Timor. *Private Collection.*

111. VOYAGE ROUND THE WORLD IN HIS MAJESTY's SHIP PANDORA. By George Hamilton, Newcastle 1813. The Surgeon of HMS Pandora wrote an account of his experiences in Tahiti, in which he described the loss of the ship and the open boat voyage. *Private Collection.*

109. PANDORA's BOATS UNDER SAIL. Pen and ink drawing with watercolour by George Reynolds. The survivors were divided into four parties with Captain Edwards in command in the pinnace, Lieut. Corner in the launch, Lieut. Larkin in the red yawl and Mr Passmore the Master in the blue yawl. *Private Collection*

112. HEYWOOD's LETTER TO HIS MOTHER. Written from Batavia, November 20th 1791. Peter Heywood remained with the mutineers, but left the Bounty at Tahiti and gave himself up when HMS Pandora arrived. In this letter he describes the mutiny, his confinement on board Pandora and the loss of the ship.

7. COURT MARTIAL OF THE MUTINEERS.

Ascending the staircase at the end of the ground floor, visitors pass under a reconstruction of the stern of HMS Duke, scene of the court martial of the mutineers. Upstairs, the gallery features a tableau of the trial, in which the ten prisoners were charged with "mutinously running away with the said armed vessel the Bounty and deserting from His Majesty's Service." Bligh was by now back in the Pacific, leaving his evidence in written form.

Lord Hood, President of the Court, together with the eleven Post Captains who

109

110. FATE OF THE MUTINEERS ABOARD HMS PANDORA. After the loss of the Pandora and the voyage in the ship's boats, Captain Edwards wrote a report from Batavia on November 25th 1791 accounting for each of the mutineers. *Public Record Office.*

113. ARTEFACTS FROM HMS PANDORA's WRECK Excavation work on the site of the Pandora wreck on the Great Barrier Reef has revealed personal possessions of the crew, ship's equipment and Tahitian souvenirs collected by the men: SURGEON HAMILTON's SILVER WATCH, ETUI, SYRINGE, MORTAR & TOURNIQUET. COOKING CAULDRON. GLASS MUG, WINE GLASS, CERAMIC MUG, BOTTLE. INKPOT, PENCIL. TAHITIAN STONE POUNDER, ADZE, FISH-HOOK. *Queensland Museum, Brisbane assisted by the Premier's Dept. of the Queensland Government.*

heard the evidence, decided to acquit four prisoners. Of the remaining six who were sentenced to death, three were reprieved or pardoned, but Thomas Ellison, Thomas Burkitt and John Millward were hanged from the yardarm of HMS Brunswick on 29th October 1792.

Supporting the tableau in the exhibition is a display of some of the original documents relating to the evidence given at the trial, and the pamphlets published afterwards by relatives of the mutineers.

116. STATEMENTS OF THE MUTINEERS. Pleas signed by each of the six men sentenced to death by the Court Martial. Of these men, three were eventually hanged: Thomas Ellison, John Millward and Thomas Burkitt. *Public Record Office*.

117. LETTER FROM PETER HEYWOOD. To Dr Scott in the Isle of Man, September 20th 1792. Heywood wrote informing him of the death sentence and maintaining his innocence of the mutiny charge.

119. MINUTES OF THE PROCEEDINGS OF THE COURT MARTIAL ON TEN PERSONS CHARGED WITH MUTINY ON BOARD HMS BOUNTY. Pamphlet by Stephen Barney, 1794. The Appendix written by Edward Christian attempts to vindicate his brother Fletcher. *Mitchell Library, State Library of New South Wales. Sydney.*

114

118

114. ADMIRAL SAMUEL HOOD, 1ST VISCOUNT HOOD (1724-1816). Oil painting by James Northcote, 1784. Lord Hood, as Commander-in-Chief of the Fleet at Spithead, was President of the Court Martial which tried the mutineers in September 1792.

115. ELEVEN POST CAPTAINS. Engravings of the Post Captains who composed the Court Martial.

118. CAPTAIN PETER HEYWOOD (1773-1831). Oil painting by John Simpson Heywood, a midshipman at the time of the mutiny, was sentenced to death at the trial, but pardoned and later rose to the rank of Captain. He is shown in Captain's full dress of 1812-25 pattern.

120. AN ANSWER TO CERTAIN ASSERTIONS CONTAINED IN THE APPENDIX TO A PAMPHLET. Pamphlet by William Bligh, 1794. Bligh produced his own evidence to cast doubt on the truth of the Court Martial minutes as recently published by Barney. The pamphlet warfare initiated by Edward Christian brought wide publicity to the mutiny issue. *British Library.*

121. LETTER TO FRANCIS GODOLPHIN BOND. From William Bligh, July 26th 1794. Writing to his nephew, Bligh remarks on the causes of the mutiny and Edward Christian's published allegations. Bond went as Ist Lieutenant of HMS Providence on Bligh's 2nd Breadfruit Voyage of 1791-3.

8. THE MUTINEERS ON PITCAIRN.

While some of the Bounty's men had chosen to remain in Tahiti and take the chance of being pursued, Fletcher Christian and the other eight sailed on in search of a safer refuge, taking with them several Tahitian men and women. Eventually they settled on the uninhabited Pitcairn Island, where the Bounty was deliberately burned in January 1790 for fear of discovery. Life on Pitcairn

compass, since lost. By this time Adams had remodelled the community and the descendants of the mutineers were living a respectable and religious life. Other ships later called at the island and reported with interest on the community, and when Captain F W Beechey visited in 1825 in HMS Blossom he was able to receive from John Adams a first hand account of the mutiny just four years before the mutineer's death on March 5th 1829.

123. CHART AND VIEWS OF PITCAIRN's ISLAND. Unsigned. Probably the original of the chart later published by Hawkesworth. The latitude of Pitcairn is incorrectly shown some 200 miles East of its true position, an error repeated by Hawkesworth. This made the island difficult to find and therefore an ideal solution to Fletcher Christian's search for an obscure refuge. *Hydrographic Department, MOD.*

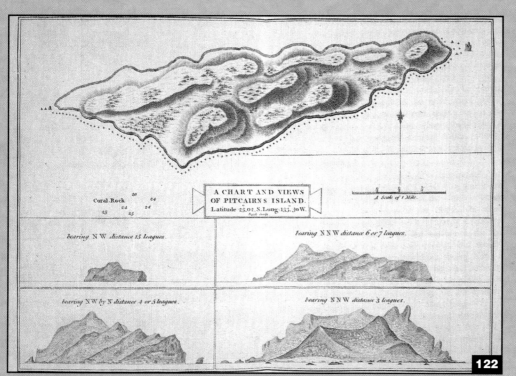

Coral Rock

A CHART AND VIEWS OF PITCAIRNS ISLAND.
Latitude 25,02. S.Long.133.30 W.

A Scale of 1 Mile.

bearing N W distance 15 leagues.

bearing N N W distance 6 or 7 leagues.

bearing N W by N distance 4 or 5 leagues.

bearing N N W distance 3 leagues.

122

124. PITCAIRN ISLAND REGISTER. A manuscript record of "Births, Deaths, Marriages and Remarkable Family Events" on the Island from 1790 to 1853. The first entry in the Register for January 23rd 1790 records the burning of HMS Bounty, followed in 1793 by the massacre of several mutineers by the Tahitians. *Society for Promoting Christian Knowledge.*

125. RELICS OF THE BOUNTY. The Bounty was deliberately destroyed by fire in Bounty Bay in 1790. The rudder was salvaged in 1933 and in the 1970s other parts of the wreck were removed. Souvenirs of the ship's timber and metal, like the worm-eaten wood, iron and copper sheathing here were taken as mementos by visitors to the island.

proved unstable and violent in the early years. There was constant conflict between the Europeans and Tahitians, and several men were murdered, Fletcher Christian probably being among them, although his fate remains uncertain.

When Captain Mayhew Folger of the American whaler Topaz of Boston discovered the island by chance in 1808, only John Adams, alias Alexander Smith, remained alive of the original mutineers. Adams presented Folger with the Bounty's chronometer, shown earlier in the exhibition, and with her azimuth

122. JOHN HAWKESWORTH's VOYAGES, LONDON 1773. Philip Carteret's account of his voyage round the world. 1766-9 in command of HM Sloop Swallow recorded the first sighting of an uninhabited island on July 2nd 1767, which he named for Midshipman Pitcairn. The Bounty mutineers, known to have had a copy of this book on board, reached the island on January 15th 1790.

126. LIFE ON PITCAIRN ISLAND. Decorated tapa cloth and pounder used by descendants of the mutineers, and other domestic tools and equipment from the Island. *Trustees of the British Museum (Ethnography)*

127. BOUNTY CANDLESTICK. Brass candlestick, part of Bounty's equipment, later said to have been used on Pitcairn Island to pound corn. *Trustees of the British Museum (Ethnography)*

132. PRAYER BOOK. Used for daily morning and evening prayers on Pitcairn by John Adams.

128. THE VOYAGES AND TRAVELS OF FLETCHER CHRISTIAN AND A NARRATIVE OF THE MUTINY ON BOARD HIS MAJESTY's SHIP BOUNTY AT OTAHEITE. London, 1798. A fictional account of Christian's shipwreck and travels in South America. *Private Collection.*

133. CHART OF PITCAIRN ISLAND. Surveyed by Captain F W Beechey RN, 1825. The chart shows the island's precipitous shores and the possible landing places including Bounty Bay. In the view below, John Adams is seen welcoming HMS Blossom to Pitcairn. *Hydrographic Department, MOD.*

129. JOHN ADAMS, LAST SURVIVING MUTINEER. Watercolour drawing by R Beechey. John Adams, previously known as Able Seaman Alexander Smith, survived the violence which had raged in Pitcairn and transformed the island into the moral and religious community first discovered by Captain Folger in 1808.
Private Collection.

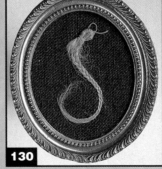

134. LANDING IN BOUNTY BAY. Oil painting, unsigned circa 1825. Showing the difficult landing in the surf in the bay where the Bounty was burned in 1790. Engraved for Frederick William Beechey's Narrative of a Voyage to the Pacific, in 1825. *Mitchell Library, State Library of New South Wales, Sydney.*

130. JOHN ADAMS' PIGTAIL.

131. JOHN ADAMS' SEA CHEST.

138. A VIEW OF THE VIL-LAGE AT PITCAIRN ISLAND. Watercolour drawing by William Smyth, Mate of HMS Blossom showing the ship's observatory set up in Adamstown. *Royal Geographical Society*.

139. CHART OF TAHITI Top by Capt. Cook, 1769: Bottom by Capt. F W Beechey Shows both the state of Tahiti when the mutineers left in 1789 and the area of Matavai Bay where Beechey landed in 1826, with news of settle-ment. Beechey subsequently helped negotiate the return of the Pitcairn Islanders to Tahiti in 1831.

140. SACRED TO THE MEM-ORY OF MR JOHN ADAMS. Lead-covered wooden board marking the grave of John Adams, the last surviving mutineer, who died on Pit-cairn Island on March 5th 1829, aged sixty five. It was replaced in the 1850s by a carved headstone sent out from England.

140

135. NARRATIVE OF A VOY-AGE TO THE PACIFIC AND BEERING's STRAIT ... IN HMS BLOSSOM UNDER THE COMMAND OF CAPTAIN F W BEECHEY RN, LONDON 1831. Beechey's narrative describes his visit to Pitcairn Island in 1825 and records the version of the mutiny and subsequent events recalled by John Adams four years before his death.

136. CAPTAIN FREDERICK WILLIAM BEECHEY (1796-1856). Oil painting by George Beechey.

137. A MEMENTO OF HMS BOUNTY. Tortoiseshell-lined box made from Bounty tim-ber. Presented to Charles Lord Bishop of Oxford by his brother-in-law Capt. F W Beechey in 1829. *Private Collection*.

142

141. ACCOUNT OF PIT-CAIRN's ISLAND. Manuscript and watercolours by George Gardener, Surgeon's Mate of HMS Curacoa, 1841. *Private Collection*.

142. VIEWS OF THE PACIF-IC. By Lieutenant Conway Shipley RN, 1851. Three litho-graph views of Bounty Bay, School House and Chapel, and Christian's House, in Pit-cairn Island.

9. BLIGH's 2nd BREADFRUIT VOYAGE 1791-3.

The mutiny did not end the attempt to transplant the breadfruit to the West Indies. In August 1791 William Bligh, now a Captain, returned to the Pacific to complete his original objective. This time the better-equipped expedition comprised two vessels, HMS Providence under Bligh's command, and a brig Assistant, Lieutenant Nathaniel Portlock. Matthew Flinders, later famed as the explorer of Australia's coast, was serving in Providence as a midshipman.

The watercolour drawings made during the voyage by Bligh and his 3rd Lieutenant, George Tobin, have survived and are shown in this section of the exhibition.

The object of the voyage was achieved, the breadfruit and other exotic plants were transplanted to Jamaica, St Vincent and St Helena, and others brought back to His Majesty's Botanic Garden at Kew. In addition, important hydrographic surveys were carried out in the Fiji Islands and the Torres Strait, following up Bligh's discoveries during the voyage in Bounty's launch.

On his return to England, Bligh received the Gold Medal of the Society of Arts, but by now he had lost favour, and became caught up in the controversy resulting from the mutiny and the campaigns of the well-connected Christian and Heywood families in particular. He never published his account of the 2nd, successful breadfruit voyage, which is consequently little known. Although eventually the breadfruit became an integral part of the West Indian economy, in the short term the transplantation was of limited benefit, since it proved unpalateable to the slaves, who preferred their native plantain.

143. SHEER DRAUGHT OF HMS PROVIDENCE.

144. DECK PLANS OF HMS PROVIDENCE. Launched at Blackwall on April 23rd 1791, Providence was fitted out at Deptford to receive breadfruit Plants with a similar arrange-ment to that for the Bounty voyage. At 420 tons and 107ft 10in. length, the ship was considerably larger than Bounty, and offered better accommodation for Bligh and the officers. Providence had an establishment of 100 offi-cers and men and Assistant, the 110 ton brig which accompanied her, had 27.

145. LIEUTENANT NATHANIEL PORTLOCK (c.1748-1817). Oil painting: Unknown artist. Having previ-ously sailed as Master's Mate with Cook, Lieutenant Port-lock was appointed to com-mand the brig Assistant. Bligh commended him after the voyage for his alertness and attention to duty, and on returning to England he was promoted to Commander.

147. A CHART OF BLIGH's ISLANDS. By William Bligh, copied by Matthew Flinders. These islands, now known as Fiji, and first seen from Boun-ty's launch in 1789, were later explored more thoroughly by Bligh in the Providence. Flinders, a young midship-man on that voyage, copied Bligh's chart in 1801.

148

146. TRACK CHART OF HMS PROVIDENCE. By Matthew Flinders (1774-1814). This chart, prepared aboard HMS Providence in 1792 shows how she found a new passage through the Tor-res Strait, and also where the Pandora foundered, having made a cautious approach to the area in 1791.

148. CAPTAIN BLIGH TRANSPORTING THE BREADFRUIT TREES FROM TAHITI. Mezzotint by Thomas Gosse. On July 20th 1792 Bligh left Tahiti with 2634 plants on board. *National Library of Australia, Canberra.*

153. RECORD OF PLANT ARRIVALS AT THE ROYAL BOTANIC GARDEN, KEW. This manuscript ledger, kept by William Aiton, Superintendent of the Royal Botanic Garden, records all the plants brought back in 1793 by HMS Providence from Tahiti, New Guinea, St Helena, St Vincent and Jamaica, including the breadfruit (artocarpus communis) *Trustees, Royal Botanic Gardens, Kew.*

152. LIEUT. GEORGE TOBIN's BOOK OF ILLUS-TRATIONS. Tobin painted more than a hundred water-colour sketches during the voyage, including views, animals, birds and fish. 152a Matavai Bay, Tahiti, 1792; 152b Bluefields, Jamaica, 1793. *Mitchell Library, State Library of New South Wales, Sydney.*

152a

149. MANUSCRIPT LOG OF HMS PROVIDENCE. By William Bligh, 2 vols., July 1791 – September 1793. Despite poor health through-out the voyage, Bligh achieved his objectives, and on successfully delivering the plants to the West Indies, he was presented with gifts of money and plate by the Assemblies of the Islands. *Mitchell Library, State Library of New South Wales, Sydney.*

150. BLIGH's BOOK OF ILLUSTRATIONS. To accom-pany the Log of the Provi-dence voyage. A volume of 58 watercolour drawings of birds, fish and views of which 36 are by Bligh and the rest probably by Midshipman George Holwell. *Mitchell Library, State Library of New South Wales, Sydney.*

150

151. MANUSCRIPT JOUR-NAL OF HMS PROVIDENCE. Kept by Lieutenant George Tobin August 1791 – January 1793. *Mitchell Library, State Library of New South Wales, Sydney.*

154. SPECIMEN OF HIBIS-CUS PLANT. Dried leaf and flower of Hibiscus ailiaceus, collected in Tahiti during Bligh's second visit there in HMS Providence in June 1792. *Trustees of the British Museum (Natural History)*

155. GOLD MEDAL OF THE SOCIETY OF ARTS. By T Pingo (Example). On November 26th 1793 the Society for the encouragement of the Arts, Manufactures and Commerce resolved "That Captain Bligh of His Majesty's Ship Providence is entitled to the Gold Medal being the premium offered." *Trustees of the British Museum.*

152b

156. TRANSACTIONS OF THE SOCIETY OF ARTS, 1793-4. Bligh's letter of December 6th 1793 thanking the Society for the award of its Gold Medal for having conveyed the breadfruit trees to the West Indies. *Royal Society of Arts.*

157. WILLIAM BLIGH (1754-1817). Drawing by George Dance, 1794. In civilian dress while at home on half-pay following his return from the 2nd breadfruit voyage. *National Portrait Gallery.*

10. WILLIAM BLIGH AND THE ROYAL NAVY OF HIS TIME.

The controversy surrounding the causes of the mutiny did not prevent William Bligh's later advancement in the Royal Navy.

Bligh had returned from the Pacific to find England at war, but he remained on half-pay at the time of the first major naval action of the Revolutionary War, the Battle of the Glorious Ist of June, 1794. However, a year later, Bligh was appointed to command HMS Calcutta, and 1797 found him in command of HMS Director, 64 guns, at the time of the Fleet Mutiny at the Nore, and the Battle of Camperdown a few months later. In addition to illustrating the events of this period with major paintings, at this point the exhibition also looks at Royal Naval equipment and discipline, in order to set the events of Bligh's naval career into a wider background.

In March 1801 Bligh was appointed to HMS Glatton, 54 guns, and fought under Nelson at the Battle of Copenhagen. His period in the Hydrographic Service is also represented by an important survey. In 1804,

while in command of HMS Warrior, Bligh had a charge of unofficer-like conduct brought against him by his 2nd Lieutenant, and at the Court Martial he maintained: "I can safely aver that at no period of my life whensoever armed with authority have I trampled on those laws which equally guard our liberty and administer redress to the oppressed."

In 1805 through the influence of Sir Joseph Banks, Bligh succeeded Philip King as Governor of New South Wales, and the exhibition includes a small display on this period of his career. His Governorship unfortunately ended amidst the controversy of the Rum Rebellion, and his arrest and deposition by Major Johnson in 1808 resulted in his return to England. Although he held no further active command, he was eventually raised to flag rank in 1811, and his final promotion was to Vice Admiral of the Blue on June 4th 1814. William Bligh died on December 7th 1817, and his tomb is in the churchyard of St Mary-at-Lambeth.

158. THE BATTLE OF THE GLORIOUS FIRST OF JUNE, 1794. Oil painting by Philip James de Loutherbourg, 1795. Lord Howe's victory over Admiral Villaret-Joyeuse's Brest fleet was the first major naval action of the Revolutionary War.

159. MODEL OF A SHIP OF 20 GUNS, SIXTH RATE, CIRCA 1795. Scale 1 1/2 in = lft. Early 19th-century model of the smallest type of rated ship, armed with twenty 9pdr guns. Such vessels repeated signals and carried despatches, playing a vital supporting role to the bigger ships of the line of battle.

160

160. ROYAL NAVAL SHIP's COMPANY OF 1777. Series of coloured etchings by Dominic Serres. Depicting five ranks in officer's uniform of the pattern worn between 1774 and 1787, and a sailor in seagoing costume. The Lieutenant is illustrated above.

161. ARTICLES OF WAR 1749. In Falconer's New Universal Dictionary of the Marine. ed. Wm. Burney, 1815. The Articles of War governing the Royal Navy laid down penalties for offences committed by both officers and men, including the death sentence for those convicted by Court Martial of mutiny, desertion, or running away with any of His Majesty's Ships.

162. REGULATIONS AND INSTRUCTIONS RELATING TO HIS MAJESTY's SERVICE AT SEA, 1787. Published Admiralty Instructions supplemented the Articles of War and gave detailed guidance to captains and officers on their conduct in action, daily duties, and discipline of the ship's company.

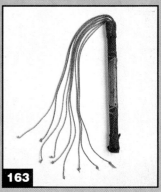

163

163. CAT O'NINE TAILS. Later sealed pattern. At a period when flogging was an accepted punishment both ashore and afloat, the seaman's concern was chiefly that it should be fairly and consistently administered when deserved, for the safety of the whole ship's company. By the standards of the age, Bligh showed marked restraint in the use of corporal punishment.

164. POINT OF HONOUR. Hand coloured etching by George Cruikshank, 1825. A rare illustration of naval punishment, showing a man seized to a grating and about to be flogged in the presence of the entire ship's company.

165. THE DELEGATES IN COUNSEL OR BEGGARS ON HORSEBACK. Coloured etching by George Cruikshank, 1797. A satire on the Fleet mutiny at the Nore, in which Bligh's ship, HMS Director, was involved. On May 19th he was ordered by the delegates to leave his ship, only rejoining her when the mutiny ended a month later.

166. EXECUTION OF RICHARD PARKER. Engraved by Harrison after Chamberlain, July 1797. Following the mutiny at Spithead, when concessions were made to seamen's grievances on pay and conditions, Richard Parker led a more serious mutiny among ships at the Nore, which ended in his execution on board HMS Sandwich on June 29th 1797.

168. PORTSMOUTH POINT. Coloured etching by Thomas Rowlandson, circa 1790. The caricature gives some impression of the bustle of a naval port prior to the departure of a warship, and emphasises the sharp distinction between the traditionally rowdy behaviour of seamen on shore, and naval discipline on board.

169. UNIFORM OF A CAPTAIN RN, 1774-87 PATTERN. Full dress uniform coat of a Captain over 3 years seniority.

170. UNIFORM OF A CAPTAIN RN, 1795-1812 PATTERN. Full dress uniform coat of a Captain over 3 years seniority.

173

167. MANNING THE NAVY. Coloured engraving by Barlow after Collings, 1790. A caricature of the press gang operating on Tower Hill. It is significant, however, that the crew of Bounty were volunteers not pressed men, and some had sailed previously with Bligh.

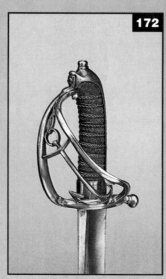

172

171. SEA SERVICE WEAPONS. FLINTLOCK PISTOL circa 1790. FLINTLOCK MUSKET circa 1790. CUTLASS circa 1800. FIGHTING SWORD circa 1780.

172. DUTCH SWORD FROM THE BATTLE OF CAMPERDOWN. Half basket open knuckle guard with anchor design. Said to be the sword surrendered to Captain Bligh on the quaterdeck of HMS Director by the Dutch Vice Admiral Reijntjes on October 11th 1797.

173. GUARDSHIP AT THE GREAT NORE, SHEERNESS. Oil painting by J M W Turner, 1809. HMS Sandwich is shown at anchor as guardship at the Nore, where she served as headquarters for the delegates during the Fleet Mutiny of May 1797. *Trustees of the late Major General R H Goulburn.*

174. BATTLE OF CAMPER-DOWN, 11 OCTOBER 1797. Oil painting by William Augustus Knell, 1848. The Dutch flagship Vrijheid is seen reduced to a wreck at the end of the action. *T E Farrar of Camperdown*.

176. MANUSCRIPT LOG OF HMS DIRECTOR. Kept by Captain William Bligh from January 1796 to July 1800. Records the part played by HMS Director in the fleet mutiny at the Nore in May 1797, and five months later at the Battle of Camperdown. Bligh's entry for October 12th describes the surrender of the Dutch flagship Vrijheid.

177. COMMEMORATION OF CAMPERDOWN. Engraved by J Parker after R Smirke with portraits of eighteen officers including William Bligh after miniatures by John Smart, 1803.

178. BOATSWAIN's CALL USED AFTER CAMPER-DOWN. Silver call by Hester Bateman, London, 1788.

174

175. BATTLE OF CAMPER-DOWN, 11 OCTOBER 1797. Watercolour over etching One of a series by Samuel Owen, 1798.

175

179. ADMIRAL WILLIAM BLIGH. Miniature by unknown artist. Wearing Flag Officer's full dress uniform 1812-25 pattern, and the Captain's Naval Gold Medal for Camperdown. Bligh was a Rear Admiral of the White in 1812, and Vice Admiral of the Blue in 1814. *Private Collection.*

179

184. LARGE SCALE SURVEY OF DUBLIN BAY. By Captain William Bligh RN, 1803. This survey carried out at the desire of the Lord Lieutenant of Ireland was the most comprehensive carried out by Bligh. Its insets show proposed harbour works off the Liffey, off Howth and off Dunlary, and include topographical details by Sir Thomas Hyde Page, Royal Engineers. *Hydrographic Department, MOD.*

180

180. BATTLE OF COPENHAGEN, 2nd APRIL 1801. Oil painting by Nicholas Pocock, 1806. After the truce which followed the British attack on Copenhagen, Lord Nelson signalled Captain Bligh to come aboard his flagship to thank him for his support in HMS Glatton.

181. PLAN OF BATTLE OF COPENHAGEN, 2nd APRIL 1801. By William Bligh. This plan of Lord Nelson's attack indicates with coloured flags the flagships Elephant and Defiance, and shows the position of Bligh's ship Glatton, the Danish fleet and the fort and town of Copenhagen. *Hydrographic Department, MOD.*

182. BLIGH FAMILY JEWELLERY. Pair-cased watch by Henry Massy of London, a pendant mounted with Tahitian pearls inscribed from William Bligh to his wife in 1790, and a gold mourning ring commemorating his death on December 7th 1817, made for his daughter Harriet. *Private Collection.*

183. MAHOGANY-CASED TELESCOPE. By Troughton of London. Inscribed "Capt. W Bligh Royal Navy" *Mitchell Library, State Library of New South South Wales, Sydney.*

182a

182b

185. SYDNEY, NEW SOUTH WALES. Aquatint views from the East and West Side of the Cove. Engraved by Clark after J Eyre, 1810. The artist John Eyre had arrived in Sydney as a convict in 1801 and became an important topographical illustrator. Bligh left England for New South Wales in February 1806.

186. HAWKESBURY RIVER. Watercolour dated 1807. On becoming Governor of New South Wales Bligh received grants of land, including 1000 acres off the Hawkesbury River, which he named Copenhagen in commemoration of his part in the recent battle. *Private Collection.*

188. HUNTER RIVER. Watercolour by William Bligh. Seaward view with soundings, showing the southern entrance to the present harbour of Newcastle, New South Wales. *Private Collection.*

192. ELIZABETH BLIGH, 1802. Pastel by John Russell. William Bligh's wife suffered from ill health in later years and did not accompany him to New South Wales when he took up the appointment of Governor in 1806. She died five years before him in 1812. *Private Collection.*

187. GOVERNMENT HOUSE, SYDNEY. Watercolour by William Westall, 1802. Presented by the artist to Governor Captain Philip Gidley King, who preceded Bligh as Governor of New South Wales. *National Library of Australia, Canberra.*

189. THE ARREST OF GOVERNOR BLIGH, JANUARY 26th 1808. Chromolithograph facsimile from the original watercolour. *Mitchell Library, State Library of New South Wales, Sydney.*

190. WILLIAM BLIGH, VICE ADMIRAL OF THE BLUE. Bligh's Admiralty Commission as Vice Admiral was dated June 4th 1814. Mr R L B Wall

193. CAPTAIN WILLIAM BLIGH RN, circa 1803. Pencil and watercolour drawing by John Smart. *National Portrait Gallery.*

194. FIGUREHEAD OF HIS MAJESTY's NEW YACHT ROYAL GEORGE, LAUNCHED 1817. The bust of George III in classical dress is supported by two male negro figures.

191. CAPTAIN WILLIAM BLIGH RN, 1791. Pastel by John Russell Bligh is shown in the full dress uniform coat of a Junior Captain. The portrait was engraved by John Conde as the frontispiece to Bligh's published Voyage to the South Sea, 1792. *Private Collection.*

VERHAAL
VAN DE
MUITERY,
AAN BOORD VAN HET
ENGELSCH KONINGSSCHIP
DE
BOUNTY,

En de daarop gevolgde rampfpoedige reis van een gedeelte van
het Scheepsvolk, het welk genoodzaakt is geweest een en
veertig dagen, in de Scheepsboot, op zee door te brengen
en, na met dezelve van TOFOA, een der VRIENDLY-
KE EILANDEN, tot TIMOR, eene Hollandfche Bezit-
ting in OOSTINDIEN, zynde een afftand van meer dan
twaalf honderd uren, gevaren te hebben, aldaar behou-
den is aangeland.

BESCHREVEN DOOR DEN LUITENANT
WILLIAM BLIGH,
Bevelhebber op het Schip de BOUNTY.

Uit het Engelsch vertaald door REINIER ARRENBERG.

TE ROTTERDAM,
By GERARD ABRAHAM ARRENBERG,
M D C C X C.

■ Dutch Edition of Bligh's account of the Mutiny 1790. *Private collection.*

Continued from page 64
direction", perhaps following the route he had intended to take in the Bounty. Later in the voyage, Bligh occasionally calculated the bearing and distance between his noon position and the few places adjacent to his route, whose positions were given in his two navigational manuals, so that he could decide what courses to steer to pass them at a reasonable distance. Thus on 13 May he calculated that Cape Cumberland, the northern tip of Espiritu Santo Island, in Vanuatu, bore S 85°W, distant 239 miles and on 23 May, Cape York, the northern tip of Australia, bore N 79°W, distant 765 miles.

As soon as the weather moderated, Bligh had a log line made up so that he could ascertain the launch's speed through the water, an essential requisite for estimating the daily distance run. A standard log line in Bligh's day was marked by knots at intervals of 50 feet, each knot being subdivided into fathoms of 5 feet. Thus when the log was heaved at the end of each hour, each knot that ran out in half a minute represented 50 feet travelled by the launch through the water

in that time. Since 50 feet in half a minute is equivalent to 6,000 feet (or approximately one sea mile) in one hour, each knot and fathom run out thus gave the speed of the launch through the water in sea miles an hour or knots, to give it its nautical equivalent. Each hour Bligh entered the number of knots and fathoms recorded by the log line and the course steered in his notebook and from them was able to calculate the distance run each day and the course made good. Then by using the traverse tables in the *Practical Navigator,* he was able to convert these figures into differences of latitude and and longitude, and after applying his estimation of the effect of leeway and current he was able to obtain a new noon position "by account" or dead reckoning.

Each noon, whenever the sun was visible, Bligh observed its meridian altitude. Taking such an observation was no easy matter in the launch, since to get an accurate altitude Bligh probably had to brace himself with one arm locked round the mainmast, standing at the same time on one of the thwarts to obtain as good a view of the horizon as possible. Although Christian had prevented Bligh being supplied with a copy of the *Nautical Almanac*, he seems to have over-

looked the fact that the *Practical Navigator* contained a table giving the suns declination for each day of the year for several years after its publication. Bligh was, therefore, able to calculate his latitude reasonably accurately for the entire boat voyage. He was, however, unable to take observations for longitude by lunar distances, since the *Nautical Almanac* contained the vital information he needed to make the necessary calculations. His longitude had to be carried forward each day by account and was thus increasingly in error as the voyage progressed. Bligh was unable to take observations from the launch to determine magnetic variation. This did not pose a serious navigational problem since he had obtained a value of 8° East for variation a few days before the mutiny and he would have been aware that its value was likely to decrease to almost zero by the time the launch reached the NE coast of Australia.

While few people will deny that it was a great achievement for Bligh to navigate the launch safely almost 4,000 miles from Tofua to Coupang, what really sets this feat apart from other notable open boat voyages, such as that of 1,700 miles by Captain Cecil Foster across the Indian Ocean in the Trevassa's boats in 1923 or

■ Bligh Cast Adrift. 19th century steel engraving from Chamber's "The Mutiny of The Bounty and Life of a Sailor Boy" nd *Private collection.*

that of some 800 miles from the Antarctic ice edge to South Georgia by Ernest Shackelton in 1916, was the discoveries Bligh made and the running surveys which he carried out during the voyage.

Bligh's decision to look for Fiji is understandable. He had heard vague accounts of these islands when he had been at Tongatapu with Cook in 1777 and during his recent visit to Nemuka had learnt that they lay NNW from that island. It is one of the enigmas of Cook's third voyage that this great navigator failed to follow up the accounts he had received of Fiji by searching for these islands. No doubt Bligh felt that it would be to his credit if he could make good this omission. On 4 May, he sighted a small island of moderate height, which has now been identified as Yangasa Levu at the southern end of the Lau Group, situated at the SE end of the Fiji Islands. More islands of this group were sighted the following day, the relative positions of which Bligh sketched in his notebook, the first of nine rough surveys which he recorded in that book. Passing through the Lau Group by a channel now known as Bounty Boat Passage, Bligh steered a course which took him right through the centre of the Fiji archipelago, sketching in the numerous islands as they came into view. Bligh also encountered numerous reefs, noting in his journal:

Many reefs are about and dangerous, as some do not show any break. The exploring these islands must, therefore, be done with caution. I have only a quadrant and a compass with me, which with the violent motion of the boat, and always wet, I am prevented from doing as much as I wish.

The following day, when about midway between Viti Levu and Vanua Levu, the two principal islands of Fiji, Bligh noted:

The lands both on the north and south appeared to be more extensive than I at first supposed them to be. They are large islands & if I were to judge of their extent as far as the looming of the land appeared, I should consider them among the most extensive Isl[s] in this sea.

However, the passage between Viti Levu and Vanua Levu is mostly shoal, with only a narrow deep-water channel running through from east to west, which lay to the south of Bligh's track, and so shortly afterwards he

suddenly got on a shoal Bank of Coral & Sand which had only 4 feet on it without the least break. It extended about 1 mile in circuit: that I could distinctly observe. Had I been here in a ship I should certainly have been on it.

Once clear of this shoal and with no land in sight ahead, Bligh steered directly out to sea, crossing an extensive area of deep water, now known as Bligh Water. At dawn the following morning, land was in sight ahead once more. This was the northernmost of the Yasawa Islands, situated at the NW end of the Fiji Islands. As they approached the Yasawas, the launch was swept close to them by the current and the crew had to use their oars to get clear. Even so, they were not out of danger since two large sailing canoes appeared and attempted to close the launch, but with sail set and with the crew pulling hard on their oars, they managed to reach the open sea and throw off their pursuers. This was a close call as there can be little doubt that Bligh and his companions would have been killed had the Fijians caught up with them.

Bligh drew three sketch surveys in his notebook as he passed through the Fiji Islands and these formed the basis of a chart published subsequently with the title *Chart of Bligh's Islands.* While the detail on this chart is somewhat rudimentary, the relationship between the various islands is shown reasonably accurately, thus showing the approximate extent of these islands for the first time. On the chart longitude is given by account, placing the eastern islands of the Lau Group 3°17' west of Tofua, compared with their present value of 3°16', while the northern tip of the Yasawa Islands, which is not so well defined on the chart, is placed 6°50' west of Tofua, compared with its present value of 6°26'. Bligh's latitudes are however reasonably accurate, being in error by no more than about 5 minutes.

From Fiji, Bligh set a course to pass north of Cape Cumberland, which was then thought to be the northern tip of Vanuatu, since there was nothing to be gained by passing through the group, as it

had been well surveyed by Cook during his second voyage. During this part of the voyage, Bligh constructed a pair of scales out of two coconut shells, and using a pistol ball found in the launch as a weight, was able to ensure that each person received the same weight of bread at each meal. By now the ration had been set at a 25th of a pound of bread and a quarter of a pint of water three times a day, though the supply of water was augmented from time to time by heavy rainfall. The wind continued to blow strongly from SSE to SE, bringing with it squally weather and high breaking seas, so that every one on board was constantly wet and suffered greatly from the cold, particularly during the night. It was under these conditions that Bligh's superb seamanship kept the launch from broaching to, even though she was continually shipping water, which necessitated constant bailing by the tired and exhausted crew.

On 14 May, when about 30 miles north of Cape Cumberland, Bligh discovered a group of islands, which he subsequently named Banks Islands, after his patron Sir Joseph Banks. Bligh drew a sketch survey of the islands in his notebook, which he later included as an inset on his *Chart of Bligh's Islands*. Although for many years these islands were thought to be a new discovery, modern historians now consider that they had been sighted in 1606 by the Spanish explorer Quiros.

For the next 14 days, Bligh's course took him through the northern part of the Coral Sea, towards the Great Barrier Reef some distance to the south of Endeavour Reef. Bligh may have been making for Providential Channel, through which Cook had taken the Endeavour in 1770. The position of this channel was not given in either of Bligh's navigational manuals, so he had to rely on the position of Cape York, the NE tip of Australia, from the *Practical Navigator,* to set a suitable course. However, unknown to Bligh, its latitude in this manual was in error, being some 33 miles south of its true position, thus making it likely that Bligh would encounter the Great Barrier Reef farther south than he intended. During this part of the voyage some very severe weather was encountered, making steering very difficult, particularly at night. On four days the sun was obscured at noon and on other days the sea was so rough that Bligh's observations for latitude could

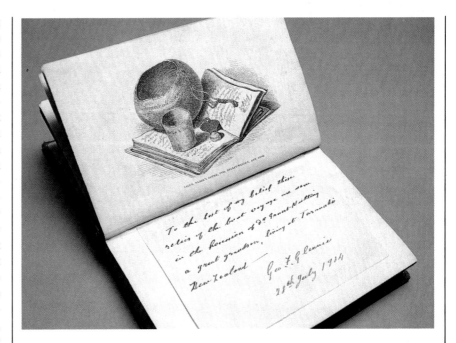

■ Cup, Gourd and Bullet Weight as illustrated in Thomas Boyle Murray's "Pitcairn: The Island, The People and The Pastor". *Private collection.*

not have been very accurate. In one respect the severe weather was something of a blessing since the strong winds were still from an easterly direction, so that even with reefed sails they continued to make good progress.

On 24 May, Bligh was forced to reduce the ration even further, by omitting the evening meal, to ensure that the meagre supply of provisions would not be exhausted should he miss Timor and be forced to sail on to Java. As if to compensate for this, some noddies, a species of tern about the size of a pigeon, came near the launch the following day and one was caught. The noddy was divided into 18 portions, which were distributed by an old fashioned method used at sea. While one person turned his back to the portions to be distributed, another pointed to each portion in turn, asking "who shall have this?" to which the first person called out one of their names. This impartial method of distribution ensured that each person had an equal chance of getting the best share. The blood was given to three of the crew, who by now were very weak. During the next few days, a number of boobies, a species of gannet about the size of a chicken, were caught and divided out in the same way. Since these birds are rarely encountered far from land, the launch was now clearly approaching the Australian coast.

At 1am on 28 May, breakers were

heard ahead and soon afterwards were sighted close under the launch's lee. Bligh immediately went about and stood out to sea, approaching the reef once again at daylight, when he was fortunate enough to find a passage through it almost at once. An island of moderate height, in line with the entrance, provided Bligh with a good leading line, causing him to name it the Island of Direction. Bligh's Boat Entrance, as it is now known, is situated just 15 miles south of Providential Channel. Bligh calculated that its longitude by account from Tofua was 40°10', which is in error by only about 50 miles in a total distance run of just over 2,400 miles.

On entering sheltered waters, Bligh's first thought was to find a suitable island to rest and recuperate, where he hoped he might find food and water. Since the Island of Direction proved to be a mere heap of stones, Bligh proceeded to the next one, situated a quarter of a mile off the mainland, where he landed and spent the next 2 1/2 days. Oysters were found here in abundance and a good supply of fresh water was also obtained. Since Bligh was able to start a fire, using the magnifying glass from his sextant, some wholesome stew was produced, which had a marked effect on everyone's appearance and morale. As the anniversary of the restoration of King Charles II occurred during his stay at this island, Bligh named it Restoration Island, noting that this name was not inappropriate to their present situation.

Shortly before leaving Restoration

Bligh's Island today.
Private collection.

Island, some Aborigines were seen on the mainland opposite, shouting and making signs for Bligh to land there, but he considered that this would be imprudent. So proceeding northwards, Bligh commenced a running survey of the NE coast of Australia. He landed on two more islands off this stretch of coast, so that he could obtain a better view of the coast for his survey. The first was Sunday Island, which he named after the day he landed there, and the second was Bird Islands, a group of small sandy cays which he referred to as Lagoon Island. On Sunday Island, Bligh's authority was challenged by William Purcell, the carpenter, who said that he was as good a man as Bligh. Whereupon Bligh, determined to maintain his authority or perish in the attempt, seized a cutlass and challenged Purcell to take one too and substantiate his claim. Purcell declined and there the matter rested. Then John Fryer, the master, who insisted in having a fire to himself, set Lagoon Island alight, thus frustrating an attempt to catch some turtle there. The same night, a party sent out to catch noddies, which had been seen in large numbers, returned with only 12, due to the misconduct of another member of the crew. It seems as though at sea, where they were under pressure, the crew were manageable, but on land the seeds of discontent were soon sown.

Bligh was able to obtain meridian altitudes of the sun on Lagoon Island, enabling him to fix its latitude accurately for his survey. He also noted the time of high water at all three islands he visited, working out the time of high water

on days of the full and new moon, noting that the time of high water became progressively later as he proceeded northwards. Peckover's watch, which had been of great service, stopped shortly after leaving Lagoon Island, but this does not seem to have affected the accuracy of Bligh's survey. On his passage north, Bligh failed to identify Endeavour Strait, because of the error in the *Practical Navigator* of the latitude of Cape York. In consequence, the name Bay of Islands appears on his running survey in the position of this strait, though Bligh suspected that it probably was Endeavour Strait. However, he discovered a channel leading to the west north of Prince of Wales Island, which he followed as far as Booby Island, where his running survey of the Australian coast came to an end.

Bligh's survey of the NE coast of Australia was carried out under much better conditions than his survey of Fiji and this is reflected in the original survey which he drew in his notebook and in his published chart. In the published account of the mutiny, Bligh wrote that his chart was not intended to supersede the one made by Cook, since the latter was better provided in every respect than he was for surveying, stating that he had only included it in his narrative to make it more intelligible and to show how the coast appeared from an open boat. However, Flinders, who had a copy of Bligh's chart when he was surveying this part of Australia in 1802 and 1803, was surprised to find that it was better in some respects than the chart produced by Cook

in the Endeavour in 1770. In an unpublished memoir, Flinders commented:

> To the west of Cape Cornwal, the islands are laid down according to my bearings and observations in the Investigator and Cumberland; and they have less agreement both in situation and appearance with captain Cook's chart, than they have with that made by captain Bligh in the Bounty's launch. It has been to me a çause of much surprise, that under such distress of hunger and fatigue, and of anxiety still greater than these, and whilst running before a strong breeze in an open boat, captain Bligh should have been able to gather materials for a chart; but that this chart should possess a considerable share of accuracy, is a subject for admiration ... my first acquirements in nautical science having been made under one [Bligh] who mostly gained his from that great master himself [Cook]: untoward circumstances shall not prevent me from repeating the name of Bligh at this moment.

The passage to Timor was a trying affair with seas continually breaking over the launch, necessitating constant bailing by the now severely debilitated crew, whose condition was deteriorating rapidly. In particular, the extreme weakness of two of his crew gave Bligh cause for considerable alarm, but he was able to sustain them with teaspoonsful of wine, which he had kept back for such an eventuality. Bligh's own condition was hardly any better and on one occasion William Cole, the boatswain, told him that he looked worse than anyone else in the boat.

At this stage, Bligh's navigation was made more difficult by his mistaking in the *Tables Requisite* the longitude of the south point of Timor Laut, situated some 200 miles east of Timor, for the longitude of Timor itself. This was an understandable mistake since Timor Laut appears in these tables as Timor Land. A different position for Timor in the *Practical Navigator* added to Bligh's difficulties. Nevertheless, Timor was sighted on 12 June, 10 days after passing Booby Island. For two days they sailed along the south coast of the island looking for a European settlement. Eventually, after rounding the SW point of Timor, off which they encountered a very dangerous

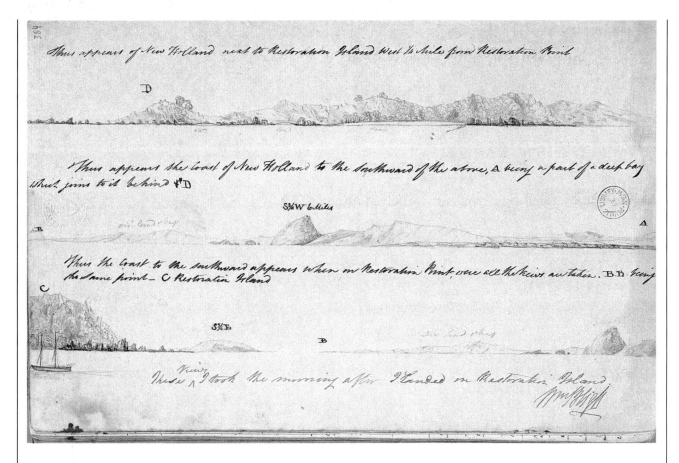

Thus appears of New Holland next to Restoration Island West ¼ Mile from Restoration Point

Thus appears the coast of New Holland to the southward of the above, A being a part of a deep bay which joins to it behind D

S¾W 6 Miles

Thus the coast to the southward appears when on Restoration Point, were all the views are taken. B.B. being the same point. C Restoration Island

S¾E

These Views I took the morning after I landed on Restoration Island

▓ View of the Coast of Australia from Bligh's Restoration Island, drawn by Bligh whilst on the launch voyage. *Mitchell Library, Sydney.*

sea, Bligh found a small sheltered sandy bay just north of the point where he anchored. Here Bligh obtained the services of one of the natives as a pilot and later that day, 14 June 1789, they finally reached the Dutch settlement of Coupang, 43 days after their departure from Tofua. Bligh had sailed the launch some 3,900 miles, at an average of 90 miles a day, during which they had, in Bligh's own words "surmounted the difficulties and distresses of a most perilous voyage, and arrived safely in an hospitable port".

Bligh remained at Coupang for more than two months, while he and his crew recovered their health. David Nelson, who had joined the expedition from the Botanical Gardens at Kew to take charge of the breadfruit plants, died at Coupang, much to Bligh's distress. Since no other transport was immediately available to take them on to Java, Bligh purchased a small, locally built vessel, which he named and manning it with his crew, sailing in her on 14 August for Batavia (Jakarta), which they reached on 1 October. Bligh remained at Batavia until the 16th of that month, when he embarked, with his clerk and a seaman, in the Dutch packet Vlydte, Captain Couvret, sailing in her for the Cape of Good Hope and Europe. The rest of his crew were instructed to follow in the next available ships.

One would have thought that Bligh might have relaxed during his voyage home and left the Dutch master to navigate his own ship, but that was not Bligh's way. Each day Bligh took a meridian altitude of the sun to obtain his latitude, which he then compared with that obtained by Captain Couvret, finding that they sometimes differed by as much as 8 minutes. He found much greater differences between their longitudes. Somehow Bligh appears to have obtained a copy of the *Nautical Almanac* in Batavia since during the voyage he was able to obtain his longitude by lunar distances, while Captain Couvret continued to rely on longitude by account. Because of this, the latter's longitude was 7 1/2 degrees in error when they sighted the Cape.

Bligh finally reached Portsmouth on 13 March 1790 and hastened to the Admiralty to report the disastrous outcome of his voyage. The rest of the launch's crew were provided with passages from Batavia to Europe in various ships soon after Bligh left Java, but not before three of them had died there. One more died on the voyage home and another was not heard of again. And so out of the 19 people who were cast adrift by the mutineers off Tofua, only 12 of them succeeded in reaching England safely.

Bligh's account of the mutiny on

board the Bounty and his subsequent boat voyage was published in July 1790. It included his charts of Fiji and the NE coast of Australia and also a chart showing the track of the launch from Tofua to Timor. His navigational achievements brought him universal admiration. An extended account of the whole voyage was edited during Bligh's absence on a second and successful breadfruit voyage to Tahiti by his friend, James Burney, and published in 1792. This account contains the three charts that were included in the earlier account and in addition his survey of Matavai Bay and Oparre Harbour drawn from memory, thus completing the cartographic record of the voyage.

How should Bligh's voyage in the Bounty and his open boat voyage be judged 200 years later? Alan Villiers, who sailed the fully rigged ship *Joseph Conrad* along much the same route that Bligh followed in the launch in the early part of this century, considered that no man before or since showed greater courage against the natural and man-made hazards of the sea. Few who have studied Bligh's notebook or read his journal would disagree.

Freewheel Around London
with a
One Day Travelcard

A One Day Travelcard is the only ticket you need for a day out in London. It allows you unlimited journeys by British Rail's Network SouthEast trains, the Underground, Docklands Light Railway and on most of London's buses for a day.

MAKE A DAY OF IT

A One Day Travelcard is ideal for a day's shopping in London or sightseeing with the children, visiting friends or relatives across town, going to an exhibition, museum or art gallery, or having a night out on the town. There's so much to see and do in the Capital - the possibilities are almost endless.

It's so convenient and the more you travel the more you save! Start your journey anytime at weekends or Bank Holidays, after 0930 on Mondays to Fridays - return home anytime same day. Tickets can be bought just before you travel or up to 24 hours in advance from any staffed Network SouthEast station or Underground station.

ONE DAY TRAVELCARD

Tahiti: paradise on earth

Bengt Danielsson, who sailed on the Kontiki expedition, reports from Papehue, Tahiti, on the life and eventual capture of the mutineers

■ IN DOZENS of books, hundreds of magazine articles and three films we have been told what the Tahitians did for and to the crew of the Bounty during their five month stay gathering bread-fruit saplings, from the end of October 1788 to the beginning of April 1789. The Tahitians treated the British seaman with such boundless hospitality and deep affection that they refused to go home, took over the ship, and returned to Tahiti to enjoy perpetual bliss in this earthly paradise.

This is, of course, an oversimplified view of the famous mutiny, but my aim here is not to correct the endless mistakes and misinterpretations of several generations of writers on the subject, but to tell instead the little-known story of what the 16 Bounty men, who spent 18 months in Tahiti *after* the mutiny, did to the Tahitians. Although they did not intend to, they irrevocably changed the course of Tahitian history.

My story, based on journals, letters and other documents preserved in British archives, begins on 22 September 1789, when the Bounty, under the command of Fletcher Christian, called for the last time at Tahiti to land the crew members who refused to accompany him any further during what they considered to be a pointless search for a safe island hideaway – which, in fact, ended successfully with their settlement on Pitcairn Island. Seven of these 16 men had not taken part in the mutiny at all, but had been forced to stay on board because there was no

room for them in the overloaded launch in which Captain Bligh and the majority of his followers were set adrift.

For these seven loyalists and nine mutineers to step ashore again at Point Venus, Tahiti, was like coming home, for during their first stay with Bligh they had all acquired many friends and sweethearts among the inhabitants of the small "kingdoms". These were stretched out along the north coast of Tahiti, corresponding to the present townships of Mahina, Arue, Pirae and Papeete. In true Tahitian style, old and new friends vied with each other to be allowed the honour to lodge them in their cool, palm-thatched houses, to feed them with delicious dishes of fish, pig, dog, bread-fruit, and tubers, baked in earth-ovens, and to entertain them daily, or rather nightly, with singing, dancing, and erotic games.

The only person missing was the chief of the Porionuu region (today the township of Arue, Pirae and Papeete), whom Cook and Bligh had believed to be the "King of all Tahiti." In fact, there were in the island 18 chiefs on equal footing. Being a born con-man, the Porionuu chief had enthusiastically assumed this fictitious role, even though it meant that he frequently had to endure a royal salute by the ship's guns, which each time scared him stiff. But then he was often compensated for his sufferings by receiving all the fancy gifts King George III of England used to send out to his royal counterpart in Tahiti. As a result, "King Otoo of Tahiti" figures prominently in Captain Cook's accounts of his voyages. Tu was the title, and not the name of this impostor, and in accordance with a widespread Tahitian custom, he changed name several times during his lifetime. During the first stay of the Bounty he was commonly known by the name of Teina, but when the mutineers returned a few months later he was called Mate. For posterity, he is Pomare I, the founder of the whole dynasty with that name.

Shortly after the departure of his protector, Bligh, in April 1789, Mate-

Pomare I began to be seriously concerned about the threat of the plundering of his treasures by the other chieftains and decided to withdraw to his brother-in-law Vehiatua's domain on the Taiarapu peninsula. According to a rumour which soon reached the Bounty men, Mate now even employed an armed bodyguard, who was said to be an English naval deserter. Mate's younger brother, Ariipaea, however, who was acting as a sort of regent during the former's absence, and who was more popular with the people, did everything in his power to persuade the 16 well-armed and well-equipped white men to settle in Porionuu. But to Ariipaea's keen disappointment, only five of them, mutineers Muspratt and Hillbrant, and loyalists, Byrne, McIntosh, and Norman, accepted his offer of a large piece of land and plenty of servants.

The other 11 men preferred to remain on Point Venus in Haapape (Mahina), the kingdom of the good-natured, easy-going Poino, where they had first been initiated into the pleasant mysteries of Tahitian hospitality. Here the loyalist Morrison, who now seems to have been accepted as the leader, was housed by none less than Chief Poino himself. The mutineer Millward also

■ Tahitienne
Private Collection.

joined the royal household as he had established a liaison with one of Poino's wives. Stewart, the loyalist midshipman, was one of the half-dozen men who had a regular mistress, and he thus settled down naturally with his "father-in-law", along with his colleague Heywood. The third household consisted of mutineer Thompson and loyalist Coleman, both of whom moved in with the latter's "parents-in-law". In a fourth hut lived the three mutineers Burkett, Sumner, and Ellison, and here it was Sumner's hospitable "parents-in-law"who prepared their food and kept house for them. Mutineer Skinner was apparently less gregarious because he went off to live alone with his girl. Finally, there was the violent and ambitious Churchill who held court in his *taio*-brother's house and brooded over Morrison's enviable position as leader of the group. Thus, the 16 men were not split up as one might have expected into loyalists and mutineers, but formed instead groups based on personal choice.

Even though the Bounty men must by this time have realized that Mate's position was not so grand and secure as they had first believed when they arrived at Tahiti, they nevertheless regarded his seven year-old-son, on whom the family title Tu had been conferred at birth, as the heir apparent to the "Tahitian throne". Thus as soon as they had settled in, they set off together to pay homage to the young crown prince. With Hitihiti, Cook's and Bligh's local interpreter, as spokesman and master of ceremonies, they shed in true Tahitian fashion the bark cloth cloaks, which they had put on for the occasion and presented Tu with a huge selection of iron tools. To round off the ceremony, they fired a deafening volley with their muskets. The young boy was understandably deeply impressed by all this, and they were consequently assured by Tu's uncle, Ariipaea, that they should consider themselves completely at home in Porionuu. Ariipaea also reciprocated by offering an elaborate feast and presenting each one of the Bounty men with a large piece of land, clearly in the hope that this gesture might persuade all the white men to desert the area of Haapape in favour of Porionuu.

To have ignored entirely Tu's father would have been a grave breach of etiquette, and since the latter was still too scared to show himself at Matavai, the Bounty men despatched a delegation under Churchill's eager command to the

King O-Too, later Pomare I, of A-Taheite, engraved by Hall after a drawing "From Nature" by William Hodges.

Taiarapu peninsula to pay their respects to Mate. Churchill returned a fortnight later together with Mate's much talked about bodyguard, an Englishman named Brown. This new acquaintance stated that he had been left behind by the British ship Mercury at his own request about a month before, and then went on to boast of the many great deeds which he had accomplished in the course of his life. He claimed that he had been a sergeant of the marine in Portsmouth, an officer in the army of the Indian Prince Hyder Aly, and captain of a ship which he had himself captured. This was all before his inexplicable decision to join the Mercury as an ordinary seaman. Although many of Brown's stories were clearly the product of a fertile imagination, there is no doubt that he had landed on Tahiti from a ship

A later engraving of Pomare, King of Tahiti. *Private Collection.*

variously called Mercury and Gustavus III. The activities of this ship have always been a mystery to maritime historians, but recent investigations have revealed that it was a privateer, and that the owner, a British merchant named John Henry Cox, had been issued with a letter of marque by King Gustavus III of Sweden. Since 1788, Sweden had been at war with Russia, and at his own request Cox had been charged by Gustavus III with the mission of hitting the enemy in the rear by attacking his trading posts in Alaska and Kamchatka, the long peninsula in eastern Siberia stretching south to Japan. This absurd project would hardly have been likely to make any difference to Russia, and Cox never made any serious attempt to carry it through. It should, however, be mentioned here that Cox, without knowing anything about the mutiny, had tried to put into Tubuai at the very time when the mutineers were making their abortive attempt to settle there. Since it was late in the afternoon and because there was an offshore wind, Cox was unable to land and continued on his way to Tahiti.

Some time later Poino, who was an intelligent man, showed Morrison a letter from Cox addressed to all ship's captains who might put in to Tahiti. It emerged from this that Brown had knifed another member of the crew on the Mercury and had simply been dumped ashore on Tahiti as a punishment for his crime. The majority of the Bounty men disliked Brown from the outset, and it was with a sense of relief that they saw him depart again for Taiarapu to resume his post as bodyguard and military adviser to Mate.

The 16 seamen had now been on Tahiti somewhat over a month and had thus had plenty of time to consider their position and to make plans for the future. The nine mutineers must obviously have been the most uneasy, since, even though they were fairly certain that Bligh and his men would not have survived, they must at the same time have realized that in due course the Admiralty would be bound to send out another ship to Tahiti to investigate what had happened to the breadfruit expedition. The wisest move would have been to follow Christian's example and make for some other island, as far away from Tahiti as it was possible to get in a large sailing canoe. But none of them seems to have thought of this, probably because they were suffering from a form of well-known and aptly named disease

■ Breadfruit Tree, Tahiti, engraved by Sydney Parkinson in 1769. *British Library*.

"Polynesian paralysis", which is still very common among European residents who have "gone native" and manifests itself in a complete inability on the part of the afflicted individual to make the effort to board a homeward-bound ship or plane.

The first person to give any any thought to how to get away from the island was, curiously enough, the loyalist Morrison who somehow felt that it was his duty to build a boat and try to get to Timor or Patavia and thence back to England. His first step was to confide in the two loyalist carpenters, Norman and McIntosh. They fully supported Morrison's audacious plan and promised their complete cooperation. But three men was far from adequate for such a project, and a few more had to be recruited at least during the construction stage. It was evident to Morrison that the mutineers could hardly be expected to show any enthusiasm for such a plan, since if he managed to reach England, he would in all likelihood disclose their hiding-place. He thus claimed that he was intending to build a boat for the fun of it, so that when it was ready they could make pleasure cruises to other island groups nearby. Presumably because they were somewhat bored with having nothing to do, at least 10 men immediately agreed to give a hand, and none but the initiated seem to have suspected Morrison's real aim, probably because it was so foolhardy.

The Boat-builders were quickly divided up into teams, and they went to work with a will. Even Brown became so interested that he made the long trip from Taiaparu to look on. Much to the relief of the boat-builders, however, he quickly tired even of this passive role and returned to his lord and master, Mate.

Habit is a potent force, and it was not long before the boat-builders fell back into their regular ship's routine with watch-keeping and the formal raising and lowering of the flat at forenoon and sunset. At the same time, Morrison began to keep a journal in which he recorded everything that happened with the same care and accuracy that Bligh used to keep Bounty's ship's log. The men felt nevertheless that they had forgotten something of importance, and in due course they realized that this was Sunday matins. From then on the service was performed

THE BREAD FRUIT.

■ 19th century steel engraving of breadfruit. *Private collection*.

regularly and piously. To balance it, another time-honoured procedure was also resumed. It had become the habit, among the large number of natives who gathered to watch the boat-building activities, for one or another of them to purloin the mutineer's iron tools. The only answer to this, Morrison resolved, was flogging, and thus it became the practice

to seize any unfortunate caught stealing and administer the requisite number of lashes. These procedures should help to dispel the erroneous claim, often heard, that the mutineers fled to Tahiti full of Rousseauesque admiration for these noble savages.

The boat-building programme soon produced innumerable knotty problems. The Tahitians were skilled craftsmen and only too willing to lend a hand, but the vessel that Morrison and his men were

■ Rudder sections from HMS Bounty, showing the fastenings now preserved in Fidji Museum, Suva, Fidji. *Bengt Danielsson.*

planning was unlike anything the islanders had ever seen. The Tahitian canoes, either a long slender hull with an outrigger or else two identical heavy hulls joined by cross-beams, were built of planks joined together by means of sennit ropes. But instead of building a large double canoe, the Bounty men obstinately persisted with their plans for a proper clinker-built schooner, and were thus forced to manage in the construction work without the help of the natives. Two other problems were the exhausting treks which had to be made up into the hills to find the right timber, and the lack of a saw large enough to make long planks. Here, however, the Tahitians were of invaluable assistance with their remarkable technique of splitting large tree trunks with stone wedges and then smoothing the planks with rough coral stones. Finally, the work was also delayed by the absence of a forge, and it was not until Coleman contrived with great patience and ingenuity to construct one from stone and clay that the boat-building project really began to make progress.

Despite all the many setbacks, they had more or less completed the frame, when, on 8 February 1790, an incident occurred which threatened to wreck the entire project. Churchill's accomplice, the unsavoury Thompson, was roundly thrashed by a native for having raped his sister. In a vicious temper after this humiliating experience, Churchill turned on a crowd of curious natives who had surrounded his hut and ordered them to go away. They were apparently slow in dispersing (the reason for which might have been that they did not understand any English) so Thompson seized his musket and fired point blank into them. The shot killed a man and the child in his arms and injured two others. All the Bounty men, with the exception of Churchill, who thought this a good lesson for the savages, were furious at Thompson's brutality and feared that Poino and his subjects would lose their patience and avenge themselves on the group as a whole. Churchill immediately offered to organize a punitive expedition which would knock a proper sense of respect into the natives once and for all.

■ One of Bounty's anchors raised by Luis Marden in 1957, now preserved in Bounty Square, Pitcairn's Island. *Bengt Danielsson.*

This vicious plan was immediately rejected by the others, and they were busily discussing the best means of making an adequate apology, when it emerged that the dead man was from another part of Tahiti, and therefore according to Tahitian law had no status whatever in Haapape. The Bounty men were relieved to hear this, everyone that is except Churchill, who in his frustration recruited his kindred spirits, Thompson and Brown, and set off for the Taiarapu peninsula, where he hoped that Mate would be more appreciative of his military abilities.

Generally satisfied with the outcome of the unfortunate episode, most of the boat-builders now returned to work with a will. But it was not long before Churchill made his presence felt again. Scarcely two weeks later a letter arrived from him, a written panegyric on life at Taiarapu and the unending goodness and generosity of Mate and his brother-in-law Vehiatua. It concluded by urging the entire group to move over to Taiarapu without delay. But Morrison and his men were sick to death of Churchill, and they did not even bother to reply. This was a mistake, because shortly afterwards Churchill showed up in person at Matavai, this time with the startling news that Vehiatua was dead, that he himself had been elected chief of the realm and that anyone who cared to accompany him back would be richly rewarded. The only ones who accepted this offer were Muspratt and Burkett, both of whom had any-

■ Another Bounty anchor lost in Toaroa Harbour, Arue, 1778. Now in the Aukland Museum. The author stands beside it. *Bengt Danielsson.*

■ Matavai Bay, Tahiti. As seen by Sydney Parkinson on Cook's first voyage in 1779. *British Library.*

way long since tired of the monotonous boat-building work. So Churchill returned to Taiarapu, obviously in a savage mood, because on the way back he shot down in cold blood a harmless native, without any apparent reason.

Scarcely a month later even more incredible news arrived from Taiarapu. In the middle of April, Brown appeared at Matavai and reported that King Churchill and his Prime Minister Thompson were dead. Since no one had any confidence in Brown, Morrison despatched one of his companions to find out what really had happened. The messenger returned with the following account which was subsequently confirmed by the natives themselves.

Shortly after his arrival at Taiarapu in the middle of March, Churchill had fallen out with Thompson, who also seems to have had ambitions to become a chief. Thompson, therefore, left Teahu-upoo on the south side of the peninsula, where Churchill had settled, and paddled round to Tautira on the north side. Here Vehiatua's uncle Titorea and the conniv-

ing Mate received him with open arms. Churchill suspected, probably on good grounds, that Thompson would make trouble for him and so, to be on the safe side, one dark night he sent agents up to Tautira with instructions to enter Thompson's residence and steal his muskets while he slept. The plan was successful, and Churchill even succeeded in assuring Thompson that he had had nothing to do with the theft. Thompson, stupid and gullible, believed this and duly moved back to Churchill's domains. Shortly afterwards, when Churchill had ill-treated one of his most faithful servants, a man named Maititi, the latter took his revenge simply by revealing to Thompson who had really been responsible for the theft of his arsenal. Thompson did not make a fuss, but merely awaited his opportunity and then cold-bloodedly shot Churchill in the back. Vendetta was a common phenomenon on Tahiti at this time and some of Churchill's subjects now felt it their duty to kill Thompson, which they did at the first opportunity by the traditional and unsavoury method of beating his brains out with large stones.

Shaken though they were by this bloody narrative, none of the Bounty men could bring himself to feel any genuine

grief over the fate of the two men involved, and in his logbook Morrison solemnly declared that it was Providence herself in the form of the native assassins who had punished Thompson for his ghastly crime.

Free now from trouble and strife, the boat-builders were able to continue their work undisturbed, and at the beginning of July 1790, the schooner was ready for launching. They had every reason to be proud of their work. The completed vessel was 34 feet long, with a 9 foot beam and able to accommodate comfortably a dozen people. The launching ceremony was carried out according to Tahitian traditions by Poino, and Morrison later described the proceedings in excellent details:

All being ready on the 5th we applied to Poino who told me that the priest must perform his prayers over her, and then he would have her carried to the sea. The priest being sent for and a young pig and a plantain given him, he began walking round and round the vessel, stopping at the stem and stern and muttering short sentences in an unknown dialect; and having a bundle of young plantain trees

brought to him by Poino's order, he now and then tossed one in on her deck. He kept at this all day and night and was hardly finished by sunrise on the 6th, when Poino and Tew, Mate's father, came with three or four hundred men. Having each made a long oration, their men were divided into two parties and the servant of Tew having received a hog and some cloth which was provided by Poino for the occasion, one of the priests went on board, and several plantain trees were tossed to him from both sides. He then ran fore and aft and exhorted them to exert themselves, and on a signal being given they closed in. Those who could not reach by hand, got long poles, a song being given, they all joined in chorus, and she soon began to move and in half an hour she reached the beach, where she was launched and called the Resolution. Tho' several trees were cut down which stood in the way, yet she received no damage, except breaking the masts in a passage of about 3/4 ths of a mile.

Christian and his party had taken all the sail cloth with them, when they left

■ ABOVE Matavai Bay, Tahiti; the landing place for Cook and Bligh. *Bengt Danielsson.*

■ BELOW Matavai Bay. Not always a safe anchorage in inclement weather. *Bengt Danielsson.*

Tahiti for the last time, and thus the only alternative for the boat-builders was to rig the schooner with mats of plaited pandanus leaves sewn together. But to their intense disappointment, this proved anything but satisfactory, since time and time again the sewn seams tore and the sails collapsed. After tackling this problem in various ways and with very little success, Morrison decided to postpone indefinitely his plans for crossing the Pacific. Nevertheless, the ship proved perfectly adequate for the alleged purpose – pleasure cruising – and everyone keenly looked forward to the first excursion. The maiden voyage of the Resolution was to be anything but a pleasure cruise, and to understand fully the circumstances it is necessary to look back a little.

When the Bounty men under Christian's leadership tried to colonize Tupuai, they had made the grave mistake of taking the side of one of the three island chieftains, thus making enemies of the other two. Despite this obvious lesson, the party who remained on Tahiti made the same error only a few months later, when they allied themselves with the Porionuu dynasty, instead of remaining strictly neutral in the island's interior affairs. Once they had more or less accepted the spurious protection of Mate, it was naturally not long before he began to make use of them. As early as April 1790, he had cautiously approached his English friends with the proposal that they should support his brother-in-law Metuaaro, an ambitious and despotic chieftain on Moorea, who was quarrelling with his neighbours. Probably with the fate of Churchill fresh in their minds, the Bounty men had on this occasion contented themselves with repairing Mate's stock of muskets and lending him their native factotum and first-rate marksman Hitihiti, who quickly defeated Metuaaro's enemies.

This was a very modest contribution on the part of the Bounty men, but the real danger lay in the fact that it could easily lead to more concessions later on. Sure enough, a few months later, a new appeal arrived. This time it was Mate's younger brother Ariipaea, who announced that the inhabitants of Tefana, immediately west of Porionuu, had revolted and asked his English friends for fire support. The Bounty men swallowed the bait, hook, line and sinker and declared themselves ready to help the "royal army" to put down "the rebellion."

It was just one of the usual border disputes which often occurred among the Tahitian chiefs. Pomare's aversion to gunfire was so intense that he had by then already fled to the peninsula, but his brother Ariipaea and his wife Itia, who were brave warriors, as usual took command of the Porionuu army, while the Bounty men fetched their muskets and cautiously formed the rear guard.

Since the enemy warriors, as the custom was in Tahiti, had neither shields nor armour and were equipped only with spears and slings, you may think that they did not stand a chance against the English crack shots. To the latter's great dismay and embarrassment, however, Ariipaea's and Itia's soldiers immediately rushed into a hand-to-hand battle, in which it was impossible for the Englishmen to distinguish in the welter of naked bodies friend from foe. They were reduced to the role of crestfallen spectators to a battle which ended with a sort of draw, when the Tefana army unexpectedly retreated.

Feeling greatly threatened after this unjustified aggression, Chief Tepau of Tefana managed to persuade the ruler of the next kingdom on the west coast, Ateluru, that his turn would soon be bound to come, and that it was in his own interest to join him in his resistance against the Porionuu expansion scheme. Ariipaea, of course, was quick to convey to the Bounty men the idea that these two chiefs had formed an alliance whose aim was to kill all foreigners. Whether they realized their initial mistake, their fate was now bound to that of the Porionuu dynasty, which meant that the only way out for them was to crush the common enemy as quickly as possible. Morrison decided to apply the classical pincer movement and attack the enemy from north and south. To achieve this, he sought the alliance of chief Temarii whose kingdom, Papara, adjoined that of Atehuru in the south. Temarii had for some time, just like Mate, been dreaming of making himself master of the whole island with the help of the English mercenaries and had already several months previously recruited Burkett and Sumner into his army. As yet Temarii felt that he was not powerful enough to take up arms against the Porionuu rulers, but had nothing against helping them to annihilate their common rivals. Ariipaea agreed to this dirty deal and to make sure that his new ally would not falter lent him his two

■ Oheitepha Bay painted on Cook's 3rd voyage. John Webber. *Private collection.*

top strategists, Hitihiti and Brown.

While Temarii's army advanced rapidly from the south, Morrison and his men encountered an unexpected obstacle in the form of a stone fortress with a high rampart strategically erected on top of a hill in Tefana. The Porionuu warriors, who were now campaigning with more discipline, allowed the Bounty men to lead the attack, yet once the enemy forces defending the fortress gave up the struggle and fled they broke order and pursued them with unprecedented fury. The Tefana and Atehuru warriors soon reassembled, however, and began preparing a counterattack. The new strategy devised by Morrison involved the use of the Resolution as a war ship. While the land forces under Ariipaea's command were to advance along the lagoon beach, the schooner, manned by the best shots among the Bounty musketeers, would keep abreast of them just off shore and in perfect safety fire on the enemy's flank. The plan was duly put into action in a slightly improved form, since the Resolution was accompanied by a fleet of 40 canoes with some 2,000 Porionuu warriors on board. Last but not least, Temarii was to attack again simultaneously from the south.

The Atehuru warriors, although roughly equal in numbers, were no match for Morrison's fire-spewing juggernaut, and it was not long before they were forced to revert to the old Polynesian defence tactics of retreating to the mountains. They collapsed completely when their merciless attackers ran amok in their villages, burning their homes and destroying their breadfruit trees and plantations. The victory was celebrated with a week of festivities back in Pare, though even then the real victor, Mate, did not have the courage to come out from his hiding place on the Taiarapu peninsula.

Having scarcely had time to observe the sea-going qualities of Resolution during her brief maiden voyage as a warship, the victors now resolved to make a more peaceful run, this time to Moorea. As might be expected, they were received with tremendous hospitality by Mate's brother-in-law Metuaaro, and also suc-

■ Oheitepha Bay today.
Private collection.

ceeded at the same time in modifying certain minor construction faults in their fast and surprisingly roomy craft. Thoroughly satisfied with the schooner, they now returned to Matavai and hauled her up on shore to protect her against the inevitable gales during the rapidly appproaching rainy season.

One of the trophies which the victors had borne home with them from the campaign against the Atehuru warriors was a belt of plaited pandanus leaves embellished with red fethers. This simple belt, known in Tahitian as a *maro ura*, had the same significance as a coronet, since it was a symbol of the bearer's position and power. When such a valuable possession changed hands – usually through inheritance, although force was sometimes used to acquire it – the event was normally celebrated by a short of investiture comparable with a European coronation. On such occasions all those chieftains who were regarded as vassals of the holder of the belt were required to attend the investiture, and so far no Tahitian chieftain had ever been so powerful as to be recognized by everyone as absolute monarch of Tahiti. After the successful campaign against Atehuru, the victorious coward Mate eventually came out of his hiding place with his head full of grandiose schemes. His first move was to send his son Tu, adorned with the belt, on a tour round the island to receive homage from every chief in Tahiti. The chances of this arrogant move succeeding were fairly good, for Mate was certain that if the worst came to the worst, the Bounty men would once again support him.

Since Mate's influence had diminished considerably on the Taiarapu peninsula after the death of Vehiatua, he wisely decided to begin his son's triumphal tour in Papara, where chief Temarii owed him a considerable debt of gratitude. The Bounty group were present to a man when this impressive ceremony took place at the end of January 1791. A newly created symbol of kingship, which was almost as sacred as the feathered belt and which was equally prominent in the procession, was a Union Flag lavishly decorated with red feathers. Equally symbolic of this new power shift, was the musketry salute fired by the English guests of honour. It is evident from Morrison's journal that the Bounty men were fully aware of and satisfied with the important part they played, for he noted that the Tahitians interpreted their pres-

ence as "a declaration on our part to support our flag in circumventing the island, as it was composed of English colours, and they made no scruple to say that war would be instantly made on those who should attempt to stop it".

In view of the white men's support for Mate, the chiefs made no attempt to prevent the curious processions from passing through their domains. Although their acceptance of it did not mean total submission, it was nevertheless a good start for Mate, and he should have been satisfied for the time being. But he was anxious to make use of his powerful allies, while they were in the right frame of mind, and he conceived a cunning plan of provoking a new war, which he hoped would establish him as overlord. He proclaimed that all the chiefs of the island were required to present themselves in Porionuu to pay homage to his son, their prince – knowing at the same time very well that many chiefs would ignore such a humiliating order.

The great ceremony took place on 13 February 1791 at a newly consecrated open air temple (*marae*) near the Toaroa harbour, where the Bounty had lain at anchor under Bligh's command some two years previously. Morrison had described the repugnant and barbaric ceremony as follows:

> Toonoeaiteatooa, the young king, being placed on the marae, a priest making a long prayer put the sash around his waist and the hat or bonnet on his head and hailed him king of Taheite, Moottooaroo then began by his orator making a long speech, acknowledging him his king, when three human victims were brought in and offered for Noorea; the priest of Moottooaroo placing them with their head towards the young king, and with a long speech over each, he also offered three young plantain trees. He then took an eye out of each, with a piece of split bamboo, and placing them on a leaf took a young plantain tree in one hand the eyes in the other he made a long speech, holding them up to the young king. The bodies were removed and buried by his priests in the marea, and the eyes put up with the plantain trees on the altar.

At this point, apparently, Morrison, who was just as interested in Tahitian customs as Bligh, took the opportunity to ask one of the priests for an explanation

of the ritual and was informed that, "the eye being the most valuable part is the fittest to be offered, and the reason the king sits with his mouth open, is to let the soul of the sacrifice enter into his soul, that he may be strengthened thereby, or that he may receive more strength of discernment from it". Some anthropologists have interpreted this very usual symbolic gesture of eating the eye as a survival from the time when the Tahitians were cannibals, and it is very possible that this is true.

Morrison continues:

> The rest of the chiefs then went through the like ceremony, some bringing one victim and some two, according to the bigness or extent of their districts, after which large droves of hogs and an immense quantity of other provisions, such as breadfruits, yams, taro, plaintains, cocoa nuts were brought and presented to the young king. Several large canoes were also hauled up near the *marae* on the sacred ground; these were dressed with several hundred fathoms of cloth, red feathers, breast plates &c., all which were secured by the priests and young king's attendants. Several large hogs were placed upon the altar, and the human sacrifices offered this day were 30, some of which had been killed near a month.

More important than the number of gifts laid at the feet of Tu on this occasion was the identity of the donors. Just as Mate had reckoned, among the chieftains who had failed to turn up were all those from Taiarapu peninsula, because through their more regular contact with him, they had seen through him and recognized his imperialistic ambitions. Mate immediately declared that the absence of these chieftains was a deliberate insult to the young prince, and consequently the Bounty men (with four exceptions), as good as their word, began to make plans for the most effective means of punishing the unfortunate Taiarapu people who had done them no harm whatever. The four men who refused to have anything more to do with Mate's disgraceful schemes were the two midshipmen Stewart and Heywood, Cole the armourer, and Skinner. In contrast to these four, Brown was once again agog with excitement, and was evidently determined to turn this new campaign into a bloodbath.

Temarii, who for opportunist reasons was still a warm supporter of Mate, produced the best plan of attack. He pointed out that the Taiarapu warriors were just as numerous and well-drilled as they, and that the only way to beat them would be by surprise. Large troop movements would undoubtedly be reported well before an attack could be launched, which meant that cunning would have to be used. He proposed that on the pretext of holding a feast for his friends he should invite all Porionuu warriors and Bounty men to Papara, and that from there in the middle of the night they should make a swift attack on the peninsula and catch the enemy napping.

Having agreed on their plan of action, Ariipaea and his men next casually put it aside and concentrated on the more immediate pleasure of eating up the vast piles of food which had been presented to Tu. The Bounty men took advantage of this welcome respite to relaunch Resolution, and once again equip the ship for service as flag-ship of his Tahitian Majesty Tu's canoe fleet. Tu, in turn, showed his gratitude in every conceivable way:

> He made us presents, and appointed each to a portion of land, being very fond of the whole of us, and desired his subjects to treat us as his relations, calling us his uncles.

In view of such wholehearted friendship and generosity, the Bounty men argued, how could they refuse the young monarch a helping hand when he needed it, even though it might entail spilling a little blood.

It was not until 22 March that the Porionuu fighting force was ready to embark for the sham festivities in Papara. They landed on the 24th and were made welcome with a tremendous banquet. Right in the middle of the meal, however, a perspiring messenger arrived with sensational news which took away their appetite: an English naval vessel, the Pandora, had anchored the previous day in Matavai Bay, and when Coleman, Stewart, Heywood, and Skinner had gone aboard they had immediately been put under close arrest. Temarii's unhappy guests were even more alarmed when they learned that two of Pandora's ship's boats were on their way to Papara with the eternal fixer Hitihiti as pilot and guide. All at once the bold conquerors became a crown of scared criminals, who were at a loss to know what to do. After a panic-stricken conference they decided, loyalists and mutineers alike, to flee in their schooner, without any idea where to go. The only sensible exception was Byrne the fiddler, who despite his blindness resolved to make his own way back to the Pandora and give himself up. When the two well-armed and well-manned ship's boats arrived at Papara,

■ The Harbour of Taleo in the Island Elmeo, by John Webber.
Private collection.

the reception committee therefore consisted of no more than Temarii and the for once innocent ruffian Brown. The schooner was still in sight, however, and the two ship's boats, one of which was commanded by Lieutenant Hayward, a former midshipman from the Bounty, took up the chase. But it did not take the Pandora men long to realize that they had no chance of overtaking the fast sailing vessel, and after a short time they returned to their own ship, taking Brown with them.

Meanwhile, the crew of the schooner, sailing aimlessly hither and thither for several days until their provisions and water ran out, returned to Papara. Temarii, who could not bear the thought of losing his valuable mercenaries just when he needed them most, begged of them to flee to the mountains and hide, promising them guides and supplies of provisions. The panic-stricken sailors, except three, accepted Temarii's offer. The three who remained on the schooner were the loyalists Morrison and Norman and, curiously enough, one of the most compromised mutineers, Ellison. It was their intention to sail round to Matavai and surrender, but when Temarii learned this, aghast at the thought of losing the fine sailing vessel as well, he

Teura; Tahitian girls then, as now, are beautiful. *Glyn Christian.*

promptly captured it and made the men prisoners.

A couple of nights later, Brown, who was now eager to ingratiate himself into the favour of Captain Edwards of the Pandora, appeared and contrived their escape. By canoe and on foot they made their way along the west coast and through the war-torn Atehuru district where, had they been discovered, they would undoubtedly have ben killed in revenge for their participation in the havoc wrought on the villages and plantations. Halfway to Matavai they came upon one of the Pandora's boats and immediately awoke the duty officer and told him who they were. To the astonishment of Morrison and Norman, Lieutenant Hayward, who turned up shortly afterwards, ordered them all to be bound hand and foot, before bundling them off to the Pandora. Their reception on board was even more disconcerting since Captain Edwards, without permitting them a word of explanation, put them in irons and sent them below to join Coleman, Stewart, Heywood, Skinner, and Byrne. Norman and Coleman, at least, whom Bligh had promised he would exonerate, should he reach England again, had good reason to complain at the treatment they were receiving. Bligh had kept his promise and informed the authorities in his report that four of Christian's companions on board the Bounty were innocent. But Captain Edwards' orders clearly stated that no distinction should be made between the men he captured, for the perfectly logical but nevertheless very cruel reason that in the eyes of the law they were all guilty until proved innocent.

Edwards toyed with the idea of holding Temarii as a hostage until the remaining Bounty men were recovered. But he was by no means certain that this would produce the desired result, and instead he despatched Hayward and Brown to Papara by boat with a force of 25 marines, while another lieutenant, Corner, and 16 men were ordered to march right across the island to hunt the fugitives out of any eventual mountain hideout.

Mate was on board almost as soon as he learned of the presence of the English warship, and as terrified as ever for his own safety he offered, without any qualms, to help hunt down the men who had served him so well. To his intense annoyance, the wily Brown proved to be a more effective Judas, since he bribed a native to reveal the mountain hideout of the hapless fugitives. He is said to have entered their cave at dead of night and checked their identity by the clever method of feeling their toes; a European's toes, instead of being spread like a native's, are crumpled and deformed. The next day, finding their hideout surrounded by marines, they all surrendered after brief and pathetic resistance. When the smaller party, who had been sent across the extremely rugged mountains from the north coast finally arrived in Papara half dead with exhaustion, they learned to their dismay that all their valiant efforts had been in vain.

The capture of the last of the mutineers not only meant that Mate had to give up his dreams of conquest at the very moment when they were near to realization, it also placed him in a very dangerous situation. His first thought was to get out altogether, and he implored Captain Edwards to take him to England. But Edwards had no use for him and ordered him to leave the ship, and Mate took to the hills.

Up to this time, there had always existed a balance of power among the chiefs, and this had effectively protected the islanders against the perils of any one tyrant or dictator. But the military help the Bounty men had given to the Porionuu dynasty permanently upset the *status quo*, and even though in his lifetime Mate – who died in 1803 – was never able to realize his dream of absolute power, he had nevertheless proved that it was possible and also shown the means of achieving it. His son Tu, when of adult age, soon followed his father's example, and by carefully cultivating the friendship of the English missionaries, who arrived in 1797, and by employing numerous sailors as mercenaries, finally succeeded in 1815, after many bloody battles and unspeakable atrocities, in establishing himself as the sole and absolute monarch of Tahiti.

His daughter Pomare IV succeeded him in 1827 and meekly accepted a French take over of Tahiti in 1842. She remained the nominal ruler until her death in 1877. Her son Pomare V lost the last shreds of control only a few years later in 1880, when the island became a French colony. He consoled himself with drink and died in 1891 at the age of 52. He was buried in an ugly mausoleum, erected in Arue at the former holy site, where his great-grand-father Tu was publicly recognized in 1791 as the first "King of Tahiti", in the presence of the Bounty mercenaries, who unwittingly had changed the course of Tahitian history.

Tragedy of the Pandora

There was more to the Navy's search of the Pacific than the capture of a few mutineers. Ronald A Coleman explains what it was

■ THE STORY of the mutiny and Bligh's epic open boat voyage of 3,618 nautical miles created an immediate sensation in England. Bligh was a hero. The mutineers, whose side of the story would not be known for two and a half more years, were the lowest of scoundrels and common pirates.

Bligh had arrived in England from the Cape of Good Hope on the 14 March 1790. Within nine days of his arrival, his friend and influential patron, Sir Joseph Banks, had obtained the King's permission for him to publish his narrative of Bounty's voyage. By Royal Navy custom, Bligh would have to face a court-martial to answer for the loss of his ship. But this would not take place for some months as the remainder of his surviving Bounty crew had not yet arrived from the Cape and they would be required to attend as well. The protracted delay would cause Bligh some anxiety. However, it would also give him time to consolidate his version of the voyage without fear of contradiction from the troublemakers Fryer and Purcell.

Unbeknown to Bligh and Banks, Secretary of State William Grenville was, at that very time, drafting orders for a secret mission to the Pacific of great importance. It was to have considerable bearing on government's eventual plan to pursue and apprehend the Bounty mutineers.

To the Admiralty, mutiny was the most serious breach of Royal Naval discipline. The mutineers could not be left unpunished. In many ways, the necessity to do something about the Bounty was a complication which might endanger Grenville's scheme. He did not want attention focused on the Pacific for the moment. On the other hand, perhaps the Bounty problem could be used to his advantage.

Two months before Bligh's return, the government had received news that two private English fur-trading vessels had been seized by Spanish warships at Nootka Sound on the north-western coast of America. The seizure was not overly alarming, but would require a routine demand through diplomatic channels that the ships be released. However, the second part of the news was electrifying. The Spanish ships were establishing a permanent settlement at Nootka.

For two centuries, attempts had been made to discover a North-west Passage between the Atlantic and the Pacific. Since Canada had become an English colony after the Seven Years' War, that the passage, if it existed, be English controlled was imperative. At virtually the same time as news of the Nootka incident was received, information was also received from Quebec which had implications of supreme importance. Fur-trapper and explorer Peter Pond had discov-

■ The sinking of the Pandora, engraved from drawings by Peter Heywood. *Private collection*.

ered what he believed to be two major rivers flowing from Great Slave Lake in central Canada towards the Pacific. The first flowed westwards and might empty into the sea near Cook's Inlet or Prince William Sound at the base of the Alaskan peninsula. The second flowed southwards through a chain of other lakes and possibly met the sea near Queen Charlotte's Sound, only 100 nautical miles north of Nootka. The southern alternative was the more desirable as it would be ice-free for longer periods of the year. If it turned out to be the passage, the Spaniards were getting too close.

Spain had traditionally clung to her ancient pretension to sovereignty over the American continents and all the seas west of a line, drawn by the Treaty of Tordesillas in 1494, which divided the world between her and Portugal. Discovery and acts of proclamation were, as far as she was concerned sufficient to secure possession of new territories. England contended that permanent settlement and active development were necessary to achieve sovereignty over a newly discovered land. This difference of opinion had caused rifts between the two countries on several occasions in the past. However, now it appeared that Spain was playing the game by England's rules and England, therefore, had no grounds for protest about Spain's claim to Nootka. But Nootka Sound was on an island (Vancouver Island) and not the mainland. If England could immediately establish a settlement on the mainland at Queen Charlotte's Sound, she could then legitimately claim possession of the coast for a considerable distance to the north and south encompassing what may be the entrance to the illusive North-west Passage. It must be done in the utmost secrecy for if the Spanish were to get wind of Grenville's intentions, they were in a position to beat England to it.

■ Portrait of Sir Joseph Banks by Sir Joshua Reynolds (1773). *National Portrait Gallery*.

In view of this, the immediate despatch of a warship in pursuit of the Bounty mutineers might be suspected by the Spanish as a pretext to pose a naval threat at Nootka and put them on their guard. Two vessels of the secret squadron, Gorgon and Discovery, were expected to sail from England within weeks and Grenville needed a distraction. Also, there was the problem that the governement needed to be seen doing something about Bounty.

In late March, the following article appeared in the London Register:

> It is said that by the express command of His Majesty two new sloops of war, one of them the Hound now on the stocks at Deptford, are to be instantly fitted to go in pursuit of the pirates who have taken possession of the Bounty. An experienced officer will be apointed to superintend the little command, and the sloops will steer a direct course to Otaheite (Tahiti) where, it is conjectured, the mutinous crew have established their rendezvous.

The article would serve two useful purposes. It would let the English public, and the Spanish know that something was being done about Bounty, but Hound being still on the stocks, could not sail before the northern summer. By then, the secret fleet would be well on its way and, it was Gorgon's orders which included the *real* plan to search for the mutineers.

Parts of Grenville's scheme had been put into effect when in the following month new information was received. Not two, but four vessels had been seized. And, most importantly, English fur-traders had established a permanent settlement at Nootka in the name of King George *before* the Spanish ships had arrived. On the face of it, the Spanish commander had invaded English sovereign territory. The Prime Minister William Pitt's government now had the excuse they needed to threaten Spain with war. England would first demand the immediate restoration of the settlement at Nootka. She would then force a resolution of the differing doctrines of colonial sovereignty on the basis that Spain had disavowed England's rightful claim of sovereignty over Nootka. This would open up all unsettled territories in the Americas and give England freedom of all the seas traditionally claimed by Spain under the Tordesillas Treaty.

Grenville's secret plan was shelved and in the first week of May the King announced to Parliament Cabinet's decision to mobilize the English fleet.

One ship to be brought out of mothballs for the purpose was HMS Pandora, a sixth-rate frigate of 24 guns.

The ship, with her masts and bowsprit, cannon and sea-going stores removed, had ridden at her moorings at Chatham since September 1783. She had been launched in May 1779 from the Deptford shipyard of Henry Adams and William Barnard to meet the needs of the American War. Pandora had initially served in the Channel Fleet during the unsuccessful French and Spanish invasion of England in 1779, then as a convoy escort between England and Quebec, and lastly, as a lone cruiser off the American east coast credited with taking at least nine rebel ships as prizes under the command of former privateer captain, John Inglis.

An Admiralty warrant now ordered Chatham Dockyard to refit Pandora for another tour of duty in the Channel Fleet. On 6 August, Captain Edward Edwards received his commission to take command of the ship. His appointment from half-pay to Pandora had been the result of a recommendation by Lord Ducie under whom he had served as First Lieutenant on Augusta (64) in the early stages of the American War. Edwards arrived at Chatham, read his orders to the crew, and hoisted his pennant on the 10th. However, the ship's original orders were not to be long lived. The following day he received a letter from the secretary of the Admiralty "directing me to attend Lord Chatham (the First Lord and brother of the Prime Minister) at the Admiralty without loss of time & informing me that a week's leave of absence was directed to be given me for that purpose."

On his return to the dockyard at Chatham on the 17th, he recorded in the ship's log that he had been "directed to fit the ship for a South Sea Voyage". Bearing in mind that the government, which, we have seen, had a penchant for finesse, was urgently preparing ships to be despatched to every corner of the globe in readiness to attack Spain and her possessions, is it mere coincidence that Pandora was now the only warship being sent to the Pacific where the cause of the conflict was centred? Possibly. The Bounty problem was still outstanding. The secret north-west coast expedi-

tion which had included a plan to capture the mutineers had been abandoned, and the story of the Hound and the other sloop had been nothing more than a red herring. Still, it is tempting to speculate on what other Pacific Ocean matters Lord Chatham may have discussed during Edwards' visit.

In September, another most curious article apeared in a publication with the impressive title, *The Lady's Magazine or Entertaining Companion for the Fair Sex, Appropriated solely to their Use and Amusement*. It was a magazine much read by wives of influential men and it said:

> The Pandora frigate is preparing at Chatham for a voyage to the South Seas; the object which the Bounty sailed from england to effect has been consigned to this ship: two botanists are to embark in her for the preservation of the breadfruit trees.

The prospect of a second breadfruit voyage had been a subject of discussion since Bligh's return. No documentary evidence has yet been found to show that Pandora was ever intended for this purpose. However, certain things do suggest that this may have been considered at some stage of the voyage's planning.

Once the ship's equipment was completed, which included the removal of several internal bulkheads to make room for 12 months' stores and victuals for Pandora's own use as well as a complete set of stores to refit and provision the Bounty, there was little room for anything else. The Ship's Surgeon, George Hamilton, was later to write:

> What rendered our situation still more distressing was the crowded state of the ship, being filled to the hatchways with stores and provisions, for, like weevils, we had to eat a hole in our bread before we had a place to lay down in; every officer's cabin, the Captain's not excepted, being filled with provisions and stores.

The Pandora then worked her way down the river to Blackstrakes where she received 20 six-pounder carriage guns and four 18-pounder carronades. An impressive armament to be pitted against the 25 mutineers, some of which, it was known, would not resist, and Bounty which carried only four "short" 4-

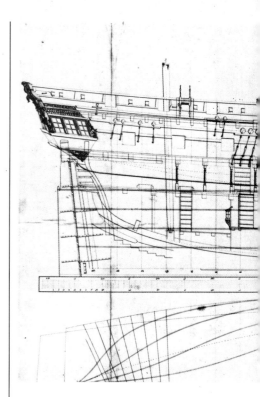

pounders. With nearly six times as many men and 12 times the fire power of her prey, Pandora might today be considered "a bit of overkill". Her presence in the Pacific would give the Spaniards something to think about.

Pandora arrived at Portsmouth on 17 October and found riding there Admiral Lord Howe's Grand Fleet preparing for war against Spain. Edwards' log entry for the 22 Ocober includes a simple statement – "… a signal was made for a Court Martial and for weekly accounts". The court martial referred to was that of William Bligh to be convened on board HMS Royal William anchored nearby. Edwards makes no further mention of the trial, but one can be assured that he took a particular interest in its proceedings and its outcome. It would appear that the relationship between the two men was less than cordial. A notation in the Rev James Bligh's copy of Bligh's *Narrative* says, "Captain Bligh told me repeatedly that Captain Edwards would never return, as he did not know the navigation of Endeavour Straits". Only Torres, Cook, and Bligh had ever navigated the Straits and the first two were dead. Was this petulance on Bligh's part?

Edwards' formal orders are dated 25 October, three days after the trial. They make no mention of breadfruit, only the capture of Fletcher Christian, the mutineers, and Bounty.

It is important to note here that on the following day, Thomas Hayward,

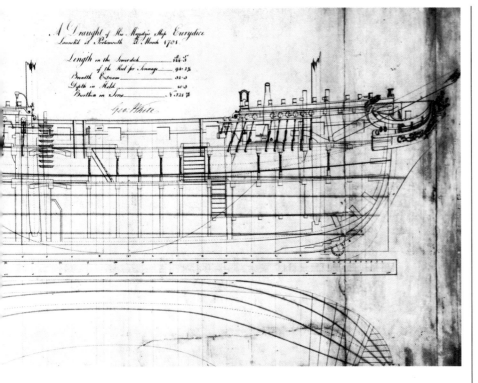

zeal in procuring and nursing such plants as might be useful at Otaheitee or the islands we might discover."

This was an activity taken directly from the journals of Cook's voyages and one of particular interest to Banks and, consequently, Bligh.

Having rounded Cape Horn without incident, Pandora passed within sight of Easter Island on 4 March 1791. Hamilton says: "We now set the forge to work, and the armourers were busily employed in making knives and iron work to trade with the savages."

Since Magellan had entered the Pacific by the same route in 1525, Europeans had found iron to be their most valuable currency among the Palaeolithic island cultures. The islanders had three basic commodities to trade for the European treasures; fresh food and water, the favours of their women, and "curiosities" such as exotic seashells and souvenirs of their cultures. The last could make a man either famous or rich on his return to England. It was the collections of Pacific curiosities which had greatly contributed to Banks rise to prominence in the scientific and social world and, there was a ready and willing market for such things among wealthy collectors of England and Europe.

After logging three other small islands as new discoveries during the next few days, the first being named Ducie's Island after Edwards' patron, Pandora dropped anchor in the transparent blue waters of Matavai Bay on the north coast of Tahiti. It was the morning of 23 March. As Pandora had slowly worked into the bay, a native paddled off and was taken on board. He brought the news that several of the mutineers were on the island, but that Fletcher Christian and eight others had left some time ago.

Shortly afterwards, another canoe came alongside bearing Joseph Coleman, armourer of the Bounty. Coleman was not a true mutineer. During the incident, he, Norman, and McIntosh had attempted to enter the launch with Bligh and the dispossessed crew, but had been stopped by Christian and Bligh had recorded their innocence in the affair.

Coleman informed Edwards that 16

---

midshipman of Bounty, and having served as a witness at Bligh's Court Martial, reported on board Pandora as Third Lieutenant. On the same day, Admiral-Cornish's fleet sailed from Portsmouth for the West Indies to prepare for an attack on the Spanish in that part of the world.

A letter (probably of the 27th and incorrectly dated the 24th) from Bligh to Joseph Banks illustrates some of his concerns at this time:

"Dear Sir, I am hapy to inform you that on Friday last I was most honourably acquitted respecting the loss of the Bounty ... I came to town on Saturday night, & yesterday morning I waited on Lord Chatham who assured me of promotion as soon as he had been with the King ... I received your obliging letter of the 4th instant, since which the cause of my not writing to you was the daily suspense I was kept in respecting my tryal ... There was at Spithead 43 sail of the line – Admiral Cornish was to sail as [of] yesterday with 5 [actually 6] sail besides Frigates ... The Pandora, if they [the Admiralty] don't forget, will sail in the beginning of the Month – she is not fitted or intended to carry any plants ..."

As mentioned, the possibility cannot be discounted that Edwards and Pandora may have, at some time, been considered for the second breadfruit mission as an adjunct to the capture of the mutineers.

In any event, it would appear that at least Bligh had not been consulted, and something had caused him to make inquiries and forward a specific statement to Banks on that issue. The probability of some animosity between Bligh and Edwards may have inspired Pandora's Captain to demonstrate that the Bounty's Captain had no monopoly on the recognition and patronage to be derived from a voyage to the Pacific. Indeed, Edwards would have been very remiss not to take advantage of the opportunity.

Pandora departed the coast of England on 7 November and set a course for Tenerife in the Canary Islands. On the 18th, Edwards cleared for action having seen a strange ship of war. It proved to be His Majesty's Sloop Shark, Lieutenant Brisac, in quest of Admiral Cornish. Brisac informed Edwards that the dispute with Spain had been amicably settled and that the English fleets were being recalled.

After Tenerife, Pandora's next port of call was Rio de Janeiro at which they arrived on 31 December. It is during their visit here that Edwards' intention to make the voyage into something other than a simple police action begins to surface. Surgeon Hamilton records in his journal:

I cannot, in words, bestow sufficient panegyric on the laudable exertions of my worthy messmates, Lieutenants Corner and Hayward, for their unremitting

of the mutineers had left the Bounty at Tahiti. Of these, two were dead Churchill and Thompson had lived with a chief in a distant part of the island. Churchill had become Tyo, or paramount friend of the chief. Upon the chief's death, by Tahitian custom he had become chief of the district. Thompson, in a jealous rage, had killed Churchill. The revengeful Tahitians had killed Thompson and, later, his skull was brought to Edwards a proof.

At 11.30 that morning, midshipmen Peter Heywood and George Stewart gave themselves up. Heywood had been not quite 17 at the time of the mutiny. Both came from well respected families and Heywood's were acquainted with the Captain. Bligh had treated Heywood as a son on Bounty and was tremendously hurt when he mistakenly perceived the young midshipman to be a part of the mutiny. In fact, Heywood's youth and inexperience had left him in an indecisive situation during the chaos of the mutiny.

Edwards' orders, and his own inherent determination to conduct an exemplary mission, allowed him no discretion to make judgments which were the prerogative of higher authority. As a consequence, all of the mutineers, whether they had been cleared by Bligh, or not, were treated equally and without prejudice. They were all guilty until proven innocent by court-martial. He delegated the responsibility of the capture of the prisoners to his officer best qualified to deal with the islanders, third lieutenant Hayward. Their confinement and maintenance was the responsibility of first lieutenant Larkan. As a result, their treatment was undoubtedly harsher than might have been if he had taken more direct responsibility. Also of concern was the fact that many of the islanders were very protective of their mutineer friends. Some had even planned a rescue attempt which Edwards could not allow. As the prisoners came aboard, they were confined in irons below decks and isolated from their islander friends and the crew while the carpenters were set to work constructing a wooden cell on the quarterdeck. This was to be nick-named "Pandora's Box."

At three o'clock that afternoon, Richard Skinner, late master's servant and ship's barber of Bounty, surrendered himself. The following day, Michael Byrne, a nearly blind fiddler who had been recruited by Bligh merely for his entertainment value, gave himself up.

Before Pandora's arrival, some of the mutineers had been engaged in the construction of a small schooner under the guidance of boatswain's mate James Morrison. The intention was to sail to the north-west coast of America or Batavia in the East Indies and from there make their way back to England. Morrison had previously been a midshipman and was mature and intelligent enough to be accepted as a leader among his fellow outcasts. Edwards received information of the group's intention to sail and dispatched two of Pandora's boats to apprehend them. They were unsuccessful. Once sighted, the schooner soon outdistanced the ship's boats. Morrison's later testimony revealed that the decision of the schooner's crew was to "not see" Pandora's boats, but to return to the island and give themselves up of their own volition thus strengthening their plea of innocence.

Once safe from immediate arrest, the schooner did return to the island. Morrison, Norman, and Ellison walked along the beach toward Pandora's anchorage and gave themselves up. The rest had taken refuge in the mountains.

Edwards again despatched two boats with a number of armed men to apprehend the remaining mutineers. On 9 April, one boat returned with Hildebrant an McIntosh as prisoners. On the following day, the other boat returned with Burkitt, Milward, Sumner and Muspratt. That made 14 mutineers captured and with Churchill and Thompson dead, only Christian and the eight others on Bounty remained to be found.

Pandora remained at Tahiti for 47 days, 18 of which had been spent rounding up the 14 mutineers. The remainder of the time was devoted to the repair of the ship, replenishing supplies of water and food, refitting the small schooner as a tender, and "refreshing" the crew. Hamilton writes a very descriptive account of the period. He mentions the collecting of curiosities and breadfruit, the establishment of gardens with the plants brought on Pandora, and he also spends some time on a description of the lifestyle and customs of the islanders.

But Edwards' main concern was where next to search for Fletcher Christian and the Bounty. Information gathered from some of the prisoner's diaries found on the island and from interviews with them had not produced a convincing answer. Christian had been intentionally circumspect about his eventual destination. He knew that someone would come searching for him.

Pandora and the tender, now named the "Matavia" [Matavai] and manned by master's mate Oliver, midshipman Renouard, and seven other men, sailed from Tahiti on 9 May 1791 to commence a four-month investigation of the most likely Pacific island groups. Only a few things occurred during the unsuccessful search which space allows mentioning here.

On 22 June off Upolu Island in the Samoan Group, Pandora and the tender were separated in the darkness. Edwards spent a month here seeking the missing schooner. With great sadness, he reluctantly gave them up for lost. Young Renouard had been the 16 year old son of Edwards' neighbour in Lincolnshire. The lad had desired to go to sea but, because of a speech impediment, his father tried to discourage him. On Edwards' appointment to Pandora, he offered to take the boy as one of his servants in the capacity of a clerk where his disability would not pose a problem. When the Admiralty ordered that all officer's servants be discharged, Edwards sought the father's permission and re-enlisted him as a midshipman.

Sailing with the prevailing winds and currents, Edwards gradually worked his way westward through the various islands until he determined that he was beyond the area where Bounty might be found and the season was getting late for a passage through Endeavour Strait before the North-westerly monsoons came. It was time to give up the search. He had every reason to be contented. He had captured the majority of the mutineers, his crew was perfectly healthy, he had collected breadfruit and curiosities, made new discoveries, and had done his utmost to discover the whereabouts of Christian and Bounty. The only task left to achieve was to find a more direct route through Endeavour Strait.

On 14 August in passing an island which is now one of the most southern of the Solomons group, Edwards named it Pitt's Island (Vanikoro Island) in honour of the Prime Minister. Sailing within a mile of the fringeing reef, Edwards observed that the smoke of fires were seen indicating that the island was inhabited. What he did not realize was that beneath the waters of that same reef were

■ The sinking of the Pandora; a watercolour by midshipman George Reynolds. *National Maritime Museum.*

resting the two wrecks of the Laperouse expedition which disappeared in 1788 and possibly the last two survivors were then on the island awaiting rescue. By the time the mystery of the Frenchman's disappearance was finally solved 35 years later, it was too late for the survivors and the details of the last months of the Laperouse expedition were lost forever.

Pandora then approached the formidable barrier of Australia's great reef. Finding his way blocked, Edwards turned southwards along the coral wall seeking an entrance. Just before noon on the 28 August, a boat was sent to examine an opening in the reef. At 2 o'clock that afternoon (which was not 29 August in the log as shipboard days commenced at midday; in fact, it was the 30th as they had crossed the international dateline), the sailing officer eased the ship in closer. At 4.30 they "hove to" to await the boat. Fifteen minutes later, the boat signalled that they had found a passage through the reef. It was 20 minutes past 7 before the boat was back under the stern of the ship and at that moment Pandora struck a submerged reef tearing away her rudder and part of her sternpost. Within five minutes, there were 18 inches of water in the hold and five minutes later, there were four feet. The hands were set to the ship's pumps and three of the mutineers, Coleman, Norman, and McIntosh were released to assist. Others of the crew bailed with buckets at the hatchways, but the leak steadily gained on them and an hour and a half later there were over eight feet of water in the hold. The weather had deteriorated and the ship felt and sounded as if she were pounding herself to pieces on the rockhard coral. The mutineers, still confined and in darkness, began to panic. Fearful that they would not be given a chance to save themselves if the ship went down, they wrenched their irons off. Learning of this, Edwards had their irons put back on and the guards doubled, threatening to shoot or hang them if they attempted to escape again. Although the situation was undoubtedly a desperate one, it probably appeared to the mutineers worse than it was. Edwards and his entire crew were fully occupied trying to keep the ship afloat and the mutineers were not the only ones who were frightened.

However, the reef was no more than 100 yards across and the depth of water over it, even at ow tide, was sufficient to allow the ship to be lifted by each succeeding wave and moved closer to the more protected waters on the lee side. Once there, at least the damaging pounding would cease and there would be a chance to stop the leak.

Two and a half hours after striking the reef, Pandora had beaten her way across it into deeper water. The small bower anchor was let go and a cable paid out. Then the best bower anchor was let go directly beneath the ship to steady her. They continued pumping and bailing for the remainder of the night barely keeping the ship afloat until daylight. But, as Pandora settled deeper, the leaks increased. The guns were ordered to be thrown overboard to lighten ship, the ship took a heel, and one gun crashed across the deck crushing a man. Another was crushed by a spare topmast falling from its stowage midships. Edwards consulted his officers and they agreed that the ship could not be saved. Supplies were thrown into the boats and everything that would float was cut loose on deck so that when she went down, the crew would have something to cling to.

At this point, Edwards ordered that the prisoners be released from their irons and brought on deck a few at a time. Armourer's mate, Hodges and the ship's corporal entered the call to release Muspratt, Skinner, and Byrne. The panic was

such that Skinner was hauled out of the box with his irons still on and the other two followed him closely. The scuttle was quickly slammed shut and barred before Hodges could get to it and he, in the meantime, removed Morrison's and Stewart's manacles. Morrison begged the master-at-arms to leave the scuttle open, but he had hardly spoken the words when the ship began to sink. The master-at-arms and the sentries rolled over the side and the prisoners could see through the stern ports that Captain Edwards was swimming towards the pinnace. The bow of the ship was underwater as far as the mainmast and the sea was beginning to flow in on them. Boatswain's mate Moulter scrambled onto the roof of the cell, pulled the bar securing the scuttle through the coamings and threw the hatch cover aside before he leapt into the sea. All managed to get out of the cell except Hildebrant as the ship went down. Morrison saw a large wooden gangway come to the surface with Muspratt clinging to it. It crashed down on the heads of several men in the water, including Stewart and Sumner, and sent them to the bottom. The top of "Pandora's Box" had floated off and on it were Heywood, Burkitt, Coleman, and first lieutenant Larkan. Heywood grabbed a nearby plank and began swimming towards one of the boats and Morrison followed his example. Hamilton records: "The cries of the men drowning in the water was at first awful in the extreme: but as they

sank and became faint, they died away by degrees."

After the boats took up as many survivors as could be found, they landed on a small sand cay about three miles from the wreck and began to take stock of their situation. A roll call revealed that 89 of the ship's crew and 10 of the mutineers had survived. Thirty-one of the ship's company and Hildebrant, Stewart, Sumner, and Skinner had been lost with the ship. Skinner and Hildebrant had still been wearing their wrist irons.

Tents were made of the boat's sails for the officers and crew, but the prisoners were kept at the other end of the cay and not allowed any shelter from the intense tropical sun. It would seem to be an act of senseless cruelty and may have been the decision of lieutenant Hayward. This would be the second time these mutineers had been the cause of his having to suffer the unpleasant trials of an open boat voyage to Timor. The white sand of the cay can be hot enough to blister bare feet and the reflected sun's rays will cause extreme sunburn within a very short time. The mutineers had been confined in the dark, sweltering cell for five months. They had few articles of clothing and their skin was soft. To try to find some relief, they buried themselves in the hot sand during the heat of the day but even so, they had their skin "flea'd from head to foot".

Two days were spent preparing the boats for the attempt to reach Timor and on the 31st they departed "Escape Key". They were now inside the outer line of the barrier and only small isolated reefs were in their path to Endeavour Straits which lay about 120 miles to the northwest. Once through the Straits, it was another 1,000 miles of open sea to Timor.

The events of the next 16 days were highlighted by an encounter with hostile natives, hunger and debilitating thirst. On arrival at Timor, Edwards arranged passage on a Dutch vessel as far as Batavia for his surviving crew, the mutineers, and a group of escaped convicts from Port Jackson who were now placed in his charge. En route, the vessel called into Samarang for repairs. To Edwards' delight, they found anchored there the missing tender and all its crew. At Batavia, Edwards divided his entourage among four Dutch East Indiamen and at the Cape of Good Hope transferred most of them to HMS Gorgon for the voyage to England where they arrived on 19 June 1792.

On 10 September, Captain Edwards, together with his officers, appeared before a court-martial held on board HMS Hector to answer for the loss of Pandora. Edwards submitted a written statement describing the circumstances of the wreck. Lieutenants Larkan and Corner and other officers swore to the truth of the Captain's account. The court then found Edwards, his officers, and men without blame for the loss of the ship.

Two days later, nearly three years and five months after the mutiny, the trial of the 10 mutineers began on board HMS Duke. Bligh was not able to attend. He was somewhere in the Pacific on his second breadfruit voyage.

During their confinement, the prisoners had worked hard to prepare their defence against the charges. Heywood carried on a copious correspondence with his widowed mother and three devoted sisters. Through their efforts, and of his uncle, Commodore Pasley and his brother all of their best family connections were brought to bear on Heywood's case. Even Captain Edwards tried to serve him before the trial. In a letter written to Mr C Christian, he refers to Heywood as an "unfortunate young man" and goes on to say: "I apprehend he did not take an active part against Mr Bligh..." and, "it is greatly to be lamented that youth through their own indiscretion, or bad example, should be involed in such difficulties, and bring ignominy on themselves, and distress to their friends."

The trial lasted for six days. As could be expected, Coleman, Norman, McIntosh, and the blind fiddler Byrne, were acquitted. Ellison, Burkitt, Millward, Muspratt, Morrison and Heywood were sentenced to death. The court, however, recommended the King's Mercy for Morrison and Heywood. It was not until 17 October that they were advized that the King had granted them his "free and unconditional pardon". Muspratt's case was discharged on a legal technicality and he was given his freedom. On 29 October 1792, the three remaining men were publicly hanged on board HMS Brunswick.

When Bligh had sailed on 3 August 1791 for his second breadfruit voyage, he was still basking in the approbation of all England. On his return at the conclusion of his voyage on 7 August 1793, he found his reception considerably cooler than he had expected. During his absence, more had been made public about the Bounty voyage than he might have wished. The trial of the mutineers had attracted widespread public interest. The witnesses, such as Fryer, Cole and Purcell, and the mutineers, had not been reticent in their mention of some of Bligh's shortcomings.

Even Sir Joseph Banks had cause to have second thoughts about Bligh's veracity. Morrison had completed his account after the trial while awaiting the King's consideration. There is evidence to suggest that Heywood at least read the manuscript and made suggestions for changes. Morrison had then sent a copy to Mr W Howell, a publisher in the Isle of Wight. Howell wrote to a Captain Phillips on 25 November 1792 stating that Morrison's manuscript was ready to publish, but that he would send it to Banks, if it was desired, as he considered that the contents might be detrimental to the reputatin of certain officers. Indeed, Morrison and by association Heywood had written things which could damage the careers of several officers, including Edwards. Howell's letter and presumably a copy of the manuscript which was later passed on to Bligh was sent to Banks. It would appear that publication may have been stopped by Banks' intervention, or possibly at the desire of the First Lord. On 5 January 1793, Banks had reason to write to Lord Chaham in defence of Bligh's qualities. It would also appear that Banks wrote to Bounty's midshipman Hallett desiring certain information about the mutineers while Bligh was away. Was he seeking verification of some disturbing details?

On his return, Bligh complained to Banks of Lord Chatham's "unaccountable conduct". Lieutenant Portlock, Bligh's second captain commanding the Assistant, gained an immediate interview with the First Lord, whereas Bligh, the expedition commander, was kept waiting for several days. On being discharged from the Providence on 7 September, Bligh was placed on half-pay and was to remain unemployed until 29 April 1795.

During 1793, surgeon George Hamilton published his journal of the voyage of Pandora. Although the slender volume contains some mistakes of fact, certain passages have been taken nearly word-for-word from Captain Edwards' manuscript account which was not published until 1915. Collaboration between the Captain and his surgeon would also explain the glossing-over of certain inci-

■ Portrait of surgeon George Hamilton with some of his instruments recovered from the Pandora wreck. *National Geographic.*

sandy bottom between two coral reefs. On the surface of the seabed can be seen the anchor which was used to steady the ship, the fluke of what is probably the Bounty anchor abandoned by Christian and recovered by Edwards at Tahiti, cannon, the ship's galley stove, and parts of the Ship's pumps at which the crew had worked so hard to save Pandora and their own lives.

Since 1983, the Queensland Museum's Maritime Archaeology Section has organized three eight-week seasons of excavation on the site. To date, perhaps 5 per cent of the wreck has been explored and recorded. By using an electronic instrument which sends sound waves down through the seabed, it has been determined that Pandora's remains beneath the sand are comparable to those of England's Mary Rose.

Apart from the usual items found on most shipwrecks, some relics of great importance have been found on Pandora which will help us to understand better one of the most significant periods of Pacific and, indeed, world history. Particularly noteworthy is a collection of medical instruments and belongings which can be identified with surgeon Hamilton. But of even more importance is a collection of "curiosities" which may comprize part of what Edwards submitted a claim to the Admiralty for on his return to England. His account was for £200 which was a great deal of money in those times.

Pandora was equipped and provisioned much the same, and in some respects better, as the expeditions of Cook and Bligh. Of all the 18th century voyages to the Pacific, only the two wrecks of Laperouse and the wreck of Pandora will ever provide us with the minute details which give substance to written history. Of these wrecks, Pandora has the most potential. Unfortunately, the excavation of Pandora has been halted due to the lack of financial support.

In 1986, the most emotive discovery of all was made. Buried in the stern section of Pandora's wreck was a human skeleton.

Ronald A Coleman is Curator of Maritime History and Archaeology at Queensland Museum, Australia.

dents and the complete omission of others. Hamilton's writing is an obvious attempt to describe Pandora's voyage in the genre of science and discovery. His forthwright descrption of the lascivious customs of the Tahitians was bound to draw criticism and attract for him the label of "licentious".

On 30 October 1793, Bligh wrote to Banks and discussed the attacks on his reputation by various people in his absence and refuted statements made in Morrison's unpublished journal which he had obviously read.

But that was not to be the end of it. In 1794, Edward Christian, brother of Fletcher, published a portion of the minutes of the mutineer's court-martial with an appendix defending his brother. The appendix included condemning state-ments supposedly made by various participants of the Bounty incident. Bligh was prompted to publish an answer to the allegations in the December 1794 issue of *The British Critic*. A detail worthy of note is that Bligh's "Answer" included a statement supposedly made by Coleman on Bligh's behalf. It is signed with an "X" and captioned "Coleman's Mark". A copy of Coleman's own written account of the early part of Bounty's voyage had been forwarded to Banks. It was not the writings of a man who could not sign his own name.

One hundred and eighty-six years after the wreck of Pandora, a group of scuba divers with the assistance of the Royal Australian Air Force, relocated the ship's final resting place. She lies in 120 feet of water buried in a gently sloping

Pitcairn: what happened

Brian W Scott looks at the lives, and deaths, of the mutineers in 'paradise'

■ IN NEED of fresh water supplies, and anxious to increase his take of seals, Mayhew Folger, Captain of the *Topaz* out of Boston, had set his course for Pitcairn's Island – first discovered by Captain Carteret in 1767. Land was seen at 1.30 pm on 6 February 1808, but it was dark when the ship reached the island. Folger therefore decided to "lay off & on till daylight" and his log continues:

> at 6 am. put off in two boats to Explore the land and look for seals, on approaching the Shore saw a Smoke on the land at which I was very much surprised it being represented by Captain Carteret as destitute of Inhabitants, on approaching Still more the land – I discovered a boat paddling towards me with three men in her.

His surprise was even greater when the canoe was paddled close in by three dark skinned youths who hailed the ship in English. He later recalled this encounter to fellow sea captain, Amasa Delano, who published Folger's description:

> They seemed not to be willing to come near to him till they had acertained who he was. He answered and told them he was an American from Boston. This they did not immediately understand. With great earnestness they said "You are an American: you come from America; where is America? Is it in Ireland?" Captain Folger, thinking that he should soonest make himself intelligible to them by finding out their original coun-

try, as they spoke English, inquired "Who are you?" – "We are Englishmen." – "Where were you born?" – "On that island which you see;" – "How then are you Englishmen, if you were born on that Island which the English do not own, and never possesed?" – "We are Englishmen, because our father was an Englishman." – "Who is your father?" With a very interesting simplicity they answered "Aleck." – "Who is Aleck?" – "Don't you know Aleck?" – "How should I know Aleck?" – "Well then, did you know Captain Bligh, of the Bounty?" At this question Folger told me, that the whole story immediately burst upon his mind, and produced a shock of mingled feelings, surprise, wonder, and pleaure, not to be described ... They informed him, that Aleck was the only one of the Bounty's crew who remained alive on the island; they made him acquainted with some of the most important points in their history; and with every sentence increased still more his desire to visit the establishment, and learn the whole. Not knowing whether it would be proper and safe to land without giving notice, as the fears of the surviving mutineer might be awakened in regard to the object of the visit, he requested the young men to go and tell

Aleck, that the master of the ship desired very much to see him and would supply him with anything he had on board. The canoe carried the message, but returned without Aleck, bringing an apology for not appearing, and an invitation for Captain Folger to come on shore. The invitation was not immediately accepted, but the young men were sent again for Aleck, to desire him to come on board the ship, and to give his assurances of the friendly and honest intention of the master. They returned, however, again, without Aleck, said that the women were fearful for his safety, and would not allow him to expose himself, or them by leaving their beloved island. The young men pledged themselves to Captain Folger, that he had nothing to apprehend, if he should land; that the islanders wanted extremely to see him, and that they would furnish him with any supplies which their village afforded. After this negociation, Folger determined to go on shore, and as he landed, he was met by Aleck and all his family, and was welcomed with every demonstration of joy and goodwill. They escorted him from the shore to the house of their patriarch, where every luxury they had was set before him, and offered with the most affectionate courtesy.

This "negociation" reveals an understandable degree of caution on both sides. Folger was reluctant to set foot ashore to meet the remnants of a mutinous crew, who might even now be armed and dangerous. Aleck, as sole survivor of the Bounty, was equally reluctant to set foot on a foreign vessel which could seize and return him to England and the due process of law.

The meeting, once arranged, must have been a fascinating exchange. Aleck identified himsel as an able seaman who

■ Rare crude 19th century engraving of John Adams after Beechey. *Private collection.*

■ Pitcairn Island. 19th century steel engraving. *Private collection.*

had joined the Bounty, under the name of Alexander Smith, nearly 21 years before. For the first time he told an outsider his version of the mutiny and the subsequent turbulent events on Pitcairn. It is only to be expected that he would explain his own involvement in the most favourable light. The passage of time and growing confidence in his own inviolability encouraged him to give more detailed accounts.

Smith, in turn, plied Captain Folger for news of the outside world from which he and his "family" had been so long excluded. He learnt of battles by sea and land – and of Nelson's famous victory at Trafalgar at which, we are told, Aleck "rose from his seat, took off his hat, swung it three times round his head, threw it on the ground sailor-like, and cried out 'Old England forever!' The total isolation of the community is highlighted by the initial inquiry to Folger: "Where is America? Is it in Ireland?" It is puzzling why Ireland should feature so prominently in the minds of the young islanders – a point to which I shall return later. On Folger's departure Smith gave him a chronometer and an azimuth compass from the Bounty and Folger summed up his impressions of the mutineer in his log:

> … he lives very comfortably as Commander in Chief of Pitcairn's Island, all the Children of the deceased mutineers Speak tolerable English, some of them are grown to the Size of men and women, and to do them Justice I think them a very humane and hospitable people, and whatever may have been the Errors or Crimes of Smith the Mutineer in times Back, he is at present in my opinion a worthy man and may be useful to Navigators who traverse this immense ocean …

However startling to Mayhew Folger and his crew, the world in general and England in particular, heavily committed to war in Europe, took scant notice of his discovery. The Topaz reached Valparaiso, in Chile, in September, but without the chronometer which had been taken by the Governor of Juan Fernandez. Folger was interviewed by lieutenant Wlliam Fitzmaurice and the information he gathered was sent as an official report to the Admiralty by Sir

Sydney Smith in 1809. It is interesting to speculate whether it crossed the desk of Sir John Barrow who had been appointed Second Secretary to the Admiralty in 1803 and whose book *The Eventful History of the Mutiny and Piratical Seizure of HMS* Bounty: *Its cause and consequences*, was published in 1831, anonymously. If it did, with more pressing matters to attend to, he took no action and Pitcairn fell once more into obscurity, even though Captain Folger wrote directly to the Admiralty in March 1813,

■ Pitcairn Island from the sea today. *Glyn Christian.*

sending with his letter the azimuth compass which Aleck had given to him.

Sir John Barrow acknowledges that this communication, transmitted by Rear Admiral Hotham, reached the Admiralty in "the latter part of 1814". It was in the same year that two British frigates, the Briton, commanded by Sir Thomas Staines, and the Tagus, by Captain P Pipon, were despatched to find and

destroy the American war ship Essex which had been marauding British trading ships in the Pacific. Again chance took them to Pitcairn where they made landfall on 17 September. As Sir Thomas recorded in a letter to Vice-Admiral Manley-Dixon dated Valparaiso, 18 October: "I fell in with an island where none is laid down in the Admiralty or other charts … I, therefore hove to until daylight, and then closed to ascertain whether it was inhabited, which I soon discovered it to be, and to my great astonishment found that every individual on the island (forty in number) spoke very good English, as well as Otaheitan." The two captains were persuaded to come ashore and the letter continues:

> A venerable old man, John Adams, is the only surviving Englishman of those who (then) left Otaheite in her; and whose exemplary conduct and fatherly care of the whole of the little colony cannot but command admiration. The pious manner in which all those born on the island have been reared, the correct sense of religion which has been instilled into their young minds by this old man, has given him the pre-eminence over the whole of them, to whom they look up as the father of the whole and one family.

Captain Pipon also wrote a very full account of the visit, but it is evident that these two senior officers were totally unaware of the events reported by Folger and therefore did not comment on the significant fact that Alexander Smith had changed his name to John Adams. The arrival of these two naval ships still alarmed him even 25 years after his role in the mutiny. Pipon writes:

> He was not, by his own account, in the small degree concerned in the mutiny, he being at the time it happened, sick in bed …

Bligh, tied to the mizzen mast of the Bounty with Smith standing guard, cutlass in hand, might have thought differently. When Adams learnt that only the two officers had come ashore, unarmed, he came out to meet them, accompanied by his wife, who was then nearly blind. Sir Thomas assured him that he had no intention of arresting him – "They were not even aware that such a person as himself existed", while Pipon observes,

"that although in the eye of the law they could only consider him in the light of a criminal of the deepest dye, yet that it would have been an act of the greatest cruelty and inhumanity to have taken him away from his little family". Indeed, when Adams expressed an interest in seeing England again "a scene of considerable distress was witnessed; his daughter, a fine young woman, threw her arms about his neck, entreating him not to think of leaving them and all his, little children to perish."

Once more, the islanders were reassured and the wisdom and understanding of these two officers is to be admired. They came ashore unescorted to see for themselves, "getting a good wetting" in the surf and were enlightened enough not to disturb an equilibrium which had only been established after years of bitter strife. Having shared a meal with John Adams they were taken back to the ships by two of the first generation Pitcairners, Thursday October Christian and George Young, who were given "a liberal supply of articles necessary for the comfort of the islanders" before Briton and Tagus continued on their voyage to Valparaiso.

When the accounts of this discovery by *English* ships reached London much more interest was aroused. Who was this "venerable old man" who so impressed Sir Thomas and his fellow captain? What was his real name? Where did he come from? Why did he sign on to the Bounty as Alexander Smith but change his name to John Adams on Pitcairn? Sir John Barrow gave his opinion, commenting on Captain Pipon's report:

> Such were the first details that were received repecting this young settlement. It may here be remarked that at the time when Folger visited the island Alexander Smith went by his proper name and that he changed it to John Adams in the intermediate time between his visit and that of Sir Thomas Staines; but it does not appear in any of the accounts which have been given of this interesting little colony, when or for what reason he assumed the latter name. It could not be with any view to concealment, for he freely communicated his history to Folger and equally so to every subsequent visitor.

Barrow's conclusion in a "classic" work, frequently republished, prolongs the uncertainty about John Adams' iden-

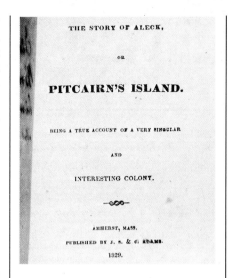

■ Probably the rarest of published Pitcairn items. *Private collection*

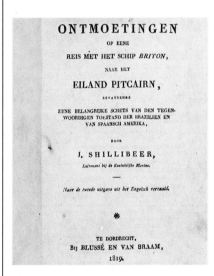

■ A Dutch Edition of Shillibeer. *Private collection.*

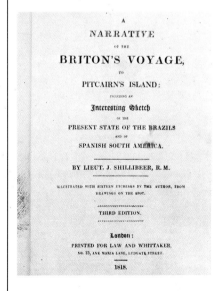

■ Account by Marine Lieutenant Shillibeer of HMS Briton's chance visit in 1818. *Private collection.*

tity. There was information closer to hand than he realized and one account published in America could have changed his viewpoint. It was particularly unfortunate since Sir John realized that Adams was not attempting any concealment of his past

Pitcairn's years of isolation were coming to an end, although Barrow was to complain: "The interesting account of Sir Thomas Staines and Pipon, in 1814, produced as little effect on the government as that of Folger; and nothing more was heard of Adams and his family for twelve years nearly, then in 1825, Captain Beechey, in the Blossom, bound on a voyage of discovery, paid a visit to Pitcairn's Island." This was not strictly the case either but lack of interest in official quarters was not for want of publicity effort by Barrow himself. In 1809, the first issue of the Quarterly Review was published on the initiative of the publisher John Murray. Barrow was persuaded to write reviews and articles for the Journal and became a prolific contributor. For the issue of July 1815 he reviewed the *Journal of a Cruize made to the Pacific Ocean by Captain David Porter in the United States Frigate Essex, in the years 1812, 1813 and 1814*, and he included an account of Pitcairn Island and the visits of the Topaz, Briton, and Tagus. Public interest was further aroused when Lieutenant John Shillibeer, an officer of Marines aboard the Briton, published in Taunton an account of the voyage in a book called *A Narrative of the Britons Voyage to Pitcairn's Island*. To his regret he did not go ashore:

No one but the Captains went ashore, which will be a lasting regret to me, for I would rather have seen the simplicity of that little village, than all the splendour and magnificence of a city.

It was philanthropic fervour rather than government action which was stirred by such accounts, with the encouragement of Sir Thomas Staines, who in his letter to the Admiralty, added:

I cannot however refrain from offering my opinion that it is well worthy of the attention of our laudable religious societies, particularly that for propagating the Christian religion, the whole inhabitants speaking the Otaheitan tongue as well as English.

In London the Society for the Promotion of Christian Knowledge were not slow to pick up the challenge, while in Hackney a group of High Churchmen, known as the Hackney Phalanx, were active in adopting charitable causes. One of their leading members, Joshua Watson, was appointed Treasurer of the SPCK in 1814. A Thomas Walters, living in Hackney, and possibly a member of the Phalanx, after reading a review of Lieutenant Shillibeer's book in the Gentleman's Magazine, decided to take action. He arranged to see John Adams' brother and then wrote to the editor of the *Gentleman's Magazine* as follows:

Hackney, Nov. 4, 1818

Mr Urban,

As your readers must have felt deeply interested in the short account rendered of Pitcairn's Island by Lieutenant Shillibeer, as noticed in your Review Vol. lxxxvii, 11, 341, I presume the few lines in addition to this may not be unacceptable.

Having been informed that John Adams, the last survivor of the Bounty's crew on the island had a brother, I desired to see him: he called on me, is a waterman at Union Stairs, wears the fire coat of the London Assurance, and is, of course, a steady character. On reading to him the lieutenant's narrative, he was much affected; said he accompanied him on board the Bounty at Deptford; but he entered in the name of Smith; and this accounts for the name of Adams not being found in the Bounty's list of her crew; that he has a sister living, older than either, who is married to a decent trademan at Derby; that he himelf has a large family. I said, "I sent for you to say if you will write to your brother in a few days, I think I shall have the means of transmitting it to him; and as you have a large family will you let your eldest son go out?" He thanked me for the offer of sending the letter, and willingly would have sent his son but an objection would lie with somebody else. Now we all know who this somebody else is, and the influence Dolly has on Johny Bull.

The letter is gone – and with it several others; but when I reflect on the surprising escape of Captain Bligh and his barge's crew, and of the events that have followed, I am not surprised that the whole is a series of interesting circumstances.

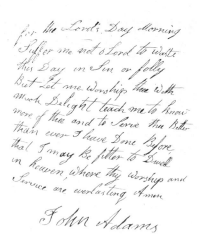

■ John Adams Prayer. *Private collection.*

Adams' brother proceeded to say: "We are natives of Hackney and were left orphans, being brought up in the poor-house." Here it was, then, that they were taught the first principles of our holy religion; here they learned what it appears, Adams in due course recollected, the Catechism he had been taught to repeat, that excellent Catechism which every child should be taught also to say.

The letter continues on a religious theme taking as a text "I will arise and go to my Father" which was reported by Lieut Shillibeer as being a prayer used on Pitcairn. The letter, which is just signed TW (Thomas Walters in Mariner's Mirror), was brought to light again by George Mackaness in his classic study *The Life of Vice-Admiral William Bligh RN, FRS*. He comments that it "is partic-

■ A miniature chest of drawers owned by John Adams. Given by his family to Admiral Lowther, on his visit to the island in the mid 19th century. *Private collection.*

ularly interesting because it contains the only information ever secured about John Adams and his home folk and also partly explains his two names". John Adams had reason to be grateful for the lively interest and initiative of Thomas Walters.

JENNY

The next significant event in Pitcairn's history was in 1817. *The Pitcairn Island Register Book* which was written retrospectively for the early years, has one entry for that year:

> William Quintal born arrived Ship *Sultan* of Boston Captn. Reynolds left this island in the *Sultan* Jenny a Tahitian woman.

It is significant for two reasons. First, Jenny was Pitcairn's first emigrant and her story combined with the various accounts given by John Adams to visiting sea captains enable a reasonable approximation of the events on Pitcairn between 1790 and 1800. Second, the visit furnished some additional information from which John Adams' true identity could be established. To understand Jenny's reasons for leaving we must first of all know how she came to Pitcairn.

Immediately after the mutiny, Fletcher Christian tried to build a settlement on the island of Tubuai for all those who remained on board. Tahiti would be the first port of call for any vessel searching for the mutineers whereas Tubuai appeared to offer reasonable

security. A discouraging reception from the natives confirmed this view. Christian continued to Tahiti to procure livestock and to persuade the women they had known previously to return with them. Among these was Teehuteatuaonoa (Jenny) who agreed to go with Aleck. The *Sydney Gazette and NSW Advertiser* which first published her "narrative" on 17 July 1819 reported:

> She has been apparently a good looking woman in her time, but now begins to bear the marks of age. She is marked on the left arm (ie tatooed) $_1^{AS}\!\!{}_{789}$ which was done by Adam Smith to whom she attached herself at first and sailed with him both before and after the ship was taken.

A VIEW OF THE VILLAGE AT PITCAIRN ISLAND

This implies, and it is quite likely that Jenny knew AS before the mutiny. The use of the name Adam Smith is curious but other names are also garbled, thus John Mills is recorded as John Main and Isaac Martin as Isaac Madden.

Christian was successful in obtaining a substantial quantity of pigs, goats, and chickens. About 28 Tahitians joined the crew but Adams was to complain later that: "We did not find as many women as we wanted. Nine only came on board ..." Having lost Jenny shortly after the Bounty returned to Tubuai at the end of June, he tried to find a local

■ Adamstown, Pitcairn, by F W Beechey 1828. *Royal Geographical Society, London.*

H.M.S. Blossom Dec.r 20.th

ADAMSTOWN ROADS, 1980

▲ Houses occupied in 1980

0   500 Feet
SCALE

replacement; he was enticed to a local chief's house where his clothes were stolen and he had to be rescued clad only in his shirt. General unrest persisted. Despite Christian's best endeavours, the settlement was almost bound to fail. At leact three of the ship's company dissociated themselves from the mutineers and realized that a return to Tahiti was the shortest route back to England.

In September, Christian was forced to call a meeting and against his advice the decision was taken to return to Tahiti once again, but with the agreement that Christian and his eight supporters should have the Bounty. For all but two, this commitment was to lead to sudden death. The 16 who chose to remain on Tahiti would receive their share of arms, ammunition and equipment from the ship.

■ Plan of Adamstown today. *Glyn Christian.*

The Bounty sailed from Tubuai (with three native men aboard) on 17 September and reached Tahiti on the 22nd. During the course of that day more men and women came aboard. Fletcher Christian's primary object was to leave no hint of his destination. If he had one in mind, he could not divulge it so he slipped anchor as soon as the night was quiet and Bounty glided silently out of Matavai Bay in search of another island sanctuary. On departure, there were 35 people on board, but one woman dived overboard to swim to shore and the fol-

■ Thursday October Christian's home, oldest in Pitcairn. *Glyn Christian.*

lowing day six other women designated by Jenny as "rather ancient" were allowed ashore at Moorea. The remaining 28 on board were:

Mutineers	Consort
Fletcher Christian	Mauatua
Edward Young	Teraura
John Mills	Vahineatua
Isaac Martin	Teehuteatuaonoa (Jenny)
William McCoy	Teio and her baby daughter
Matthew Quintal	Tevarua
Alexander Smith	Obuarei
John Williams	Faahotu
William Brown	Teatuahitea
Tahitians	
Teimua	} Mareva
Minarii	
Niau – a boy	
Tubuaians	
Oher	} Tinafornea
Tetahiti	
Raiatean	
Tararo	Toofaiti

The search was to last almost four months. Christian found an edition in Bligh's cabin of Hawkesworth's Voyages with the brief description of Pitcairn's Island given by Captain Philip Carteret. It was small, remote, uninhabited and covered with trees and had "a small stream of fresh water running down one side of it, I would have landed upon it, but the surf, which at this season broke upon it with great violence, rendered it impossible ... it is probable that in fine weather landing here may not only be practicable but easy". To Christian, it sounded like the perfect refuge, but his first problem was to find it since the island had been charted incorrectly. The reward of his perseverance and skilled navigation came on the evening of 15 January, 1790, when the mutineers saw Pitcairn for the first time.

THE DARK DECADE
Fletcher Christian took an armed party ashore in the cutter and this preliminary excursion confirmed that the island was uninhabited and had all the natural resources needed. The Bounty was brought close in shore and with the weath-

■ Pitcairn Island's register, detailing visits, and interesting events. Note the entry on 23 January 1790: 'H.M. Ship Bounty burned'. *SPCK, London.*

er favourable was stripped of all that could be put to good use. A site was selected for the settlement at the top of the cliffs and during the feverish activity there was discussion about what should be done about the Bounty itself. With no hidden anchorage, the vessel would be visible for miles All we know for certain is that within a few days of the landing, the ship was set on fire and destroyed. This action has been attributed to Matthew Quintal, but we can only speculate on his reasons. It may have been for fear of the ship being sighted, but it certainly meant that the mutineers were stranded.

After long months at sea the novelty of their new surroundings must have created a great sense of freedom and exhilaration, but the seeds of discord were sown immediately by Christian's decision to divide the island among the nine whites, leaving no land for the Polynesians – thus creating the roles of master and slave from the outset. The community began to develop and in October 1790 the first child was born on the islands. A son to Fletcher and Mauatua, they named him Thursday October – later changed to Fri-

day when it was pointed out that the Bounty en route to Pitcairn had crossed the date line.

Within a few months of arrival, John Williams "wife", Faahoto, died – according to Jenny "of a scrofulous disease". He thus became the only white man on the island without female company and his initial demand that one of the women shared by the Polynesians be handed over to him was rejected. This grievance festered for some time until, according to Jenny's account: "The Europeans took the three women belonging to the natives, Toofaiti, Mareva and Tinafornea and cast lots for them, and the lot falling upon Toofaiti she was taken from Tararo and given to Jack Williams. Tararo wept at parting from his wife and was very angry. He studied revenge ..." Tararo was the only native to have a woman of his own. By now all the natives were little more than labourers for the dominant white landowners and Tararo was easily able to raise support for an uprising. However, the plotting was overheard by some of the women who then informed the whites. Christian acted swiftly and ruthlessly.

Births, Deaths, Marriages, and Remarkable Family Events

Date	Parties Names &c.
1790 January 23	H M Ship Bounty burned at Pitcairn Island
October –	Same year died Faoto wife of John Williams Thursday October Christian born
1791 & 1792	This year Matthew Quintal, Daniel McCoy & Elizabeth Mills born & Charles Christian
1793	Massacre - of part of the mutineers by the Tahitians. The White men all killed, part by jealousies among themselves, the others by the remaining Englishmen. Mary Christian born
1794	A great desire in many of the women to leave the Island a boat built for the purpose of removing them. launched, and upset. Fortunate for them that she did so for had they launched out upon the ocean where could they have gone or what could a few ignorant women have done by themselves drifting upon the waves but ultimately have fallen a sacrifice to their folly

Four of the natives, under threat of death, were sent to find and kill the two ringleaders, Tararo and Oher, who had fled from the village. Oher was murdered by his fellow Tubuaian, Tetahiti, and Tararo by Minarii.

The four remaining natives were now in an even worse situation. Not only were they outnumbered by more than two to one but the native women had constantly favoured the white men. Even Toofaiti, now named Nancy, seemed happy with her new partner. So the resentment of these men isolated in the community and cut off from their own people and culture soon grew to bitterness and hatred. The balance was savagely redressed in 1793. Plotting with more cunning and secrecy and taking advantage of the mutineers laxity in keeping the arms and ammunition secure, they planned a concerted attack while the Englishmen were working on the land. There are discrepancies in Adams' and Jenny's accounts of that

■ Interest in the Pitcairns even extended to the Police Gazette.

day, but the sequence of events was broadly as follows. It appears that Teimua and Niau had been able to steal guns and Tetahiti borrowed one "under the pretence of shooting hogs" before joining them. The sound of the first shot which killed Williams would therefore not have aroused any alarm and the conspirators then asked if Minarii (who was working alongside Mills in his garden) could come with them to help carry in the wild hog which they pretened had been killed. Next they set out to find Christian and shot him dead "whilst digging in his own field". Mills was shot and wounded and his head cut off with a hatchet. Martin, also wounded, was beaten to death and Brown was the last to die. The two whom the natives perhaps feared most, Quintal and McCoy, managed to escape to the wooded interior. Adams, who was warned by Quintal's wife, escaped inland, but having returned to obtain food and clothing was shot and wounded in the neck and shoulder and his hand was injured fending off a blow from the butt end of a musket. Making his escape again

Adams was persuaded to return when the women pleaded his cause with the natives.

There has been much speculation as to how Midshipman "Ned" Young managed to escape unharmed. He too was a favourite with the women and they may have given him prior warning. Jenny records: "Ned Young's life was saved by his wife and the other women." The native men had won the battle, but not the war. With five mutineers killed the numbers were even but the victors fell out over the spoils and Minarii killed Teimua in a jealous rage and then fled inland where Quintal and McCoy were still in hiding. By some means a message was sent to them urging them to kill Minarii. They did so, but were still reluctant to return to the village while the two remaining natives were still free. Again the women took matters into their own hands. Resentful at the murder of their white husbands they sought revenge and according to Jenny:

> Next day ... about noon, while one of the Otaheitan men was sitting outside of the house, and the other was lying on his back on the floor, one of the women took a hatchet and cleft the skull of the latter; at the same instance calling out to Young to fire which he did, and shot the other native dead.

Adams in his accounts confirms that Young shot Niau leaving four men on the island, but these were not to be the last violent deaths.

Some time before the massacres, John Adams had lost his wife Obuarei when she fell from a cliff when searching for birds eggs. There were no children of this union. Now with only four men remaining on the island some adjustments in the living arrangements were made. Adams was joined by Vahineatua (Prudence) who already had two children by John Mills (Elizabeth and John). She and Adams had three daughters born between 1794 and 1800: Dinah, Rachel and Hannah. In 1804, Adams' only son George was born. His Mother was Teio (Mary) who came on the Bounty with William McCoy and the baby Sarah.

There followed a period of relative calm although Quintal and McCoy were

■ View near Matavai Bay, from original drawing by Webber.
Private collection.

131

a disruptive influence with a reputation for harsh and brutal behaviour. The women were so discontented that there was even an unsuccessful attempt to build a boat to escape from the island. Then on 20 April 1798, it is recorded in the Register Book:

> McCoy distilled a bottle of ardent spirit from the Te-root. The copper of the Bounty made into a still, frequent intoxication the consequence, McCoy in particular upon whom it produced fits of delirium, in one of which he fastened a stone to his neck, threw himself from the rocks, into the sea and was drowned.

The next entry in the Register recalls the death of Matthew Quintal in 1799. In this year, Tevarua (Sarah) who had four children by him (Matthew, Sarah, Arthur and Jane) also fell to her death while looking for birds eggs. Although there were other women available, it is conjectured that Quintal wanted Teraura (Susannah), because she bore him a son Edward after his death. When this was refused Quintal became threatening. In a signed statement to Captain Beechey of HMS Blossom dated 5 December 1825, Adams says:

> In consequence he vowed an oath that he would be the death of us; which was foiled in one attempt: and as we considered that our own preservation depended upon the death of this man, it was resolved to put him to death which was consequently done by a Pole Axe.

This claim of justifiable homicide is John Adams' only admission of violence. In less than 10 years, 13 men had died and now only Ned Young and John Adams remained. They had always been friends and the close ties continued in later years when Young's daughter Polly married George Adams and his son George married Hannah, Adams' youngest daughter. Young was a well educated man and together they began the process of reformation. Unfortunately Young survived for only a short time and died in 1800 of a long lasting asthmatic complaint. As for Jenny, it is hardly surprising that she wanted to leave the island. Her husband had been murdered, she was childless and she had lived through 10 unhappy years. Another 17 years were to pass before she persuaded Captain Reynolds of the Sultan to take her away.

School House and Chapel, Pitcairn Isd.

ADAMS OR SMITH?

The discovery of the refuge of the mutineers was news in America as well as England. The Sultan, like the Topaz before her, was an American ship and was on a trading voyage to the Pacific; it is due to the enthusiasm of Mr Samuel Topliff, a New England Publisher, that we have the details of the ship's visit to Pitcairn. His letter to the editor of *New-England Galaxy* was not published until 12 January 1821:

> Sometime in December 1819 I learned by accident that the ship *Sultan* of Boston, C Reynolds, Master, which arrived here the 6th Sept of the same year, from Canton had, during her voyage, touched at Pitcairn's Island, and wishing to gratify my curiosity to know what transpired relative thereto I immediately went in quest of Capt R … but found on enquiry that he had gone to Dighton.

Nor was the first officer, George Newell available, having left for Canton in the Cordelia, but Topliff discovered that Newell had left his private journal of the voyage with a relative. He borrowed it and copied down details.

Topliff gives a succinct summary of all the events relating to the mutiny, commenting... "A particular and interesting account of the visits of Capt Folger, and Sir Thomas Staines, may be found in the voyages published by Capt Amasa Delano in this place a few years since." The article continues with the extract from Newell's private journal,

School House and Chapel, Pitcairn by Conway Shipley. *National Maritime Museum.*

written in diary form: "Oct 17th, 1817. At 2 pm made Pitcairn's Island bearing E. by N 7 leagues distant. At 5 pm hove too off the North side of the Isle, where we discovered a small village situated among a grove of cocoa nut trees. I went in with the boat but could not land on account of the surf which beat with considerable violence on the shore."

Newell recounts that ten young men seeing "we were not disposed to land leaped into the surf and swam off to the boat". He invited four of them on board the Sultan for the night, whose conduct "was such as excited the admiration of every person on board the ship". The weather was very boisterous, through the night and by the next morning they were out of sight of land. "In the morning the weather became more moderate, when we turned out the reefs and got up the top gallant yards, and made all sail".

On reaching the island again, two boats were sent ashore "for refreshment". Newell went ashore himself on two occasions, once bringing John Adams back to the ship. Replenishment of the ship's stores continued over two days and the journal records: "We obtained from these happy people 18 pigs, 5 goats, 3 dozen fowls, some eggs and a large supply of yams, cocoa nuts and some sugar cane etc, all of which they have in great abundance." The islanders fared well in return – being presented with the ship's jolly boat

and "a number of other valuable articles". With the Sultan ready to depart John Adams and the young men with him gave three cheers as the ship "bore up to *ESE* under full sail, the wind at *NNW*." They also said goodbye to Jenny who was on her way "home" at last, but it was to be a long voyage. The first officer makes no mention of Jenny in his journal, but Topliff's curiosity was not yet satisfied and he managed to contact Mr Downs, second officer of the ship, and garnered more interesting news items. Downs informed him that:

> They received on board the ship, an old woman who was very desirous of return-ing to her native place, Otaheite; and as she was very earnest in her entreaties to be taken away, and having neither hus-band, nor children, nor anything else to attach her to the island, Capt R consented to take her on board.

From Pitcairn the Sultan sailed to Coquimbo in Chile and it was not until May 1818 that she was landed at "Nooa-heavah" – probably Nuku-hiva in the Marquesas and from there she had to make her way south west to Tahiti. Downs also had news of John Adams describing him as "a fat stout man, with a bald head; his beard had been extracted" and he "was quite elated when he came on board, pulled the rigging and sang several songs, and appeared perfectly happy". Most important of all Downs told Topliff that Adams had presented Captain Reynolds with an old spy glass and *two blank books which belonged to*

the Bounty. Persistant as ever, Topliff made inquiries and found "that Capt Reynolds had presented one of the books to Mr Greenwood, proprietor of the New England Museum, to whom I applied, and he politely loaned it to me".

Topliff reminds his readers that when Capt Folger visited Pitcairn he found that the only survivor was Alexan-der Smith but "when Sir Thomas Staines visited the island, he passed by the name of John Adams which name, it appears by the above journal, he still held when the Sultan visited the island". Confused by the evidence in front of him Topliff, like Sir John Barrow, expressed his opinion:

> I think there can be no doubt that the name of Adams was assumed by him, for reasons best known to himself and that his real name is Alexander Smith ... I find in the book now in the possession of Mr Greenwood that Smith had attempted in four places to write a hist-ory of his life; but finding himself unequal to the task, gave it up. Mr Downs assured me, that the writing was in Smiths own hand, and to show that he was incapable of writing his own history, as well as to remove all doubts concern-ing his name and place of birth, I here introduce a copy, verbatim et liberatum, of all I find in the book relative to the subject. Alexander Smith, alias Adams I was was Born at Stanford Hill in the par-rish of St John Hackney Middellsex of poor But honast parrents My farther was Drouned in the Theames thearfore he left

■ Old Courthouse in the square, Pit-cairn where Christian's second wife and son are buried. *Glyn Christian.*

> Me and 3 More poore Orfing Bot But one was Married and ot of All harmes In another part of the book he writes as fol-lows. The Life Of John Adams Born November the 4 or 5 in the Year Sixty Six att Stanford Hill in the parrish of St John Hackney My father was sarvent to Danel Bell Cole Marchant My father was drowed in the River Theames.

This may be one one the shortest autobiographies ever written and it was obviously a disappointment to Samuel Topliff who considered Adams "inca-pable of writing his own history". It does, however, reveal a lot about the character of the man and contains a lot of information. He had heard nothing of his family in England since joining the Bounty under a false name in 1787, nor they of him. His reason for changing his name was not to hide his identity, but exactly the opposite – to reveal his real name so that his family, who must have assumed that he was dead, might hear of his existence. He had to provide as much evidence as he could to prove his identity. The visit of Sir Thomas Staines and Cap-tain Pipon had given him the reassurance that he was no longer a wanted man and thus relieved of anxiety he must have desperately wanted to tell his story, but without Ned Young there was no one to help him write it. He therefore wrote

down the essential information as best he could, and gave it to the Captain of the next ship to arrive at Pitcairn, an American. It must be remembered that in his 27 years on the island only three ships had called before the Sultan and Adams had no means of knowing when another English ship would call.

Adams says that he was born on 4 or 5 November 1766 in the parish of St John, Hackney, Middlesex, and that he had three brother or sisters one of whom was married. We know already from Thomas Walters that he had a brother and a sister older than either, who had married "a decent tradesman at Derby ..." By linking this information together and examining the parish register of Baptisms for St Johns Hackney the family names were revealed by the following entries:-

Rachel D of John Dinah Adams bap
    Dec 4 1754
Dinah Jemima D of John Dinah Adams
    bap Feb 2 1757
John S of John and Dinah Adams bap
    Dec 4 1767
Jonathon S of John and Dinah Adams
    bap Apr 13 1774

The strength of the family bond is revealed by the names he gave his children on Pitcairn: Dinah after his mother and sister and Rachel after his eldest sister. But why was his third daughter called Hannah? She in due course married George Young and two of her daughters were called Dinah and and Jemima. John Adams' son George and his wife Polly named their first two children John and Jonathan.

As John Adams was born in November 1766 he was still only 20 (as recorded on the Muster Roll) when he joined the Bounty on 7 September 1787. But why join under an assumed name? Dr Mackaness quotes as follows:

This man's real name was John Adams, but having deserted from another ship he entered himself on board the Bounty as Alexander Smith – Rev James Bligh's note on his own private copy of Bligh's voyage.

Such an authority must carry weight and it is certainly a likely reason – which was picked up by subsequent writers on the subject – but was there another reaon?

■ Bounty Bay by Conway Shipley.

In the same Register of Baptisms, the entries for September 1787 include: "Sarah. d. of John and Hannah Adams. 21." Parish '21' indicates the date of the month so the baby was baptised just two weeks after "Alexander Smith" joined the Bounty. Did John Adams name his third daughter on Pitcairn after the mother of his daughter in England? The marriage is not recorded at St Johns and parish indicates that mother and child were in receipt of parish relief and lacked paternal support. There is also circumstantial evidence that his father, also John, came from Ulster but a John Adams was born in the parish of St Johns Hackney on 30 May 1731. He in turn was the son of Jonathan and Rachel Adams and with the continuity of family names this seems to be a more likely line of descent.

Jonathan was the youngest of the four children and was only 13 when the Bounty sailed and his life is an interesting contrast to that of his brother. Thomas Walters, "having been informed that John Adams had a brother ... desired to see him, is a waterman at Union Stairs, wears the fire-coat of the London Assurance and is of course a steady character". The archives of the Corporation are held in Guildhall Library and its history was written by Bernard Drew.

By the time Thomas Walters "desired to see him", Jonathan had served as a Fireman for 15 years – hence the emphasis that he was "of course a steady character". Walters suggested to Jonathan: "if you will write to your brother in a few days I think I shall have the means of of transmitting it to him." He was familiar with the work of the SPCK and probably knew Joshua Watson, the Society's Treasurer. Watson was instrumental in the appointment of Dr Middleton (a member of the Hackney Phalanx) as the first Bishop of India and it was this connection which Thomas Walters envisaged as the link with Pitcairn. He went further and asked whether Jonathan would let his eldest son go out. The rejection of this proposal he attributed to "the influence Dolly has with Johny Bull" – perhaps a veiled reference to Jonathan's wife Margaret. Her name is found in the Parish Registers of St John, Wapping. A son Andrew Stedman Adams was born on 26 November 1797 at Upper Gun Alley.

By 4 November 1818, a letter, "and with it several others", was on its way to Pitcairn via India.

THE PATRIARCH
For John Adams, the next arrival at Pitcairn came sooner than he had dared to hope. The Sultan carrying his brief life history was still at sea when the Hercules, sailing to Calcutta, called at the island. Captain Henderson's account was published in the *Calcutta Journal* on 20 July 1819. He describes his arrival at Pitcairn on the morning of the 18 January 1819:

After breakfast I went on shore at 7 am and was received on the rocks by old Mr Adams, and all the other inhabitants of the Island; but not before the Islanders that were in the boat with me had given a shout or cry peculiar to themselves to signify my being a friend. I delivered to Adams the box of Books from the Missionary Society of London, and a Letter from Adams' brother, who is still living at Wapping in London. I read this Letter to him, giving him a description of his family, mentioning the death of one sister, and the prosperity of another. This affected him much, and he often repeated that he never expected to see this day, or indeed one of his countrymen more.

One can imagine the turmoil of emotions which engulfed Adams on hearing this first news of his kith and kin. The letter from Jonathan has never come to light, but the reply dated the same day, and no doubt written with Captain Henderson's assistance, was published in the Calcutta *Government Gazette* for 27 July 1820 – a year after the Hercules reached Calcutta:

To Mr Jonathan Adams, Wapping.
My Dear Brother,
I this day have the greatest pleasure in my life since I left my native country, that is of receiving your letter, dated the 13 October, 1817. I have now lived on the island 30 years, and have a wife and four children, and considering the occasion which brought me here, it is not likely I shall ever leave this place. I enjoy good health, and, except the wound which I received from one of the Otaheitans when they quarrelled with us, I have not had a days sickness. I understand it is the intention of the Missionary Society of London, to send a person here to instruct us in the Christian Religion; I can only say I have done every thing in my power to instruct them in the path to Heaven, and, thank God, we live comfortably and happy, and not a single quarrel has taken place these 18 years. Should this reach you in time, that is before the gentlemen come out which is intended by the Missionary Society, should it be in your power to send me any useful articles, they will be received with many thanks and kindness. Inform the Missionary Society I have received the box of books by the last India ship, Hercules, Captain Henderson. Wishing you every health and happiness this world can afford you, I remain, my dear brother, your very affectionate brother,
JOHN ADAMS
Pitcairn's Island,
South Seas, Jan. 18. 1819

We must assume that the letter did reach Jonathan safely; certainly, the contents reached England because they were quoted in *Felix Farleys Bristol Journal* dated 11 March 1820. When the Hercules reached Calcutta in July, the Calcutta Journal placed an "Advertisement" on the front page of its issue dated Tuesday 13 July 1819: "Captain Henderson ... who had communication with the Descendants of the Crew of the Ship Bounty ... and intending to call again at Pitcairn's Island," has stated that the islanders require iron tools and agricultural implements and "has offered to take charge of any articles that may be confided to him for that purpose". The advertisement urged "any philanthropic Gentleman to make their contributions to Mr Matthew Smith of Clive Street and suggested that "dona-

■ View of Bounty Bay, Pitcairn in the 1960's before recent modernisation of the jetty. The Bounty lies just off top left of the picture.
Private collection.

tions of elementary books in English would be exceedingly useful and acceptable".

The public response was generous and the Diocesan Committee in Calcutta under its President, Dr Middleton, was also active: "It having being intimated that a supply of bibles had been furnished by another Committee, the Diocesan Committee made such a selection of other books and tracts as appeared most suited to the situation of these people, which together with New Testaments, Prayerbooks and children's books were placed under the care of Captain Henderson ..." For John Adams, a man of limited learning, the delivery of yet more religious material might have been rather overwhelming, but strangely, with so much information on the first visit, there is no record of the Hercules having touched at Pitcairn a second time. Bad weather may have prevented a landing and frustrated the good intentions of Captain Henderson and the citizens of Calcutta.

The visit of the Hercules was a turning point in Pitcairn's history and ships began to treat the island as a normal port of call. For the American whalers in particular it was a useful source of fresh produce while the islanders benefitted from all the foods bartered in exchange. Inevitably, there was an element of curiosity and novelty so that accounts of the island and its inhabitants are numerous from 1819 onwards. Captain Raine of the Surry was captivated by all the beauties of the island: "The young women generally speaking are all handsome fine figures, with beautiful teeth and fine hair; and being in a state of native simplicity, combined with apparent innocence, they have an effect upon the mind which is not easy to describe", but from Captain Henry King of the Elizabeth we learn that even the daughter of a Patriarch can fall from grace. Human nature still flourished on Pitcairn and Dinah Adams and Edward Quintal had an illegitimate child: for this "sin" their marriage was forbidden by Adams. The story ended happily, however, as King persuaded him to relent and provided "some porter, wine, and spirits, to regale themselves with at the wedding".

The Elizabeth arrived at Pitcairn in March 1819, less than two months after the Hercules and during the visit a book of devotions published by the Religious

■ First day cover from Pitcairn on 15 October 1940. *Private collection.*

Tract Society was presented to John Adams by one of the officers – an inscription in the last page reads: "John Adams his book given him by Samuel Henry Rapsey of the ship Elizabeth 5 March, AD 1819" Many years later in 1853, the Rev W H Holman acted as Chaplain on Pitcairn when George Hunn Hobbs was being ordained in England. On his return to England, the book was given to the Museum of the United Service Institution. It contained a label in the Rev Holman's writing claiming that it was used by Adams for public morning and evening prayer. Adams' favourite prayer was: "I will arise and go to my Father and say unto him: Father I have sinned against Heaven, and before thee, and am no more worthy to be called thy Son." He also composed a prayer for the Lord's Day Morning – a copy in his own hand is held in the London archives of the SPCK. Recognition of the piety and good manners of the islanders is a constant theme in the various accounts, and the influence of John Adams should not be underestimated.

Family prayers were said every morning and evening and no meals were taken without grace being said. Schooling was introduced for the growing number of children and responsibility for all this fell on Adams alone. It was not until the arrival of John Buffet in December 1823 and then George Hunn Nobbs in November 1828 that the load was shared. As H E Maude says of Adams in *Pitcairnese Language*, "… he was no scholar and at first could read only with difficulty and write hardly at all." Cynics have implied that he acted thus to save his own skin but Maude is more generous: "He was essentially a good and kindly man however, and his supreme achievement was to knit the community into a large but united family of which he was the revered and beloved patriarch and the unquestioned arbiter in all disputes". Adams' great granddaughter Rosalind Amelia Young, author of the delightful *Story of Pitcairn Island 1790-1894* recalls: "One gold ring, the property of Edward Young, played an important part in the wedding services performed in those days, and continued to be used until somewhere in the forties." Adams hav-

ing to officiate himself had never had the satisfaction of a service for Mary (Teio) and and himself and at his request Captain Beechey performed the marriage service in December 1825.

In his declining years, Adams was able to hand over much of his work to John Buffet who took over as schoolmaster and helped with the religious services. His position was to be usurped by the older and more dominant George Hunn Nobbs who arrived at Pitcairn unexpectedly in 1828 and who was to guide the destiny of the islanders for many decades. John Adams died a few months later on 5 March 1829, aged 62 and his wife very shortly afterwards. Perhaps the last word on John Adams, Patriarch of Pitcairn should be left to the Rev Thomas Boyles Murray: "… he left a name the memory of which is cherished beyond the borders of his little island". A fitting epitaph for any man.

John Adams' brother Jonathan died on 30 July 1842 at the age of 68. He was then living with his daughter Mary at 6 Knights Court, Wapping. She had married John Berry and they had four children: John James, Margaret, Mary Ann, and Ann Louisa.

Turning a mutiny into legend

Christian or Bligh? Misunderstood captain or wholesale tyrant? Writers still take sides as if the Bounty sailed yesterday. Gavin Kennedy reports on some books

■ OF THE 46 men and boys who sailed on Bounty from Spithead on 23 December 1787, two died before the mutiny (one of blood poisoning, the other of alcoholism), 10 were murdered after the mutiny (by each other, or by Polynesians), four drowned while prisoners, three were hanged (another three were pardoned), and five died from disease or the after-effects of the open boat voyage. (Details of the entire Bounty crew, including those who deserted before she sailed, are provided in D Bonner Smith's article, "Some Remarks about the Mutiny of the Bounty", *The Mariner's Mirror*, vol 23, no 2, 1937).

For the survivors, the mutiny disrupted but did not destroy their careers. William Bligh was promoted to Post Captain and died a Vice-Admiral of the Blue in 1817; Midshipmen Thomas Hayward and John Hallett were promoted Lieutenants, but later drowned in sea tragedies; Midshipman Peter Heywood, found guilty of mutiny but pardoned, rose to Post Captain's rank, and retired after a distinguished career; John Fryer, Bounty's Master, rose to become a Master of the 1st Rate, and served at the battles of St Vincent and Copenhagen; Robert Tinkler, "midshipman" (and Fryer's brother-in-law) became a Lieutenant and Commander (and also served at Copenhagen); and James Morrison,

Boatswain's mate, drowned in 1807 while Gunner on Admiral Troubridge's flagship, HMS Blenheim.

The mutiny, however, put at risk the reputations of all concerned from the moment the world heard what had happened from 4 am of that fateful morning, 28 April 1789. That the Admiral was bound to be interested in what had happened on any of the King's ships was predictable – it could be concerned about events more trivial than mutinies, as any ship's log shows – but that the world continues to be fascinated by the mutiny is a matter of some curiosity, given the relatively unimportant, mission Bounty was engaged on and the tumultuous events then happening in Europe and North America. Moreover, that the men involved, particularly William Bligh and Fletcher Christian, can excite such passions after 200 years, that supporters and detractors mobilize behind one view or another of those involved, that pamphlets and letters of abuse cross the globe, with personal motives questioned – indeed reputations rubbished – and dark allusions made to personal dishonesty and scholarly ethics, is probably a greater mystery than the causes of the mutiny itself.

The literature about the fatal voyage of HMS Bounty is already vast, and there is no sign that it has ceased growing. True, more is known about the men and the mutiny now than at any time previously, but gaps remain in the historical record, and tantalizing hints of hidden literary treasures occasionally surface. Not least among the latter is the complete absence to date of any material directly written by Fletcher Christian himself (his only known signature is among some Bounty papers in the Mitchell Library in Sydney). We know that he sent letters to his family from the Cape in May 1788, before the mutiny, but no trace of them

has been found (his letters to his brother, Charles, would be of special interest). We know that he destroyed some of his papers immediately before the mutiny (in case of they were used as evidence against him if he failed?). If Christian took advantage of the opportunities he had after the mutiny to record his version of why he mutinied – he had charge of all Bounty's writing instruments and papers (including boxes of Bligh's lifetime collection of navigation and sailing books and personal records) – he hid his efforts to well, or too carelessly. Hence, we have to rely on second-hand reports of his reasons from Peter Heywood and James Morrison, who were among Christian's party who stayed behind at Tahiti, and John Adams (aka Alexander Smith), the last survivor of the bloody murders on Pitcairn.

For the other figures in the mutiny, the literary record is extensive despite the gaps. Some of the original manuscript logs and journals are accessible to the public, without the necessity of expensive trips to the libraries where the originals are preserved in London and Sydney – even highly priced special and facsimile editions of logs and journals still incite a seemingly inexhaustible market for *Bountyana*. In addition, a number of books is also available, for much the same reason as with the manuscripts, and can be found in good public libraries: The Bounty's Log has been published in two limited editions: the first was transcribed and edited in two volumes by Owen Rutter in the Golden Cockerel Press series in 1937: *The Log of the Bounty, being Lieutenant*

137

William Bligh's Log of the Proceedings of His Majesty's Armed vessel 'Bounty', on a voyage to the South Seas to take the breadfruit from the Society Islands to the West Indies, now published for the first time from the manuscript in the Admiralty records; the second was a facsimile of the official log, published as a limited edition in 1975 by Genesis (London) as: *The Log of H.M.S. Bounty*. A popularly priced transcript of the log was published in 1978 as *Mutiny!! Aboard H M Armed Transport 'Bounty' in 1789* by R. M. Bowker and by Lt. William Bligh, RN in his official log (with illustrations including real charts). A facsimile and transcript of Bligh's pocket-size journal which he kept in the open boat was published in 1986 by the National Library of Australia as a limited edition: *The Bligh Notebook: Facsimile and Transcription: 'Rough Account – Lieutenant Wm Bligh's voyage in the Bounty's Launch from the ship to Tofoa & from thence to Timor, 28 April to 14 June 1789'. With a draft list of the Bounty mutineers,* edited by John Bach (a popularly priced edition of this interesting literary treasure was published subsequently in the United States).

Bligh's own versions of the mutiny, first published in 1790 and 1792, have seen numerous modern editions in several languages. Partly, this has been encouraged by the interest in Bligh as one of the early, and typically controversial, Governors of the Colony of New South Wales (where he suffered another mutiny), which has motivated various Australian libraries to collect almost anything connected with Bligh. Many of the important manuscripts of witnesses to the mutiny have also been published within the past 50 years, while those who are able to visit the Public Record Office at Kew, or the Mitchell Library in Sydney, will find most of the rest of the material needed to form a view of the men and the mutiny.

Views about Bligh and the men onboard HMS Bounty have changed more than once over the two centuries since his second-in-command placed him under armed arrest and put him over the side into one of the ship's boats. To a large extent, these public moods follow the publication of books and articles asserting this or that version of each man's motives. Indeed, it was Bligh's own effort to explain the mutiny to the wider public that prevented it from

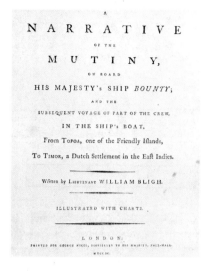

■ First Publication of Bligh's First Account of the Mutiny, Published in London, 1790. *Private collection.*

■ Pirated Dublin Version of no. I, published in 1790. *Private collection.*

■ Authorised French Account of Mutiny, Published Paris 1790. *Private collection.*

becoming merely another footnote in the history of the Royal Navy.

Bligh's *Narrative of the Mutiny on board His Majesty's Ship Bounty ; and the subsequent voyage of part of the crew in the ship's boat from Tofoa, one of the Friendly islands, to Timor, a Dutch Settlement in the East Indies* (1790) gave his version of the events from the mutiny to the successful conclusion of the open boat voyage to the Dutch East Indies. This version, it must be said, was less than candid.

In journalistic terms, Bligh had a story to tell, especially after surviving the rigours of the open boat voyage, but he also had another motive: to explain why a mutiny had occurred on his ship, and why he was unable to prevent it, or having failed to prevent it, why he, or some of the loyal men in the crew, were unable to put it down. His career, if not his pride, depended on how convincing was the explanation he gave to the Admiralty and to the wider public.

Certainly, Bligh's overt behaviour the night before the mutiny supports his later claim to have been totally surprised by it – he slept without a sentry outside his cabin; he was unarmed, having given his pistols to John Fryer, the Master; and he had not secured the key to the arm's chest, having delegated that task to Fryer, who in turn had delegated it to Joseph Coleman, the Armourer. Thus, Bligh showed that he had no idea that a mutiny threatened, because otherwise he would have taken steps to prevent it. This led him to imply, therefore, that the men who mutinied were able to do so only because they had engaged in a deeply hidden conspiracy. But this left the question: why did Christian mutiny? If Bligh swore that there was no obvious cause for the men to mutiny arising from his own behaviour as captain, he had to have a convincing alternative to account for the fact that nevertheless they had done so. He found this in the spectre of sex:

> It will very naturally be asked, what could be the reason for such a revolt? in answer to which, I can only conjecture that the mutineers had assured themselves of a more happy life amongst the Otaheiteans, than they could possibly have in England; which, joined to some female connections, have most probably been the principal cause of the whole transaction.

That there might have been a sexual motivation among some of the men who mutinied, and in some of those who were none too zealous in putting it down, is plausible, but this does not explain Christian's behaviour (nor does Bligh claim that it does – he did not allude directly to Christian's motives in the above explanation, referring instead to the motives of "the mutineers" in general). That some of the men had formed sexual attachments during their five month's stay in Tahiti is undisputed (Heywood, Stewart and Morrison, for example), as is the probability that some of the mutineers may have been seduced by their recent memories of Tahitian women into seizing the opportunity of Christian's mutiny to return to them, undeterred even by the gruesome punishments of the Articles of War for mutiny.

While not explaining Christian's behaviour, Bligh's 1790 *Narrative* provided an explanation for the mutiny that did not require, if it was accepted, further enquiry into Bligh's general conduct and fitness for command. Men regularly deserted Royal Navy ships, and not always in places as attractive as Tahiti. Some did it to escape from naval service or to avoid punishment; many for other reasons unconnected with the way they were managed by their commanding officers. The punishment, if caught, was severe – death or a heavy flogging. That seamen would run for sex and a life of plenty (however illusory in fact) was plausible and, in the absence of contrary evidence, it absolved Bligh from public ignominy. The fact that the sequel to the mutiny was the open boat voyage across the Pacific more than justified the credibility of his claims to have been a good commander who was the innocent victim of a dastardly plot by base men led by base officers. There is no doubt that this is how Bligh saw the mutiny and his role in it. He was never aware of how hurtful or destructive his manner could be to those whom he commanded, particularly those of whom he had the greatest hopes.

The impact of Bligh's *Narrative* on the reading public was considerable, and in so far as he expressed the same convincing views to the Admiralty, and to the relatives of those who had mutinied, he was assured of no repercussions on his career. But, if it was a conscious effort on his part to mislead, if only by omission, it was flawed in one key respect: that there were other survivors who had been witnesses to the transactions he had made public.

For the moment at least, Bligh's version swept all before it. His Court Martial for the loss of Bounty acquitted him of any dereliction of duty, and a grateful Sovereign had him promoted from Lieutenant to the coveted rank of Post Captain (the Admiralty having to pull some awkward procedural strings for this to take effect).

John Fryer, the Bounty's Master, was one potentially hostile witness to Bligh's version of events. He had been much criticised by Bligh during the voyage, mainly on grounds of his alleged professional misconduct Bligh's personal journal and log (preserved in the Mitchell Library, Sydney), written before the mutiny, contains numerous references to the alleged failures of the Master. None of these was made public by Bligh, nor were they included in the official Log he deposited at the Admiralty on his return (preserved in the Public Record Office, Kew). A possible explanation for these omissions lies in quarrels Bligh had with his Master abut his expense books. John Fryer, with Bligh in the open boat, was refused a copy of Bligh's log of the voyage and "therefore in my own Defence I am obliged to write the best my memory will allow me". And write he did. The fact that he wrote in his own "defence" echoes his fears that he was vulnerable to Bligh exacting professional revenge on him once the Bounty affair died down.

Fryer's account of the boat voyage was written after Bligh's *Narrative*. In it he gives a different version of the events in the open boat, largely playing-down Bligh's presentation of himself as the sole source of the success of that dangerous journey. Whatever Fryer's motives, his original manuscript account was not published until 1934, and then only as a limited edition by Owen Rutter (editor) in the Golden Cockerel Press series: *The Voyage of the Bounty's Launch, as related in William Bligh's Despatch to the Admiralty and The Journal of John Fryer*. Rutter followed this limited edition with another in the same series in 1939: *John Fryer of the Bounty: Notes on his Career Written By his Daughter Mary Ann..* In 1979 Genesis published a contemporary transcript of Fryer's original account, edited by Stephen Walters, as *The Voyage of the Bounty Launch: John Fryer's Narrative*.

Fryer's explanation for the mutiny contradicted Bligh's, "from what they [the mutineers] said I suppose they did not like their Captain". Pointedly, he also denied that Christian had a specific female friend while at Tahiti, and suggested that the treatment the boat party received when ashore at Tofoa (where John Norton was murdered) was in revenge for Bligh's treatment of some islanders at nearby Annamooka.

Fryer's 1790 manuscript made the first reference to the "coconut" incident the day before the mutiny, which suggests that all was not as tranquil on Bounty as Bligh evidently believed, or as he portrayed in his *Narrative*. There had been a row over allegations that members of the crew during the night had helped themselves to some of the coconuts which were stored on deck (it was a hot night and men may have quenched their thirst from the coconuts strewn around the deck). Bligh, in his dual role as captain and purser, intended these to be issued during the voyage as part of the crew's rations. He believed that the men had stolen some of these nuts and that the officers had either been neglectful or in collusion with the thieves. In the row that followed, Fryer states that Bligh demanded of each officer that they account for their stores of nuts and threatened the men that if the thieves were not found the yam allowance would be cut from 1 1/2 lbs to 3/4 lb day. Interestingly, Fryer, writing in 1790, only mentions one officer by name, Edward Young, midshipman, and does not mention Christian at all. Yet, in the next four years, the coconut incident came to play an increasing central role as the explanation for Christian's mutiny.

Fryer had clashed with Bligh throughout the voyage. In October 1788, after leaving Adventure Bay (in modern Tasmania) Fryer refused to sign the ship's expense books. Bligh bullied Fryer into signing the books and entered details of Fryer's act of dissent in his personal journal and log. There were other incidents between them at Tahiti before the mutiny (and Bligh recorded them, perhaps with a view to preferring charges against Fryer after the voyage). At Sourabaya, Dutch East Indies, in September 1789 after the open boat voyage, which had been occasioned by several rows between them, Fryer was again in trouble with Bligh. According to Bligh, Fryer and others had milled

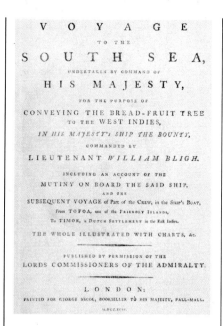

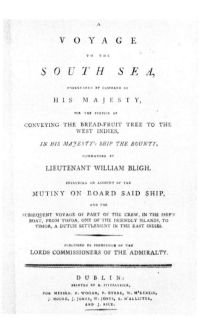

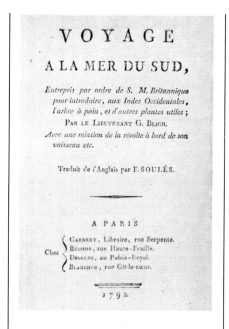

■ Bligh's Full Account, edited in his absence on HMS Providence by James Burley. *Private collection.*

■ Dublin Pirated of No 4, Published in 1792. *Private collection.*

■ Authorised French Version of No 4, published in Paris 1792. *Private collection.*

around the deck in a "tumultuous manner", and Bligh had them arrested by the Dutch authorities. If Bligh had hopes of court martialling Fryer on the serious charge of open defiance, perhaps even mutinous assembly, they were soon extinguished in this mysterious incident. Bligh fully reported his version of what happened, including details of Fryer's gross insubordination, in his personal journal and log, but in the official log, presented to the Aduralty, he made no reference to the "tumult" at Sourabaya, merely providing a description of the Dutch settlement as "one of the most pleasant places I ever saw".

Bluntly, Fryer claimed he had evidence that Bligh had fiddled his expenses at Coupang in Timor (as with the expense books at Adventure Bay?). He reported his evidence to the Dutch officials who passed on to Bligh the substance of Fryer's charges. These included a list of the prices Bligh claimed to have paid to Dutch merchants for subsistence and the fitting out of the vessel he had purchased, and what Fryer claimed was the actual price list for these same items given to Fryer by the Dutch authorities at Coupang (it is possible that the merchants reported to the authorities lower prices than they charged Bligh to avoid the local sales tax, thus causing a discrepancy). Bligh certainly fumed about his "honour" and berated the Dutch to see the "villiany" of Fryer in trying to entrap his commanding officer. Negotia-

tions continued, however, and the outcome was that Fryer apologized in writing to Bligh. But the apology has to be set beside the fact that Bligh did not make any charges against Fryer at the Court Martial for the loss of the Bounty, and exercized his prerogative to refrain from making any negative references to Fryer in the official log. Whatever he agreed with Fryer (under the duress of the evidence against him, or because he was advized that it would be unseemly to court martial his second-in-command?), he court martialled William Purcell, the irascible ship's carpenter, with whom he had clashed on numerous occasions (the court found the charges in part proved and reprimanded him). However, Fryer, in return perhaps for Bligh's restraint, or because it would damage his career, did not raise any criticism of Bligh when invited to do so by the Court Martial.

While both men stuck to their alleged agreement in respect of the Court Martial, they certainly did not do more than this. Bligh refused Fryer a reference when Captain Riou asked him for one in 1790, and Fryer, while refraining from public criticism of Bligh, not only wrote his journal for private circulation in 1790 (smarting from Bligh's refusal of a reference?) but also collaborated extensively with Professor Edward Christian (Fletcher's brother) in 1794 to make public certain aspects of Bligh's style of command of Bounty in general and his treatment of Fletcher Christian in particular.

Meanwhile, Bligh had left on his second Breadfruit voyage in HMS Providence, and had handed over the editing of a fuller version of the Bounty voyage to his friend, Captain, later Admiral James Burney. This appeared in 1792 as: *A Voyage to the South Seas, undertaken by command of His Majesty, for the purpose of Conveying the Bread-Fruit Tree to the West Indies, in His Majesty's Ship the Bounty, commanded by Lieutenant William Bligh.* This gave an account of the voyage prior to the mutiny and repeated the 1790 account of the mutiny from the *Narrative.* Like its predecessor, the *Voyage* has been published many times, including facsimiles of the original 1794 edition (for example one was published by Hutchinson in Australia in 1979) plus numerous paperback editions. Closely following the official versions of Bounty's log, the *Voyage* contains a great deal of interesting material on the customs and culture of the Tahitians. This has given Bligh a reputation as a contributor to the social anthropology of the unique cultures of Tahitian society at the time of their first contacts with Europeans (a role also accorded to James Morrison, Boatswain's Mate, from the accounts he gave in his *Journal* from his long stay on Tahiti after the mutiny). But if Bligh had hopes that the mutiny would fade into the background and that he would continue with his career as a navigator in the steps of Captain James Cook, he was to be sadly disappointed on his return to Britain in 1793.

■ The Crew of HMS Bounty landing at Otaheite, 19th century Engraving. *Private collection.*

In Bligh's absence, the Royal Navy had captured the survivors of Christian's party who had been left behind in Tahiti in 1789, and had brought them home for trial (less the four who drowned in the sinking of HMS Pandora in 1791). Whatever crimes the men had committed they were entitled to a fair trial from the Admiralty, and they could rely on the firm support of their families irrespective of their guilt or innocence. That some of the men had more influence than others, and had greater family resources at their disposal to see that a conviction was made more difficult, only reflects the social structure of the 18th century. With some of the mutineers still at large, including the leader, Fletcher Christian, there was also the possibility that the precedents set at this first trial might be applied at a second, or third, trial should other mutineers be captured. Full details of the trial, including transcripts of the evidence for the prosecution and the defence, were published in 1931 by Owen Rutter (editor), *The Court-Martial of the "Bounty Mutineers"*, in the Notable British Trials series.

The prosecution had Bligh's sworn testimonies, the evidence of the Court Martial of Bligh and the men who returned with him, and the evidence of those who had returned and who were still in England in 1793. Bligh was not expected back until 1794. The defence could either press to postpone the Court Martial until Bligh returned, or press for its early opening before he did so. Which to favour depended on what view was taken of Bligh's likely stance on the guilt or innocence of individuals. He had cleared four men – Joseph Coleman, Armourer; Thomas McIntosh, carpenter's mate; Charles Norman, carpenter's mate; and Michael Byrne, seaman (actually a semiblind fiddler) – of complicity in the mutiny, in his logs and in his publications. They were safe with Bligh's testimony and might have preferred a postponement. Others were less certain of their fate. By implication, all others left on board were mutineers, but some of them, such as Peter Heywood and James Morrison, had hopes of a defence that they were held on board against their will.

James Morrison, boatswain's mate, was a man of more than average intelligence and scholarly inclination. He had been a midshipman for a short period before joining Bounty as Boatswain's Mate. His position on board in no way reflected his abilities and he set these abilities to work to save his life and to expose Bligh's unfitness for command. His literary contributions to the Bounty story are preserved in the Mitchell Library, Sydney, and consist of two manuscripts, one entitled '*Memorandums and Particulars respecting the Bounty and her Crew*' and the other, known as,'*Morrison's Journal*' The *Memorandums* manuscript is a copy of the original (now lost) and was presented to the Mitchell Library by one of Bligh's descendants. It was written by Morrison during his confinement with the other prisoners on HMS Hector during September – October 1792. It consists of a short critical account of life on Bounty under Bligh, plus a sharp criticism, in the form of an open letter, of his life as a prisoner on Pandora, and afterwards, under Captain Edward Edwards (an altogether more ferocious disciplinarian than Bligh). The *Journal* is a more ambitious project, consisting of 382 pages in Morrison's own handwriting, giving a full account of the voyage under Bligh, the mutiny, and the aftermath, first under Christian and then in Tahiti while awaiting the Royal Navy's inevitable search for the mutineers. It was written after Morrison's release (he had been pardoned for mutiny by the King on the court's recommendation) during November 1792 and early spring 1793. Originally it had a Tahitian vocabulary (possibly compiled by Peter Heywood) attached, but this is now lost.

The *Memorandums* manuscript was circulated among influential public figures after the trial and conviction of the mutineers in September 1792. Its purpose was to secure a pardon for Morrison and Heywood, and perhaps a commutation of the death sentences for the others. While no excuse was possible for mutiny – a man could be convicted for failing to overthrow a mutiny – Morrison intended to show that the man responsible for the mutiny occurring, and, by his earlier conduct, failing to inspire anybody to overthrow it once it had begun, was Lieutenant William Bligh. He did this by reporting incidents that showed that Bligh was a bad commander: alleged misuse of his powers as purser (poor food, fiddled accounts, small rations, theft of some cheese); of having numerous rows with his officers (he details the public dissent of Fryer over the signing of the expense books, his quarrels with Purcell, his dispute with Christian at Annamooka and his row about the coconuts the day before the mutiny). In short, he presents a different picture of the voyage from the one in Bligh's *Narrative* and *Voyage*.

That this helped to influence the court is seen in its recommendation of Heywood and Morrison for pardon (though this recommendation was not unconnected with the fact that Heywood had a relative by marriage, Captain Albermarle Bertie, among the officers of the court and could draw on men of considerable influence, such as Commodore Pasley to speak informally to the other members and to the Admiralty, as well as having inherited a sizeable fortune while

a prisoner). These efforts, verbally and in writing, plus the evidence that emerged in the trial itself certainly turned official opinion against Bligh, not least because it exposed his own publications, which detail the many innovative and humane changes he made to the management of a ship on a voyage of discovery, to the charge that they were in error, at the very least by omission, and, more damagingly, perhaps also by deceit.

Sir Joseph Banks, the leading botanist and influential friend of the King, read Morrison's *Memorandums* and passed a copy to Bligh, on his return, for his comments. These Bligh made in a number of letters to Banks (some of which with some detailed notes are preserved in the Mitchell Library under *Remarks on Morrison's Journal*. These were published in 1937 as a limited edition by Owen Rutter (editor) in the Golden Cockerel Press series: *Bligh's Voyage in the Resource and his Remarks on Morrison's Journal*. Bligh survived Morrison's criticisms, largely because they had such a restricted circulation at the time, and because his defence of his conduct to Sir Joseph Banks and others, in naval disciplinary terms, was robust. The *Memorandums* circulated for a short while, but were not published and Morrison's larger *Journal* remained almost unknown except to a few people, largely missionaries, whose interest was confined to the information about Tahiti and its customs and language, rather than to the events on Bounty. However, some of the criticisms of Bligh in Morrison's manuscripts appeared in 1820–21 (Bligh died in 1817) in the *Sailor's Magazine and Naval Miscellany* , under the title: 'The Authentic history of the mutineers of the Bounty'.

By the 1820s, Peter Heywood had possession of Morrison's Journal (how he acquired it is not known) and its contents were gradually revealed in a number of publications. In 1825, a biography of Captain Peter Heywood was published in John Marshall's (editor) *Royal Naval Biography or, Memories of the Services of all the Flag Officers, Superannuated Rear-Admirals, Retired Captains, Post-Captains, and Commanders, Whose Names appeared on the Admiralty List of Sea Officers at the commencement of the present year, or who have since been promoted.* (1823–35). Heywood's entry contains detailed extracts from Morrison's manuscripts and acknowledges

their source. In 1831, Sir John Barrow (Secretary to the Admiralty), using papers provided by Heywood, was the anonymous author of *The Mutiny and Piratical Seizure of HMS Bounty: its Cause and Consequences*, which included more extracts from Morrison's manuscripts and gave them a wide circulation. Barrow's book, since republished in numerous editions, is perhaps the fairest account of what happened (the Folio Society) In 1870, Lady Belcher, Peter Heywood's step-daughter, and the estranged wife of Admiral Sir Edward Belcher (she had accused him of giving her VD on her wedding night and of submitting her to other indignities) published *The Mutineers of the Bounty and their Descendants in Pitcairn and Norfolk Islands*. This included extracts from Morrison's *Journal*, then in her possession. Lady Belcher not only made Morrison's account of the mutiny and his views on who caused it, widely available in her own book (which was also published in the United States) she also lent Morrison's manuscript to William Fletcher, who used to give a public lecture ('Fletcher Christian and the Mutineers of the "Bounty"', in *Transactions of the Cumberland Association for the Advancement of Literature and Science, Part II, 1876–77*, Carlisle) to an audience in Christian's home town of Cockermouth. Thus, within 80 years of Morrison writing his version of the affair, his views were well known to anybody interested in the Bounty.

It was not, however, until Owen Rutter edited a limited edition of Morrison's Journal in 1935 in the Golden Cockerel Press series *(The Journal of James Morrison, Boatswain's Mate of the Bounty, Describing the Mutiny & Subsequent Misfortunes of the Mutineers, Together with an Account, of the Island of Tahiti)* that Morrison's story was published in full.

While Morrison's manuscripts failed to become widely known until long after his death in 1807, and then largely due to the efforts of his friend, Peter Heywood between 1825 and 1831 (Heywood died in 1831), the substance of his version of events on Bounty were of immediate interest to Christian's family (who naturally sought information about the fate of their relative and what had caused him to mutiny). Peter Heywood's family were friends of Fletcher Christian's family, both sets living in the

Isle of Man at the time of Bounty's departure for Tahiti. Both families also shared the experience of suffering a sudden financial crisis. In Heywood's case, his father had lost a well-paid post just before Bligh was collecting his crew for the Bounty voyage. Bligh responded to requests from Heywood's family to take the young boy with him (Bligh's wife, Elizabeth Betham, also from the Isle of Man knew the Heywoods). Fletcher Christian's case was more severe and ultimately might provide the full explanation for his emotional outburst that fateful morning. His mother had lost her family's fortune largely through ill-advised investments and had been forced to leave Cockermouth for the Isle of Man to escape pestering creditors. She also had to terminate the costly education of two of her sons, Charles and Fletcher, and send them prematurely out into the world to earn their living. Charles went to sea as a surgeon with the East India Company (during which voyage he mutinied against the "tyranny" of his captain) and Fletcher, the youngest, was sent to sea first as a midshipman in the Royal Navy (he completed one voyage) and then as a "young gentleman" with Bligh in the merchant service. What degree of resentment Fletcher felt at the interruption to his career, and at his elder brother Edward (who had completed his expensive education before the crisis) we cannot but conjecture. In my view, his disenchantment with his future, and his realization of his unsuitability for life as a naval officer, played some part in his rash decision to mutiny over a row with his captain, instead of following Fryer's advice to suffer in silence on these occasions.

When Heywood was released after his royal pardon, he immediately contacted Fletcher's brother, Edward, who was a professor of law. Edward Christian was an intelligent man. He knew that there was no point in trying to exonerate his brother. Three men had hanged for participating in a mutiny led by his brother, who would have no defence, if he was captured, whatever the behaviour of his captain. Unable to save his brother's life, he could, however, save his reputation. To do this he had to undo Bligh's. He did this, using a brilliant

■ The Mutineers seize Captain Bligh, 19th century broadsheet Engraving. *Private collection.*

device. Christian invited individual Bounty men to meet him and be questioned. To demonstrate the truth of what he reported, without having to disclose what he left out, he arranged for at least one other gentleman, sometimes more than one, to be in attendance. These gentlemen were named by Christian, and an impressive list they make too. However, he was less than candid in explaining their relationships with him and his brother. Those whose relationships can be identified turn out to have close local, family, or political ties with Edward Christian. Their politics show them to be radicals, much impressed with the early phases of the French Revolution (full details are given in C S Wilkinson, *The Wake of the Bounty,* 1953 this is the best source for material on the alleged escape of Fletcher Christian from Pitcairn and his return to Cumberland). Edward Christian had not set up an independent tribunal; it was a legal snare for Bligh, but one into which he did not fall.

Christian's report of his conversations was published as an Appendix to the prosecution minutes of the Court-Martial of the mutineers taken down by Stephen Barney: *Minutes of the Proceedings of the Court-Martial held at Portsmouth August 12 [sic] 1792 on ten persons charged with mutiny on board His Majesty's Ship Bounty,* London, 1794. The text of Barney's minutes, its Appendix by Edward Christian and Bligh's reply, were published in the Everyman's Library series in 1938, and reprinted in 1981, edited by George Mackaness, as: *A Book of the 'Bounty': William Bligh and others*

It was the *Appendix* which caused the stir. In it are detailed pages of criticism of Bligh's style of command and of the opinions of the crew (not always named) regarding Fletcher Christian. John Fryer and William Purcell feature in it more often than anybody else who is named, and they made good witnesses. Fryer, as Master, the senior officer after Bligh, makes telling points about how Fletcher conducted himself the night before the mutiny. Five years after the event, the coconut incident has assumed a central role in the final collapse of Fletcher Christian into mutiny. Fryer and Purcell testify how badly Fletcher Christian took Bligh's accusations that the officers had colluded with the thieves of the ship's nuts. Interestingly, in the *Appendix* it is Fletcher who is the man

143

singled out for Bligh's abuse and not Edward Young, as Fryer first reported in 1790. The extraordinary drama of Christian planning to jump overboard with some planks and swim 30 miles to the the nearest island, Tofoa, becomes public for the first time; as do the events on Tubuai, where Christian first tried to make a settlement. This is portrayed in an exceedingly bland light when it fact it was a bloody mess from start to finish. Christian's party murdered several score of islanders, and abducted and raped various women (behaviour which repeated in the smaller community in Pitcairn cost Christian and the others their lives).

The *Appendix* contained a serious embarrassment for Heywood – its disclosure of midshipman George Stewart's role in suggesting to Christian that it was possible for him to seize the ship, rather than commit suicide by jumping over the side ("When you go, Christian, we are ripe for anything", p.71). Heywood's defence at his Court Martial rested entirely on his claim that he and Stewart were kept below by the mutineers against their will, and that Bligh, unaware of this circumstance, had misunderstood their absence from his side. Now, if Stewart had in any way suggested to Christian anything at all that could be construed as an incitement to mutiny, then this made risible the notion of Heywood and Stewart as gallant loyalists. Years later, when Captain Beechey visited Pitcairn and interviewed John Adams, he too received this damning version of Stewart's role, and he wrote to Heywood in 1830 asking for his comments on the contradiction between Adam's story and Heywood's own in his 1825 biography. Heywood denied the claims of Adams (reported in Sir John Barrow's account). Yet the record shows that not only did Adams claim in 1825 this to be Stewart's true role, but so did the Bounty men interviewed by Edward Christian in 1792–4, and also James Morrison in his *Journal* of 1792–3. Morrison went further and claimed that Christian had also told "Hayward", which was clearly a reference to Heywood, as Christian was not talking to, let alone confiding in, Hayward at that moment (the two names were often misspelt in the manuscripts). Apparently, Bligh was not the only Bounty man given to economizing with the truth.

Bligh, however, comes out very badly in the *Appendix*. Whatever follies Christian had committed, Bligh is shown

to have been ultimately responsible for them because of his bullying of Christian. Far from the mutiny being the conspiracy that Bligh made it out to be, or of it being motivated by the lure of Tahiti, the mutiny is seen to be the result of one man breaking another's sense of duty through personal insults and provocations beyond the latter's capacity to endure. That this view says nothing about Christian's emotional state as a result of his personal reactions to his family circumstances, nor anything about whether it was reasonable for a man aspiring to be a First Lieutenant in the Royal Navy to crack under his captain's pressure to lick him into shape, is of little comfort to Bligh's reputation. This particular man did crack under this particular captain's pressure, and as far as Edward Christian was concerned it explained, without necessarily justifying, what had happened.

On his return from the successful voyage of Providence and Assistant, which completed the bread-fruit voyage interrupted by the mutiny on Bounty, Bligh was forced to reconsider his career prospects. Edward Christian had used much of the time between receiving Heywood's letter praising Fletcher and meeting other members of the Bounty and Bligh's return to lobby against Bligh (he contacted Sir Joseph Banks, for example). The Court Martial had also led to the Admiralty reappraising Bligh's future as a commander (though, given the Post-Captain system, with everybody's progress dependent solely on the attrition rate of those above them, it is not surprising that others would encourage a removal of Bligh from the list, if that would make way for them, or for their protégés).

Bligh felt the cold on his return and set about to reply to the *Appendix*. This duly appeared in *An Answer to Certain Assertions contained in the Appendix to a Pamphlet ...* , London, 1795 (also contained in the Everyman's Library edition of 1981). It was not a full and decisive reply to the *Appendix*. Bligh seemed to assume that all he needed to do was to produce other documents showing contradictions in the moral standards of some of his critics and to imply that Edward Christian, as the brother of a mutineer, was an unreliable witness of what persons unknown, or unidentified, asserted about their commander. Bligh was a career naval officer who saw his duty as carrying out his King' and the

Admiralty's commissions and as such was not given to justifying himself to subordinates, disaffected or otherwise. The Admiralty wanted the bread-fruit transplanted from Tahiti to Jamaica and it was his duty, and that of everybody on board Bounty, to comply with that request. Any man who failed to carry out his duty was, in Bligh's view, beyond the pale and not worthy of a hearing on any complaints he might have about his officers. Thus, while we can see why Bligh approached the task of his *Answer* in the way he did, we must conclude that he missed an opportunity of ensuring his reputation in posterity. Certainly, Edward Christian felt that he had won the contest, for he published *A Short Reply to Capt. William Bligh's Answer* (1795).

Bligh has had a number of biographers, of which two should be mentioned here as being head and shoulders above the rest. Owen Rutter has been mentioned several times in connection with making available key documents relating to the Bounty story in the 1930s. He also wrote a perceptive biography of Bligh in 1936: *Turbulent Journey: A Life of William Bligh, Vice-Admiral of the Blue* Long out of print, Rutter's assessment of the issues involved in the mutiny remain close to the good order and discipline view: at stake is the issue of *duty*. In so far as men have difficult, even tyrannical, commanders, the good of the service and in the ultimate the defence of the realm depend on their unquestioning professional obedience. Legalistically, Rutter comes down on the side of Bligh as a commander and places Bligh's personality in the context of his "turbulent" career.

The Australian historian, Dr George Mackaness, published the first serious biography of Bligh in 1931 (two volumes): *The Life of Vice-Admiral William Bligh, RN, FRS*. A revized one-volume edition also appeared in 1951. Mackaness was undoubtedly the leading scholar on Bligh and the Bounty mutiny throughout his life. As an historian, Mackaness brought the skills of his profession to bear on what was, and remains, a historial topic of wide public interest. Using the original materials available in the Mitchell Library, Sydney, and several collections held by Bligh's descendants, Mackaness put together the first scholarly biography of the man at the centre of the Bounty controversy. He quotes extensively from Morrison's manuscripts and the large Bligh and

■ Mutiny On The Bounty, 19th century frontispiece. Drawn by Dickens' illustrator, Phiz. *Private collection.*

Banks correspondence that has survived. Since 1931, much more material has come to light; indeed, Mackaness was instrumental in making available new key documents, in particular, the important manuscripts of Lieutenant Francis Godolphin Bond (Bligh's relative and his First Lieutenant on HMS Providence).

Like many other writers on Bligh (for example, Dr H V Evatt: *Rum Rebellion: a study of the overthrow of Governor Bligh by John Macarthur and the New South Wales Corps,)* Mackaness was also caught up in historical debates about Bligh's role as a governor of New South Wales in 1808–10 and, incredibly, what it meant for modern Australians in the 1930s (there was a political controversy about the Governor's powers in New South Wales at the time), and this tended to colour his, and his critics', judgments about Bligh as the commander of Bounty 1787–89. The issues in these disputes over Bligh's role as a colonial governor rumbled on well into the 1950s,

and unfortunately became very acrimonious and bitterly personal. A flavour of the debate can be leaned from reading M H Ellis's biography: *John Macarthur* (1955), which takes a polar opposite view on the overthrow of Bligh to that of Evatt and Mackaness. Recently, the National Library of Australia published Bartrum's minutes of George Johnston's Court-Martial in 1811. Edited by John Ritchie, *A Charge of Mutiny: The Court-Martial of Lieutenant Colonel George Johnston for deposing Governor William Bligh in the Rebellion of 26 January l808* (Canberra 1988), gives a clear account of what happened in the 1808 rebellion and why (and who – John Macarthur – was behind it all) by presenting verbatim the evidence of prosecution and defence.

Turning to the contemporary debate about the mutiny, it is necessary to consider the scholarly studies of Rolf Du Rietz of Uppsala in Sweden. Du Rietz has taken over from Mackaness as the leading scholar on Bligh and the Bounty, and, in a series of monographs and articles published since 1962, he has done a great deal of analytical work on the

mutiny and the original manuscripts and contemporary accounts. His more important studies have been published in two series of papers (unfortunately, so far, in limited editions only). The first was *Studia Bountyana,* published in 1965 and 1966. They were occasioned by Madge Darby's *Who Caused the Mutiny on the 'Bounty'?* (Angus and Robertson, Sydney, 1965), which put forward a psychological explanation for the breakdown of the earlier good relationship that there had been between Bligh and Christian. Darby argued that Christian's mutiny was not explained by Bligh's intolerable conduct as a harsh disciplinarian but by some Freudian defect, even a frustrated or guilty homsexuality in Christian. She also argued that midshipman Edward Young was the decisive influence in the crucial moments of the mutiny. Apart from the reference to Young in Fryer's *Journal,* he is totally ignored in all other accounts, and Darby found his role more sinister on this score alone. (Certainly there is cause for grave suspicions about Young's role in the bloody massacres on Pitcairn, as there is for the last survivor, John Adams).

Du Rietz did not agree that the mutiny needed an explanation of this kind, and he launched a thorough, often ill-tempered, polemic (which is his style) against Darby's theses: *The Causes of the Bounty Mutiny: some comments on a book by Madge Darby (Studia Bountyana,* vol 1). The Du Rietz thesis on the mutiny, which he bases on his unrivaled knowledge of the historical evidence (he is a professional bibliophile), is that it is fully explained by Bligh's conduct; in short, Bligh drove Christian to mutiny. His most telling point is to compare the effect on Christian of Bligh's style of behaviour as commander of Bounty, with its effect on Lieutenant Bond on Providence. Bond was Bligh's step-sister's son and sailed on Providence in the same role as Christian sailed on Bounty. From a experimental viewpoint, what greater fortune could a historian have: two closely related events in which the object of the experiment is served by a change in the critical variable the captain's subordinate, and observing the reaction of each to the same influence, Bligh's conduct.

Bond's reaction to his relative's style of command had been made public by George Mackaness in two small papers published 1953 and 1960 respec-

tively (*Fresh Light on Bligh: being some unpublished correspondence of Captain William Bligh, RN., and Lieutenant Francis Godolphin Bond, RN. with Lieutenant Bond's manuscript notes made on the voyage of HMS "Providence," 1791–1795*, and "Extracts from a log-book of HMS 'Providence' kept by Lieut. Francis Goldolphin Bond, RN ...", *Journal and Preeceedings of the Royal Australian Historical Society,* 1960. In Du Rietz's view, Bond corroborates the evidence of Bligh's tyrannical behaviour given in Fryer's *Journal*, Morrison's *Memorandums* and *Journal*, Edward Christian's *Appendix* and Heywood's entry in Marshall's biographies. Bond's criticism of Bligh bears on his general behaviour: "imperious", "want of modesty", an "ungovernable temper", "envy and jealousy" and "unparalleled pride". Bligh exposed Bond's alleged deficiencies as a navigator in public, demanded he attend to his duty rather than compose a journal of the voyage, kept him on duty watch, demanded he be acquainted with every transaction on board, and to check with him every order he was about to issue. The list of complaints is as extensive as it is repetitive: in short, Bond was driven hard by Bligh and he resented it. Unlike Christian, he did not mutiny. Du Rietz is convinced that this solves the so-called problem of the mutiny: Bligh caused it.

Darby was by no means convinced by Du Rietz and she replied in *Studia Bountyana* 2: *The Causes of the Bounty mutiny: a short reply to Mr Rolf Du Rietz's comments* (1966). She quotes Bligh's extremely good personal and professional relations with Lieutenant Portlock, captain of the Assistant, sister ship of Providence on the voyage, and a comment from Lieutenant George Tobin, third lieutenant of Providence: "For myself I feel I am indebted to [Bligh]. It was the first ship in which I ever served as an Officer – I joined full of apprehension – I soon thought that he was not dissatisfied with me – it gave me encouragement and on the whole we journeyed smoothly. Once or twice indeed I felt the unbridled licence of his power of speech – Yet never without soon receiving something like an emollient plaister to heal the wound." She also quotes from others to show that Bligh's foul language was by no means unusual among officers at the time (though it might still have shocked the unworldly Christian).

The second set of monographs written by Du Rietz consist of three volumes in his *Banksia* series. Again they are polemical, but as always Du Rietz also contributes important material from the historical records on the Bounty men. His *Thoughts on the Present State of Bligh Scholarship (Banksia 1)* set out an historian's methodology for coping with the issues raised by the Bounty mutiny and was extremely critical of my own approach in *Bligh*. (1978). *Banksia 2: Fresh Light on John Fryer of the 'Bounty'*, and *Banksia 3, Peter Heywood's Tahitian Vocabulary and the Narratives by James Morrison: some notes on their*

■ Portrait of Bligh in Captain's uniform in later life. *Private collection.*

origin and history, make significant contributions to the history of the manuscripts and views of these important witnesses to the mutiny, and show where a lot of Bounty authors have made wrong inferences from wrong facts in the past It would be a fair summary of Du Rietz's work to say that he has demolished the image of Bligh as portrayed by himself in his two books and as developed by other authors since, without (only just) going over the top and condemning Bligh altogether out of sight. Compare this approach with Alexander McKee in his *The Truth About the Mutiny on the Bounty* (1961), in which he portrays Bligh as an unprincipled swindler and liar. Du Rietz's approach can be seen in Bengt Danielsson's *What Happened on the Bounty* (1962) (to which Du Rietz contributed a lot of the material), while

Danielsson added a lot of information about Tahitian society at the time of Bligh's visits.

Where does the historical record leave Bligh and the men of the Bounty? In one sense, not very much closer to the truth than was known (or accepted) in the years immediately after the mutiny. We know how some of the men involved saw the event and how they rated the principal figures involved. While Christian has left nothing in writing for historians to argue over, his views on what happened have been reported in detail by Morrison. Fryer's assessment of what happened is also available. None of the men whose views have so far been discovered has any doubts about who caused the mutiny: universally they blame Bligh. Their assessments, of course, have nothing in common with the imaginative presentations of scriptwriters and film makers.

Bounty was not a happy ship, but not because of a physical tyranny by a stereotyped 18th century commanding officer – Bligh was never a flogger in any sense that would enrage an 18th century ship's crew. Nor did Bligh overstep the norm as a nagging officer. The Royal Navy had far worse martinets than Bligh, and many more who did not have any of his redeeming features. But Bligh did overstep the mark with Fletcher Christian – it was not Bligh crushing, so much as Christian crumbling, that brought things to a head. More than one seaman has deserted, even committed suicide, sometimes simply by disappearing over the side, because he could not take the petty bullying or constant mockery of a shipmate. Men in close confinement on long voyages were faced with intense psychological stresses hardly understood today, let alone in the 18th century (the incidence of sea-borne insanity was put down to the men banging their heads on the low beams). That Christian was highly stressed (Morrison thought him insane on one occasion) is beyond historical doubt. That he contemplated jumping overboard and becoming a statistic – "man lost at sea" – is also beyond doubt (in which case hardly anybody would have heard of HMS Bounty). But he did not go through with his plan (as, perhaps, many other young men facing similar stresses decide as their fury cools). Instead, he set about arranging his seizure of the ship. The rest, as they say, is history, but none the less mysterious and rivetting for that.

Film-makers and Bounty

You have read the books, now see the films. Glynn Christian finds too much of Hollywood and not enough truth

THE BOUNTY story has been a godsend to entrepreneurs from the day Bligh landed at the Isle of Wight and first told the story. That was 14 March 1790, and with the undue haste that scandal excites in the Thespian world, London's Royalty Theatre speedily dramatized the events with The Pirates or The Calamities of Captain Bligh. Right there on stage you could wonder at Bounty sailing down the Thames, thrill to an Otahetian Dance, watch the seizure of Bligh, share the distress of the boat at sea, celebrate its miraculous arrival and friendly reception. The dramatic licence we expect from movies clearly has its roots in the stage. Those latter scenes were actually set at the Cape of Good Hope (which would indeed have been an open-boat journey) and thus the final tableaux were of Hottentot departure ceremonies. The Bill of Players, stuffed with superlatives and bursting with promises, ended with a guarantee that the drama was "rehearsed under the immediate Instruction of a Person who was onboard the Bounty, Store-Ship". A short time later, a Parisian company went the whole hog and set the entire spectacle to music. At the time the French felt they had some prior claim to Tahiti and things Polynesian.

There was a small number of theatrical productions during the 19th century, but the avalanche of pamphlets and good works thrust down the missionary-dominated throats of Victorian society was enough of a good thing. It was not until the 20th century that media other than the

"Outstanding" reviews for the "Spectacular" 1962 film Mutiny on the Bounty. *Private collection.*

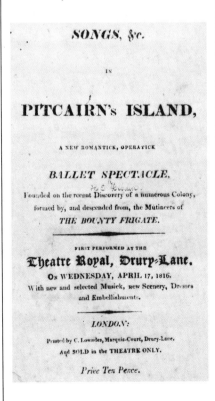

Song sheet sold at the Theatre Royal, London. *Private Collection.*

printed page turned again to the story. It was moving picture time, and from the start the mutiny was associated with firsts. Most astonishingly, the first film which springs to the mind of my generation, that starring Laughton and Gable, is not the first Bounty based film. Those honours are held by an Australian production: two in fact. Then in 1930 the Chauvels followed, and made Australia's first full-length feature film with sound. *In the Wake of the Bounty* was made as a pioneering drama documentary, essentially concentrating on the contemporary life of the Bounty descendants on Pitcairn Island. It is almost impossible to conceive the problems experienced by the Chauvels as they humped the huge sound and camera equipment of the time to Tahiti and then to Pitcairn Island. The film is gorgeously archaic and sentimental, hauntingly lit as only old black and white movies seem able. But there is much more of interest to the film buff than pictorial quality. Interspersed with the documentary footage are dramatised scenes of the mutiny and of early life on Pitcairn Island. In another first, the Chauvels cast a swashbuckling young Tasmanian as Fletcher Christian – Errol Flynn. Complete with colonial

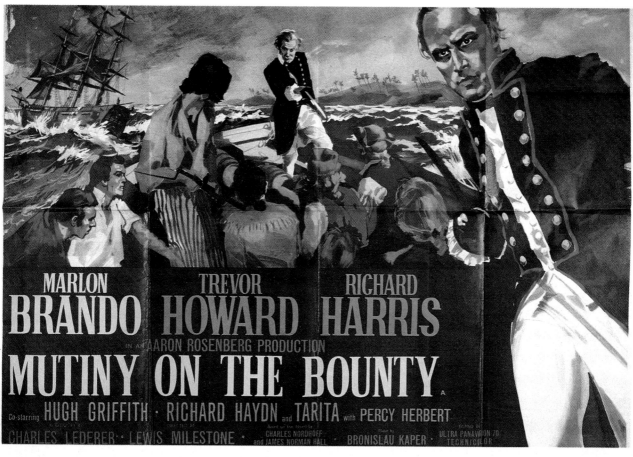

■ Far Left Theatre Royal poster announcing the new production of 'Pitcairn's Island'. *Private collection.*

■ Left Charles Laughton as Bligh in the 1936 MGM film. *Kobal collection.*

■ Right "The Greatest Adventure ever lived becomes the Greatest Adventure ever filmed.". *Private collection.*

accent, Flynn is said specially to have enjoyed the role, for his mother's family claimed descent from the mutineers.

The film was shown for just a few weeks in a number of Australian capital cities and then bought lock stock and barrel, by MGM. They scuppered Flynn's new career by excizing all his scenes and using the documentary portion as pre-publicity for their Laughton Gable production. The full version has thus never been seen in the Northern Hemisphere, but because television did not exist when the original was bought and not included in the contract, it has been seen on television in Sydney and it is available for telecasting internationally.

The famous Laughton – Gable film, released by MGM in 1936, has never been bettered for drama, but in the greatest of Hollywood traditions it is far from the truth. The infamous keel-hauling scene could never have happened, as it had long been banned by the time Bounty sailed – indeed if Bligh were really as tough as this film made out, there might not have bean a mutiny. Bligh ruled by tongue not lash: the reverse may well have served him better. Gable's charm in this film was ... well, Gable, and I am sure that if Christian's social abilities were remotely like this lots of men would have followed him anywhere. Essentially though, this is a film *based* on the story and not *of* it. The inclusion of Christian's father in the last scenes (when he had died in 1768) is indicative of its underlying "inventiveness". But who cares ... it is a great and entertaining movie, made on and off Santa Catalina.

■ Left One of the many posters advertising the 1962 'Brando' film. *Private collection.*

■ Right A still from a dramatic moment in the 1962 film. *Private collection.*

MEL GIBSON · ANTHONY HOPKINS

THE BOUNTY

After 200 years, the truth behind the legend.

DINO DE LAURENTIIS PRESENTS
MEL GIBSON ANTHONY HOPKINS
"THE BOUNTY" ALSO STARRING EDWARD FOX LAURENCE OLIVIER AS ADMIRAL HOOD

Unis dans la tourmente. Ennemis au paradis.

MEL GIBSON ANTHONY HOPKINS

LE BOUNTY

200 ans après, enfin la vérité

DINO De Laurentiis PRÉSENTE
MEL GIBSON - ANTHONY HOPKINS
"LE BOUNTY" avec EDWARD FOX - LAURENCE OLIVIER
Musique composée et dirigée par VANGELIS Scénario de ROBERT BOLT
D'après le roman "CAPTAIN BLIGH AND M. CHRISTIAN" de RICHARD HOUGH
Produit par BERNARD WILLIAMS Réalisé par ROGER DONALDSON

Produced by BERNARD WILLIAMS
Directed by ROGER DONALDSON

Distributed by Columbia-EMI-Warner Distributors

ON · ANTHONY HO

BOUN

THEY BEGAN
THEIR EPIC VOYAGE
AS FRIENDS......IT
ENDED IN HATRED
AND BLOODSHED.

NS

TY 15

AFTER 200 YEARS,
THE TRUTH BEHIND
THE LEGEND

The Brando – Howard version of the early 1960s has the twin advantages of colour, and spectacular Tahitian and Moorean scenery. What it lacked was a script, and thus the production and the 178 minutes of the final film dragged an a bit. The fay character Marlon Brando made Fletcher Christian to be was possibly close to some of the truth, but this screen toughie did not fully explore the great physical strength for which Christian was famed, or reveal the revolutionary thinking that saw him run Bounty by committee decision. It is a half portrait and Brando's screen death, blistered and mumbling while Bounty burned was a catastrophe, at least it was for me – even good friends believed that because they had seen it in the movies it must be true, and I could not possibly be descended from this man. Christian had two sons, Thursday October and Charles, and a single daughter who remained unmarried. She was first celebrated as the Maid of the South Seas, then died a crabby old maid and was buried on Norfolk Island. Brando married his co-star Tarita, bought a Polynesian paradise island, and called a son Christian. The gravelled crabbiness of Trevor Howard and his vituperative delivery was never balanced with a view of Bligh's exceptional talents. He was far too old for the part, and the wrong colouring too.

The latest feature film starring Anthony Hopkins and Mel Gibson has much to say for it, though its claim to be telling the truth for the first time was off the mark. The ages of the men playing Bligh and Christian were indeed closer to the truth, but not that much. The Bounty replica built in Whangarei, New Zealand. is a pretty exact exterior copy, whereas Brando's version was about 20ft longer than the original (you can visit it in St Petersburg Florida; the NZ ship sails from Sydney, New South Wales with paying passengers and is visiting Pitcairn Island in 1990 to celebrate the community's bicentenary commanded by Lt. Commander Gerrie Christian, RAN, another descendant). This production used Rarotonga for location work, believing it looked more like Tahiti than Tahiti. That is probably true, too, but that is about it. Otherwise, the film fairly and squarely struck a bullseye by evenly insulting everyone, Bligh, Christian, the Admiralty,

■ A selection of posters advertizing the more accurate 1983 film.
Private collection.

151

■ A still from the 1983 film, perhaps the most accurate and spectacular so far. *Private collection.*

the crew – especially the Tahitians. The idea that Bligh finally brought the mutiny on himself by wanting to sail back via Cape Horn is a travesty of the truth and profoundly insulting to him, who followed orders whatever the cost – his orders were to return via the Cape of Good Hope. I have given up expecting Fletcher Christian to appear remotely like himself, but you expect that in films. But I still cringe at what they did to my Tahitian ancestors. The New Zealand Maori they used to play the Tahitian King (there was no such thing at the time) smiled in close-up to reveal rotted, discoloured teeth, whereas 18th century Tahitians were famed for their perfect teeth. It is only the past few generations, eating European foods, which have developed dental problems.

Then London thrilled to David Essex's mammoth 1987 musical Mutiny,

starring him, Frank Finlay and a stunning, bucking, pitching, rock 'n' rolling ship set which required tranquillisers merely to watch. I know David and his team worked diligently on adding verisimiltude where they could, and it is a sad measure of the critic's lack of interest in the truth about anything that Frank Finlay was criticized for playing Bligh as mercurial with ever changing moods and no definable character. To me, it was by far the best and most accurate portrayal of Bligh and the impossibility of dealing with him no matter how much you admired his undoubted skills. Of course, Finlay and Essex were too old by far, and why the musical arrangers felt obliged to change the blood-quickening Tahitian music and rhythms to anodyne strummings of their own escapes my comprehension. I long for Mutiny to be produced again, with the Tahitian scenes played to real Polynesian rhythms against the voluptuous waterfall-backed tropical forest recently seen in South Pacific at London's Prince of Wales Theatre. David really should not have changed his mind

and covered the breasts of the Tahitian women after a few weeks.

Despite the millions of pounds, dollars, and other currencies spent, the story of Bounty still awaits factual transferral to large or small screen. This is a story where truth is far more spectacular than the fictions of scriptwriters. The truly fantastic story of what happened to Christian and his band after the mutiny – high adventure, discovery, drunkenness, debauch and as many rapes, murders and mysteries as you choose to stomach until his island became the 19th century's most God-fearing community – is barely known at all. A most interesting game to play is that of casting the actors who might best and most accurately portray the chief protagonists. Who is there to fascinate us with a Bligh of light West Country accent, acid tongue, scientific mind, porcelain complexion, blue eyes and black hair, early 30s? And who to play Christian, swarthy and well muscled, slightly bandy, revolutionary, early 20s, classically educated.

Elizabeth Bligh - her beginnings

The account of the William Bligh Trust's Bicentennial Commemorative Voyage beginning on 28 April 1989 by Jasper Shackleton

A WHILE ago I decided to build a launch like that used by William Bligh and follow the route he took during his gruelling open-boat voyage. The idea came to me forcefully during a cruise on a large sea yacht in the Pacific.

On my return to England, I immediately started work on the project. First, we needed a lines plan: I applied to the National Maritime Museum and one month later a copy of the original draft, from which the Bounty's launch was built, found its way into my hot little hands at a cost of £3.45p. Funds … oh yes, we'll need some to pay for the project, but don't worry, it will be okay … I just could not wait to get cracking at my drawing board: the first thing to do was to redraw the lines plan and make a table of offsets (reproducing drawings distorts the paper so you cannot rely on measurements taken from them as being accurate). The scale on the original was also a bit strange, so I redrew the lines to 1 1/2":1' 0", a nice big scale and made my table of offsets. The next problem was somewhere to build the vessel, and of course some cash to pay for it.

It was at this stage that Captain John Wells DSC CBE RN (retired) came onto the scene. Captain Wells, a retired naval captain, had for some time been working on the restoration of HMS Warrior at Portsmouth, but fortunately this project was just coming to an end. When I asked him if he could help, he replied that he was supposed to be retired and what with

Warrior and the rest, he really could not … but he has been a staunch supporter ever since, and has kept reminding me that we need money and organization the whole way through. My natural priority was of course the building of the launch, for without this and a crew, there was no way the voyage could be done. Captain Wells suggested that I contact the Maritime Workshop in Gosport as they had done some work on one of the Warrior's boats, and had the expertize and facilities for this sort of job, the only trouble being that I was determined that I should build her myself with the assistance of a shipwright and apprentice.

I went down to the Maritime Workshop and met a director of the yard, Peter Hollins. He seemed keen on the idea of building such a boat but not too enthusiastic about my playing a large part in the construction of it, but I am happy to say that he came round in the end. Peter Hollins is also a trustee of the William Bligh Trust. Work began on the lofting in December 1987. I had not built a boat before, so I was unsure of the amount of hired labour that would be required, but it emerged that I did most of the construction myself. I did however require help with the planking and "fitting out" inside. Adrian Redman, on the Youth Opportunities Scheme, was extremely useful in helping me with this work, and he worked with me for perhaps three of the six months the launch took to build.

I am no stranger to woodwork, having been involved in my own business for some years designing and making furniture "one-offs" in English hardwoods, and I treated Elizabeth Bligh in just the same way as any other one-off. The prospect of building a boat is rather daunting until you hoist aboard the fact that it is a simple question of straight measurements from centre and datum lines. Obviously it is important to be accurate in these measurements and to keep everything fair, that is to say in smooth curves. On completion of the

lofting, which involves drawing the lines of the vessel full size on the floor, a scrieve board is made: this shows the transverse sections of the hull from which the actual frames are made. This is a tedious process of checking and fairing coordinates from datum and centre lines. Once completed, it is a guide to the amount of curve required on the frames of the boat.

I had already decided to use grown oak crooks and to saw the frames from the natural curve in the timber. I made a few inquiries to timber contacts I had down in the south, but they all reported that nobody wanted bends or curves and most of this sort of timber was either logged up for the home or burnt on bonfires at the tree felling site. It seemed a far cry from the days of wooden ships when the foresters used to peg down the branches of oak trees to obtain a naturally grown curve in the timber specifically for this purpose. I had a hunch that perhaps Yorkshire was the place to go and travelled up north with the idea of searching it out. Thirty-six hours later I had found pretty much what I wanted: the logs had all been felled for a number of years and showed a good deal of curve. Johnny Walls, the owner of this small yard, was delighted to get rid of this bent stock and dropped all other jobs he had in hand and converted the crooks under my supervision

Research had shown that it was probable that the planking of the launch would have been larch. I managed to find two good logs, also in Yorkshire (it is believed to be better to use northern-grown larch for boats as it grows more slowly and is more durable). I found some excellent oak in Wiltshire to make the keel, hog, and keelson in single lengths. The main frames were to be made in three pieces, one floor timber with an ear to either side hook scarfed together. All the frames were sawn 2" x 4" over the keel, fairing out to 2" x 2" at the heads (gunwales), and spaced at 14" centres along the length of the vessel.

BERGEN

STAVANGER

OSLO

INVERNESS

ABERDEEN

BERLI

NEWCASTLE

BELFAST

TEESSIDE

DUBLIN

MANCHESTER

AMSTERDAM

CORK

LONDON HEATHROW

LONDON GATWICK

SAARBRUCKEN

JERSEY

PARIS

INNSBRU

ZURICH

BERNE

TOULOUSE

MONTPELLIER

LOURDES
TARBES

NICE

PERPIGNAN

MADRID

LISBON

MAHON

IBIZA

For complete network details please refer to timetabl

The closer we come to '92, the more you need our business connections.

As Europe progresses towards the single market, so Dan-Air Scheduled Services progresses towards the network of routes business travellers will rely on in 1992.

Indeed, we are already the second largest British scheduled airline to Europe.

We fly you direct from Gatwick to capital business centres like Paris, Madrid, Lisbon, Berne, Dublin and Zurich.

The prosperous South West of France is also Dan-Air territory, with flights to Toulouse, Perpignan, Montpellier, Lourdes and Nice.

Our new Class Elite business service is already in operation on all flights to Paris and Nice.

With special check-ins, custom designed seats, superb cuisine and complimentary champagne, Class Elite is our way of ensuring that business travellers arrive refreshed and ready for a day's work.

This service will be offered on many more routes during 1989.

But don't wait until 1992 to fly Dan-Air. Contact your travel agent for details of our European schedules. Or you can telephone Dan-Air Reservations on LinkLine 0345 100200.

You'll find we already have the right connections.

The secret is service.

■ Main framing set up, she's beginning to take shape.

By the beginning of March 1988, I had the centre line structure set up, including transom, stern post, keel, deadwoods, stem, apron, and all the main framing bolted securely in place, the whole resembling the skeleton of a whale. The next job was to fair the frames for planking, a laborious job of many hours spent with adze, plane, chisel, and batten making sure the planks fitted each frame in succession, horizontally and diagonally. Planking was the next step: the planks are made in pairs, starting by the keel. The first plank is called the garboard and is generally quite a wide plank, the section through the frames at this point being fairly flat. We had decided to plank her in an unusual way as it had been very hard to establish just how the original launch was planked. I had spoken to a number of people about this, and was inundated with conflicting advice: some said "carvel" and some said "clinker, without

a doubt" , and one expert told me she was double diagonal as he claimed that a section of the original launch had been found at Samuel White's yard in East Cowes when it closed, and the part in question had been double diagonal. Further research on the issue revealed that the original launch had been sold in the Dutch East Indies, and although Samuel White built a lot of double diagonal hulls, this technique had not come into use until a good time after the Bounty left England.

I think it is worth mentioning at this point that the Maritime Workshop premises in Gosport were known as "White's Slip" at the time of the Bounty. The yard was worked by a man named Thomas White who used the premises for fitting out ships. Conveniently situated for Portsmouth Harbour, we believe that White built the original launch and there is a good chance that it was built on the Gosport slip.

All the conflicting information made a decision on the planking difficult, and I determined to go to the National

Maritime Museum to see if there were any contemporary drawings showing the planking detail. I explained my predicament to the very helpful draftroom staff, and they discovered a drawing of a launch of similar type which was carvel underneath and clinker on the top sides.

I jumped at this compromise, believing it would keep everyone at least half happy. People have often asked me the probable reason for this type of construction, and I can only come up with a couple of suggestions: I think it is fair to say that a ship's boat would spend a good deal of its life on deck, and it is not good for any wooden boat to be left high and dry, so water would almost certainly have been put inside to stop the planking drying out. This water would have sloshed about and kept the bilges wet, although a boat would never be filled right up to the gunwales. In carvel construction, the planks are butted together edge to edge and then caulked in the joint with either oakum or cotton, depending on the size of the hull. If the planks were to dry out and shrink, the caulking would tend to fall out. If, however, the top sides were clinker, which has no caulking and relies entirely on the fit of a plank overlapping the one below, clinker topsides would eradicate this problem, as if the planks were to dry out, the fastenings could if necesary be tightened, though when the boat was put into the water, the topside planks would soon take up.

Another possible reason for this type of planking could be that when the ship's boat is in use, going alongside docks and shipping would tend to damage the topsides. It could simply be that the shipwrights of the time thought it easier to change clinker rather than carvel planks. My own feeling is that if it looks right, it is right, and I am pleased with the visual effect of the clinker strakes.

Fitting planks to a hull is a somewhat repetitive but satisfying task. Rather like wallpapering, you cover a chunk at a time and see the almost finished shape appear behind you. On a good day, we could fit almost a pair of planks: this would include spiling the shape from the plank below, marking off the widths, fairing it with a full length

■ Larch planking almost complete; note the first clinker plank fitted.

batten, cutting the strake out of the larch boarding, hand planing the edges, and so on. Each carvel plank has to be hollowed and rounded to fit the shape of the frames, the amount of hollow depending on the width of the plank together with the amount of curve on the hull. For example, the planks on the bottom tend to be wider and there is less hollow due to the flatness of the bottom. When one gets to the turn of the bilge, the planks are considerably narrower and there is more "hollow". The hollowing process is all done by hand with a rounded plane. When I selected the larch for the planking, I tried to guess the amount of "shape" (longitudinal) that would be in the planks as they progressed. I must admit that this was good luck rather than

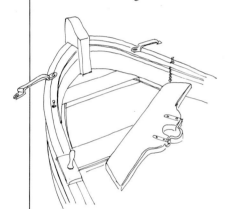

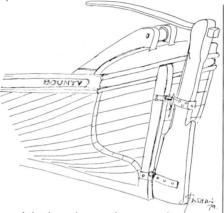

■ There have been many interpretations of the launch over the years; here we see one example of the stern and forward sections.

judgment for I was able to cut all the planks in one piece: there were only two joints on Elizabeth Bligh's planking, and these were both the results of snapping a plank while bending it round.

I cannot tell you of the irritation of snapping a plank after several hours have been spent fitting it: the remedy is either to scarf a new piece on, or, and I favour this method, to place a butt strap behind the joint and butt the two ends together, We got pretty good at bending in the end, and found that by soaking the forward end of the plank in the creek, and using a wrapper (a thin piece of wood laid over the forward end of each plank covering its full width) that casualties were kept to a minimum.

When it came to a decision on the best method of fastening the planking onto the frames, I decided that silicon bronze screws were the only feasible

solution. I am sure that originally all the planking would have been nailed with wrought iron or similar nails. Wrought iron is one of the materials we seem to have overlooked in our modern society. This very durable material is almost impossible to obtain. When we came to think about the rudder fittings, I decided that they should be forged out of wrought iron. I had what I thought was a very good idea and got hold of some old cart tyres, two and a quarter inches wide, and five sixteenths thick and some 4' 6" in diameter. I gave these to the yard's blacksmith together with a pattern of what was required. It was not a success. I was in his bad books for a while. So as not to concede defeat, I took the remaining iron to a friend, also a blacksmith with considerable forging experience: he managed to get the shape required but the iron delaminated in the process,

much to our mutual displeasure. A poorer substitute was eventually used.

It would be untrue to say that the construction of the launch went like clockwork. There were many small problems, most of which could have been avoided with logical forward thinking and a bit more experience in the boat building field. Bill Puddle, the yard foreman, could not have been more helpful. When morale was low, he would step in and get the show back on the road.

The spring of 1988 progressed, and so did the Elizabeth Bligh. The planking complete, gunwales, stringers, and risers fitted, breast hook and quarter knees, thwarts, floor boards, and side benches, the hull was caulked, splined and the dreadful job of fairing the hull for painting dawned. This is just plain hard graft: getting all the irregularities out of every square inch, often lying on your back with showers of shavings dropping in your eyes, the only prospect being that when this was finished, the whole hull had to be sanded. But eventually, the great day came to start painting.

I was not quite sure where the water line would be so I decided to float her and finish the painting later. I cannot describe the feelings of doubt that come to nag one before your first boat is launched for the first time: did that dead wood fit properly? Will she leak through the keel bolts? Do those inaccessible stop waters fit well enough? Will she float with a list to starboard? Will the trim be all right? Shall I have to bale flat out

157

■ Time is drawing near to leave Gosport; Elizabeth Bligh on the slip at The Maritime Workshop.

until the tide leaves her stranded on the mud? It just shows how one's paranoia can get the better of any situation.

She was launched one rather cloudy day in June by crane over the side of the quay. I stood there watching as she was slowly lowered into the water. I had left all the floor boards out to see where the water came pouring in, but suddenly she was afloat and the slings were cast off. I peered in, expecting the worst, but "she's dry!" – there was not a single leak.

Over the next few weeks, the launch had a lot of finishing touches put to her, and I started making masts and spars. We could not find a sail plan of the launch. The forward mast step was shown on the lines plan, but we knew she carried two masts and there was no sign of the mizzen step. We also knew that she carried a dipping lugsail.

I got in touch with Commander Morin Scott who had a fair bit of experience of sailing old naval boats with dipping lugsails during his days in the Navy. He then persuaded Colin Mudie to become involved who very kindly came up with two sail plans, both similar but one showing 250 square foot of sail and the other just under 200 square foot. I decided on the latter, less height to the masts and a slightly more "stable" looking design. I suppose that if one had to describe the rig, she would be called a dipping lug ketch, two-masted – mainsail and mizzen, the mainsail being a dipping lug and the mizzen a standing lug with a boom kin over the transom to which to sheet the mizzen. This rig has been very successful and the only change I have made is to add another set of reef points in both sails.

From reading accounts of Bligh's voyage, I had learned that he fitted shrouds to his launch. We thought and thought and could not come up with a way of doing this that did not involve another crewman to release one shroud and secure the one on the opposite side during each tack. In bad weather, shrouds would be necessary. In the end, I devised a system, admittedly somewhat unorthodox, as I had read somewhere that the halyard was often secured to the weather

■ She's a natural. Elizabeth Bligh conducting sea trials.

side to act as a support to the mast. The only problem with this system is that you have to lower the yard to such an extent, pass the halyard over the yard and proceed to pull the yard back up, bearing in mind that while you are doing this that the rest of the crew are trying to dip the yard. The result is that the after end (the end over which you are trying to pass the halyard) is tending to point upwards making the halyard operation very difficult, to say the least. My invention, like most good inventions, was simple – a double halyard, one to either side, the advantages of which were enormous, mainly that you always have support to the mast and the leeward halyard has enough slack to be pulled clear of the sails and therefore will not allow any chafe.

In addition to the sails, the launch carries six oars. Even a supposedly simple question such as the rowing arrangements on the Bounty's launch drew varying opinions: the oarsmen would have been double banked, that is to say two men side by side on each thwart. No, no,

no, they were of course staggered – one man to a thwart sitting on the opposite side from his oar lock. We tried both and found that staggered oars were simply not efficient; for example, when rowing in a seaway, the surface of the sea on one side of the boat is often much higher (or lower) than the other. With staggered oars, all the men, port and starboard, have to pull together and there is a good chance that there may not be any water to pull in on one side, and too much on the other. With the double banked arrangement, the oars are shorter and more manageable, and although each side has to pull together (meaning all port oars or all starboard oars), this system gives the oarsmen a chance of a better contact than thin air.

All these techniques and systems were tried out during the summer of 1988 after the official launching in July. As I have already mentioned, Elizabeth Bligh was built at Gosport: the plan was to base ourselves at Chichester Harbour for all sea trials and crew selection. The

great day finally arrived when it was time to leave Gosport and a party of keen volunteers was gathered to come on the maiden voyage. We had never set any sail on the Elizabeth Bligh before, and I was dying to see how she would handle. We rowed rather stiffly out of Forton Lake and into Portsmouth Harbour, set sail and off we went, a close reach under full sail out of Portsmouth Harbour (against the tide) , bearing away to make for Chichester Harbour entrance.

I cannot describe what an exhilerating feeling it was to be sailing what up to that moment had been just a 23-foot woodwork project. There was a fair sea running that day, she seemed a natural and handled it beautifully, and to my relief everybody aboard looked happy and content. As far as the project was concerned, we now had the main component and what was more, she was a tremendous success.

Sea trials continued all summer and late into the autumn. On the early trips, it was not unusual for me to have a completely new and fresh crew off a list of crew applicants; some took to it, some did not come back for more within a couple of months. Basically, the same faces returned and procedures on board became more fluent, going about, jibing and rowing, cooking and of course sleeping. My original plan had been to have a crew of six in addition to myself: this would make for three watches of two and one man floating to fill any gaps; as far as rowing went, six oarsmen and a coxswain.

How on earth Bligh managed with 18 men on board, I will never know. The suffering must have been extreme, especially when you bear in mind that relationships were strained for a lot of the time.

After much thought, I decided to cut the total complement down to six, deciding that one less man made the accommodation much more comfortable for all, to say nothing of the food, water, and equipment that the extra man would need. The crew who have been selected are a bit of a mixture: a sailor, a doctor, an accountant, a fireman and a foundry worker.

One thing that the reader must realize is that this project is not designed as a stunt. Bligh may have been a very difficult man, but it does not alter the fact that he was a brilliant navigator, hydrographer, and seaman, and deserves any tribute one sees fit to bestow on him.

There have been many books written about the mutiny: I have read some of these, but do not pretend to be an expert on the subject. There are so many facets to the story that I think it best, for those interested, to read one of the excellent accounts available, including this catalogue. I would, however, like to say a little about events relating to the open boat voyage as I feel that these are relevant to the general conception of this project.

In our modern world, it is hard to imagine a time when you could not just pick up the telephone and talk to someone on the other side of the globe, or pull out an atlas from the bookcase and flick to a finely detailed map of, for example, the Cape York area of Australia. When Bligh was cast adrift in his heavily over loaded launch, he had none of these facilities: he did have a sextant and tables and the gunner's watch (which stopped), but he had no charts or safety equipment, very little food and water with the prospect of the nearest help some 3,600 sea miles distant, through virtually unknown waters. He did, however, have one very valuable asset, his incredible memory.

Bligh had been Captain Cook's sailing master on Cook's last voyage aboard HMS Resolution, whose main purpose was to discover a north-west passage many miles from the Great Barrier Reef. Bligh remembered much vital information about the north-eastern coast of Australia and Endeavour Strait. From discussions with Cook, he knew the position of a pass in the Great Barrier Reef and also of Timor in the then Dutch East Indies. You must bear in mind that the first colonists had only just arrived in southern Australia, and there was no prospect of help in the northern part.

One interesting point is that Bligh and his launch full of half-starved men were the first Europeans to set eyes on the Fiji Islands: Bligh naturally drew sketches of these islands and the pass between the islands is still called Bligh Water. Having left Tofua in the Tongan Islands, Quartermaster Norton having been murdered by natives on the beach, Bligh decided not to stop at any inhabited islands for fear of further attacks on his vulnerable party. While passing through the Fiji Islands, fires could be seen on shore and some canoes even put out to sea in their pursuit. Although Bligh and his party did sight land, they sailed non-stop from Tofua to Restora-

tion Island off the Australian coast, a distance of approximately 2,200 nautical miles, before continuing northwards up the Cape York peninsula and on to Timor. A further remarkable fact is that apart from Norton who was murdered on the beach at Tofua, all the rest of the crew survived the ordeal.

My party aboard Elizabeth Bligh will be off Tofua on the 28 April 1989, 200 years to the day that Bligh and his 18 officers and men were cast adrift. I often wonder what Bligh would have to say about a group of men volunteering to undertake such a voyage?

THE WILLIAM BLIGH TRUST AND ITS AIMS
The William Bligh Trust was established in 1987 (charitable status applied for) to administer the planning of the open boat voyage and the trustees include a naval historian, a solicitor, an accountant, and marine artist. When the project was in its preliminary stages, the question of what to do with the launch after the voyage was raised. It seemed a great shame not to put her to use, and it was decided to put all the expedition's assets into a scheme to try to make the lives of disadvantaged children more enjoyable by running day and weekend trips with the emphasis on fun. We hope, finances permitting, to hire a part-time skipper and mate (or even to use volunteers with suitable qualifications) to run the trips and to assist in keeping Elizabeth Bligh seaworthy. The need for funds has been mentioned. A project of this type is expensive to mount: private donations have been very generous as have donations from certain trusts , and equipment has been given or generously discounted. However, we are still badly in need of more money. If you feel you would like to help with the project financially, or would be interested in getting involved with Elizabeth Bligh on her return from the Pacific, please contact the Trust for further information: – The William Bligh Trust, The Coach House, Portland Square, Liss, Hampshire GU33 7LA

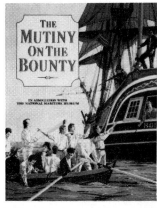
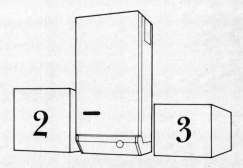